The Oxford

Australian Love Poems

The Oxford Book of
Australian
Love Poems

Edited by Jennifer Strauss

Melbourne

OXFORD UNIVERSITY PRESS

Oxford   Auckland   New York

OXFORD UNIVERSITY PRESS AUSTRALIA
Oxford   New York   Toronto
Delhi   Bombay   Calcutta   Madras   Karachi
Kuala Lumpur   Singapore   Hong Kong   Tokyo
Nairobi   Dar es Salaam   Cape Town
Melbourne   Auckland   Madrid
and associated companies in
Berlin   Ibadan
OXFORD is a trade mark of Oxford University Press

National Library of Australia
Cataloguing-in-Publication data:

The Oxford book of Australian love poems.

Includes index.
ISBN 0 19 553650 9.

1. Love poetry, Australian. 2. Australian poetry.
I. Strauss, Jennifer, 1933– . II. Title: Book of
Australian love poems. III. Australian love poems.

A821.0080354

Publication of this title was assisted by the Commonwealth Government
through the Australia Council, its arts funding and advisory body.

Typeset by Solo Typesetting, South Australia
Printed by McPherson's Printing Group, Victoria
Published by Oxford University Press,
253 Normanby Road, South Melbourne, Australia

CONTENTS

INTRODUCTION

'Australian love poetry? Will it cover more than a postcard?' So often did such a reaction greet early announcements of this project that discouragement might have prevailed if I had not come fresh from intensive study of Gwen Harwood. No writer has done more to strengthen my conviction that we cannot identify our own cultural baggage, nor understand the joys and sorrows, the tenderness and violence of our social life, until we have achieved a better grasp of what we have made in this country of 'the nature and the names of love'.

Harwood's phrase from 'David's Harp'—a poem, ironically enough, crowded out in the final selection processes—provided a structural plan. And it was easy enough to think of likely sources for love poems: clustered near in time to Harwood were James McAuley, Judith Wright, A.D. Hope, while I could rapidly summon up both earlier poets (Mary Gilmore, Lesbia Harford, R.D. Fitzgerald) and later ones (Gig Ryan, John Scott, Dorothy Porter).

I knew, however, that random acquaintance, while it might confirm that sufficient material existed to justify an anthology of love poetry, would not be adequate if I wanted to map the layout of Australia's Garden of Love, not merely pick a pretty posy of sentimental—or even profound—blooms. I set out on a comprehensive scanning of collections and of journals (past and present) publishing poetry, but was ill-prepared for the sheer number of volumes of poetry brought into being by commercial publishers or determined authors over Australia's two hundred years of English-language publication. Without funds from the Australian Research Council, and the energetic research assistance of Kathryn Henderson, I could not possibly have scanned the 3000 or more books (individual collections and anthologies) that have fed this project, let alone the journals and newspapers. My hopes of finding a neglected genius in the latter were not fulfilled; with the exception of some recent work, nearly every journal poem selected for serious consideration turned out to have been published in book form. Given, however, that something like 75 per cent of the books scanned contained one or more love poems, I had thousands of poems from which to choose: in fact, far more material than could be used, and more than enough to put to rest any assumption that Australian poets (whether native-born, immigrant or expatriate) do not write love poetry.

So where had this assumption come from? What had muted the

audibility of what is demonstrably a major thematic strand of Australian poetry? Was the stereotype of national identity that casts us as a pragmatic bunch, laconic to the point of emotional illiteracy, so powerful as to be impervious to counter-indications? Had that particular mythic stereotype been re-enforced in the twentieth century by a general diversion of the rhetoric of passion into one of irony?

It seemed that one clue existed in the indexes of those survey anthologies which have, over the years, been major instruments in constituting 'Australian poetry', partly for readers in general, but above all for readers (teachers and students) in educational institutions. For although mine was an anthology conceived from the beginning as primarily one of poems rather than poets, its organisation—by poets in chronological birth order—inevitably created something of a cast list. And as the cast list of my anthology took shape, it did not look extraordinarily different from other comprehensive anthologies, despite the presence of some little-known names and the absence of some highly regarded poets who have simply written little or no love poetry. The noticeable differences were not so much in the canon of authors present as in the poems by which they were represented.

I began to wonder whether there had not been a process whereby, in the anxious project of constructing a 'national' poetry, love poems had been selected out because they were perceived as offering too little that was distinctively Australian. Love's old songs (both sweet and sour) migrated to the Antipodes with highly conventional trappings, and much of the sentimental verse which abounds in the nineteenth and early twentieth centuries could have been written— with equal lack of distinction—anywhere in the English-speaking world. While observers of social mating customs such as Charles Thatcher might record in 'Love on the Diggings' a mine of novel material, those who wrote about the psychic processes of love or its abstract nature were more likely to feel that they were speaking of universals, and even after local idioms and rhythms began to make an Australian accent available to Australian poetry, that accent tended, in much love poetry, to be muted rather than broad.

This has been perhaps especially true of those poets for whom traditional mythology has been a crucial resource. A.D. Hope's 'The Wandering Islands', despite local references to Cook or Quiros, has little that is uniquely Australian in its modern themes of existential alienation, the failure of the old narratives, the desire for an order of things in which Eros functioned to construct and unify both individual lives and society. The castaway survivors of heroic/ romantic quest narratives may dream that sexual contact will still fulfil the narrative of rescue, but in this poem mere nature is not enough; sexual congress, while it may retain primal energy, cannot of itself re-create the lost world of mythological wholeness and significance.

The tradition of Eros as unifier, however, co-exists with a powerful antiphonal perception of Eros as destroyer. Many poems in this collection put one view or the other; but the tensions generated when both views exist at the same time are particularly visible in the work of Gwen Harwood. There the Psyche myth informs poems in which love's desire to know and be known is both irrepressible and dangerous, so that we may have to accept with trust love's visitations in the dark ('The Wine is Drunk'). Love's riskiness is addressed in an ironic version of the traditional *carpe diem* motif, where the speaker presents herself as a sacramentalist, incapable of the carnal hedonism that would make possible a *safe* surrender to the seduction to seize the day. The conclusion—'I give my body to be burned'— expresses the persistent notion of love's consuming of the lover, a narrative motif which expresses our deep anxiety that the price of love's promised fulfilment of the self will be the annihilation of the existing individualised self. Burning and eating: that the traditional symbolism of consumption deployed in 'Carpe Diem' has not exhausted its resonance is demonstrated in the witty grotesquerie of Chris Wallace-Crabbe's 'The Amorous Cannibal'.

There are many poems in this collection that I would like to speak about, but most must speak for themselves. There was a stage when I contemplated an anthology that would include many forms of love—parental and filial, friendship, love of country, love of nature, love of God. It soon became apparent that this would be altogether too diffuse, and that there was ample material to sustain an anthology which took as its particular focus those attachments between adults which are, or have been, sexually charged—attachments which may range from casual lust to passionate devotion, from the ephemeral to the permanent, from the socially legitimate to the irregular. While there was no intention to privilege poems of heterosexual love, it was no surprise to find that these were very much more numerous. What did surprise me was that it proved easier to find overtly lesbian poems than explicitly homosexual ones; perhaps the established codes of the love poem as the male poet's declaration to, or about, the object of his affections have allowed for the development of an ambiguous sexual rhetoric from which male-to-male love poems find it more difficult to break free.

In the event, I have tried to make a selection that will show a broadly conceived 'love' in the variousness of its manifestations: the characteristic situations and emotions of its processes of yearning, wooing, gaining, losing; its voices of celebration and disappointment—even of fear, loathing and disgust; its psychic consolidations or disintegrations of lover and beloved; its invitations to speculative thought; its social contexts and consequences. In such a framework, a poem about infanticide (Mary Gilmore's 'Down by the Beach') may be a less predictable presence than one about an old-fashioned wedding (Peter Porter's 'Old-Fashioned Wedding'), but it is not an irrelevant one.

Despite my intention of establishing limits to the territory, my final selection retains poems in which, either through the nature of experience or through the nature of language, no simple borderline can be drawn between sexual love and other loves of the kind mentioned earlier. Charles Harpur's 'The World-Birth of Love' exemplifies the idealistic strain which sets human affections within the music of divine harmony. In the nineteenth century writers were more given to writing poems about Love as an upper-case abstraction, which can lead to readerly doubt as to whether the poem's addressee or subject is indeed human or divine, with consequent peevishness about vague religiosity. But uncertainty can be rich as well as vague, so it was not unduly disconcerting to find myself quite unable to disprove a challenge that it was divine rather than erotic love that 'came so lightly' in John Shaw Neilson's 'Love's Coming', one of the earliest poems considered for selection.

The fortunate married lovers of Gwen Harwood's 'Iris' have found a place within the territory of love as the divine covenant of creation and within the territory of loving friendship inhabited by those who are long-term collaborators on a common task. They have come out on the positive side of the complex substitutions, negations and equations that occur between self-love, passionate love and family love. In James McAuley's 'Father, Mother, Son', however, it is the negative side, 'the sad geometry of family love', that is registered by the son who contemplates in his father's life and death that compromise of selfhood which is associated with love itself in Harpur's 'Self-Liberty' and with love's institutionalisation in Lesbia Harford's 'I'm like all lovers'.

Not surprisingly, since interchanges between the language of mortal love and the language that speaks of Nature are a traditional part of English poetics, there are poems straddling the borders of love poetry and landscape poetry. Many of these operate at an extremely simple level: when Dorothea Mackellar writes, in her over-exposed 'Australia', 'I love a sunburnt country' we are not likely to be confused about the existence of erotic sub-texts. When, however, she writes of 'an opal-hearted country,/A wilful, lavish land' we see, in a woman poet's enunciation of this stereotype of the unpredictable mistress, the power of traditional rhetoric to elide Nature and Woman as the two major non-divine significant others in the experience (and the self-definition) of the males who have been for generations the cultural literati, the arbiters of language. It is, however, not surprising that the feminised and eroticised landscape should be more common in the work of male poets. Nor is it surprising that, of the threateningly seductive versions found in Brian Vrepont's 'Night' and Barcroft Boake's 'A Wayside Queen', it is Boake's earlier poem which is more consciously 'Australian'.

One might indeed argue that the most interesting early Australian love poetry is not that concerned with human relationships, but that concerned with the colonial imperative to transform the strangeness of a new land into a familiar (and familial) home — to conquer or tame it, to possess, to penetrate, to make fertile, to domesticate, to husband it. And if some of these poems display all the *odi et amo* ambivalence of one branch of traditional love poetry, others commit themselves enthusiastically to an eroticising of the landscape as a project of Australian literary nationalism.

It is for this reason that my starting point is Charles Harpur's 'Country Lovers', a naive courtship ballad which adapts the conventions of the love-language of flowers to define the lover's allegiance to a new 'glowing type' of girlhood analogous to the wildflowers of the native woodlands. This 'Australian lassie' foreshadows those fictional Little Bush Maids whose specifically Australian brand of femininity was an element in the dream of a new, healthier, more natural society. While Edith Mary England's 'The Bush Girl' shows the survival of the type well beyond its heyday, its major poetic deployment is in the verse melodramas of George Essex Evans, whose long leisurely narratives, unfashionable as they may be in style and genre, are a storehouse of material illustrating Australian versions of nineteenth-century mythologies of love.

Constrained by space to a single extract, I have chosen the opening of 'Loraine' to illustrate Evans's vision of the Australian pastoral place as an Eden in which the two young lovers are matched in affection, interests, social and economic status and in their complementary physical qualities of feminine grace and masculine sturdiness. They are not, however, to be matched in narrative activity, for 'Loraine' strongly encodes contested male possession of the love object as the essential narrative element, and there is considerable irony in the hero's reflection, early in the poem, that his happiness is complete in his untroubled possession of two elements often stressed in Australian experience as incompatible: 'What more to a man,' he asks, 'can the high God send/ Than the fairest maid and the firmest friend!' The latter, as it happens, will, after a half-hearted attempt at murder, leave the hero to die of a fever in the wilderness and trick his sweetheart into a marriage that leads to her death in childbirth.

Although changing fashions in diction and in themes may make it difficult to respond with full sympathy to work of an earlier period, some themes seem almost indestructible. Waiting for a letter holds its own remarkably well even against the variant of waiting for a telephone call, but contemporary readers probably find 'The Fallen Woman' an alien topic, just as a nineteenth-century revenant would probably consider 'unnatural' such contemporary post-separation 'division of the spoils' poems as Jenny Boult's 'i'd like to know about the fruit bowl'.

The Fallen Woman was one of the most notable Victorian mythological configurations of the female: in religious terms, a daughter of Eve in her descent into a world of unsanctified appetites; in psychological terms, a scapegoat figure, through whose casting out society could assuage its own guilty awareness of, and participation in, a sexuality dualistically split between flesh and spirit, lust and 'true' love. In Australian literature, as elsewhere, it was left to writers of radical persuasion to go beyond a sympathetic tempering of judgement to the assertion of a counter mythology, insisting that prostitution had to do with the commodifying of sex in a market where the providers were driven by economic necessity not romantic betrayal or personal moral frailty. Henry Lawson's weary but golden-hearted whores are figures in socialist mythology, victims of, and a reproach to, capitalist greed.

Other conventional concepts of love and sexuality are contested as well as celebrated. Thomas Shapcott and Barbara Giles refuse to cede the territory of love exclusively to the beautiful and young. Ada Cambridge, Anna Wickham, Dorothea Mackellar, and Lesbia Harford are early rejecters of that icon of desirable femininity, the passively receptive, pure, family-centred woman. Their stance is maintained in the high-spirited, sometimes angry, work of Dorothy Porter, Gig Ryan, and Ania Walwicz, while denial that the personal sphere is primary for women takes on a specific political significance when Oodgeroo (formerly Kath Walker) insists in 'My Love' that personal affection must take second place to her love of, and service to, her own Aboriginal people.

It is understandable that love poetry as we derive it from our European literary heritage and colonial experience should not have been a priority for writers needing to articulate a whole culture and history previously unspoken in English. Nonetheless, through Jack Davis, Lionel Fogarty, Bobbi Sykes, and Mudrooroo (formerly Colin Johnson), Aboriginal voices are finding their own distinctive idioms and themes for writing about love. And even as White audiences are hearing these voices, they are being made aware of the rich storehouse of Aboriginal love poetry contained in the tribal song-cycles translated by anthropologists such as Ronald M. Berndt.

These translations remind us how remote our society has become from ritual celebration of the sexual act as an impersonal instrument of fertility. They remind us, too, of how uneasy our poetic diction is with the abundant supply of linguistic terms for the sexual parts and their interaction. When Judith Wright dramatised recognition of the impersonal force of generative sexuality in 'Woman to Man', she relied entirely on symbolism rather than sexual explicitness. Readers who responded enthusiastically to that poem will suffer no stylistic shock from Song 27 of the Goulburn River Cycle, in which intercourse is represented by the capture of a mouse by a gull. But such readers may well be shocked—poetically if not morally—by the anatomical directness of some other songs from the Goulburn and Rose River cycles. If I have not presented such examples here, it is not from prudery, but because I think that they need to be seen in the context of the complete cycles. The decision to place these poems at the date of their translation was for two reasons. One was Ronald Berndt's statement that these were not timeless 'primitive' songs, but living and evolving forms at the time he translated them; the other was that it was at this stage that these translations, and others appearing from this time onwards, caused English-speaking audiences to make adjustments to their notions of the constituent elements of 'Australian' culture.

Questions of checks and balances in representativeness became increasingly important as my voluminous list of possible poems had to be reduced to a practicable size, and I am well aware that I am unlikely to have satisfied all demands for generic, let alone individual, representation. Many hard choices had to be made, especially in limiting the representation of the more prolific love poets in order to achieve breadth of representation. A rough and ready rule of no more than six poems per poet did little to help with the problem of the long poem. If we are convinced that love poems are short lyric or dramatic pieces, this may well be because such poems are the ones most easily chosen for anthologies; but there are long love poems, and these may be qualitatively as well as quantitatively distinctive. In the case of Kenneth Mackenzie and A.D. Hope, for instance, I deliberately set aside numerous shorter poems to allow the inclusion of 'The Moonlit Doorway' and 'An Epistle: Edward Sackville to Venetia Digby'. It is from the latter, Hope's major poem of reconciliation between the joys and grief, the sexual and spiritual realities of love, that I take an envoi for this anthology, in the hope that its readers, like Edward Sackville, can feel

> Now like the garner ant when frosts begin,
>   I have my harvest heaped within;
> Abundance for my year to come, a feast
>   Still cherished, still increased.

Although the final responsibility for the contents of this anthology is entirely mine, I am grateful to the many friends and colleagues who offered advice and admonishment while it was in the making. More formal thanks are due to Monash University, which provided me with time through Outside Studies Leave and to the Australian Research Council for the funding that enabled me to obtain the services of Kathryn Henderson, whose industrious and intelligent research activities brought to my notice several of the poems finally selected. Chris Wallace-Crabbe and Peter Rose first proposed the project to Oxford University Press, and both were supportive but unobtrusive sources of sound advice and encouragement. And finally, Jo McMillan was as efficient and sympathetic an in-house editor as anyone could wish for.

Jennifer Strauss

Charles Harpur

Country Lovers

She— Where have you been all the day?
    Tell me where, Australian laddie!
Were you near or far away?
    Truly say, Australian laddie!
He— Where the cloistered echoes play,
Where the glens wind far away,
Hunting have I been all day,
    My fair Australian lassie.

She— Tell to me what you have seen,
    Tell me all, Australian laddie!
What most charmed you in each green
    Woody scene, Australian laddie?
He— Tulips wild, in virgin pride,
Bashfull bells, in blushes dyed,
And many a glowing type beside
    Of thee, Australian lassie.

She— Passed you by old Alen's cot
    As you came, Australian laddie?
Tow'rd his boasted garden plot
    Looked you not, Australian laddie?
He— Yes, and saw his Julia there,
Fairest of its roses fair,
Rubies are her lips, her hair
    Is gold, Australian lassie.

She— Ever thus I hear anew
    Julia's praise, Australian laddie!
Yet how often to be true
    Vowed have you, Australian laddie!
He— Yes, till this fair moon shall strew
O'er my grave her silver dew,
Vowed have I, and so have you,
    My fair Australian lassie.

He— Wilt thou wander forth with me,
    Fairest girl, Australian lassie?
She— I will wander forth with thee
    Trustingly, Australian laddie!
Both— Let us stray thus, side by side,
Near old Hawkesb'ry's placid tide,
O'er which gentle airs now glide,
    Like dreams o'er sleeping beauty.

Rhymes to a Lady with a Copy of Love Poems

Many and many a day and night
Have taken their uncared for flight,
Since this wild Wreath, mid scenes afar
   Was woven for delight.
And long it was ere I could deem
The glowing, and so grateful star
Of Morning love did only beam
To gild, alas!—a morning dream.

But so it was;—although she'd die
The Maiden vowed, if Fate our lot
Cast separate; nor in vows was I
   Behind her a single jot!
But Fate, in the vile shape of pelf,
At length between us thrust herself;
And yet (however strange to tell)
We both lived on—and—even got well!

Alas! a tear is in mine eye
To think our very truth was—what?
   A golden lie!
And hence, although I will it not,
The Real is battling from my head
All—all the dear romance that shed
O'er other days, and other nights,
Such heart-perceived auroral lights;
And caution dinning me the while
With—have a care of Beauty's smile,
For though a thing so rosy-rich,
It is the perilous stuff of which
Is woven passion's painful thrall.
Yes: of the love that left me lonely,
Such, Lady, is the sequel only,
   And such the profit all!
And for the days that bore it by
These lines are one long *written* Sigh.

The World-Birth of Love

Off from all Being, as a worn-out part,
The husk of time's indifference is hurled,
And the brute earth becomes a dreaming heart,
So soon as Love is born into the world!

The Old hath passed away, and in the New
Nothing is undelightful, nothing mean,
But all life passions into Beauty through
A purple morning-light before unseen.

A sudden concord runs all Nature's round—
Runs through the utterance of all vocal things:
Yea, Music wheresoever there is sound
Doth spirit-gift it with her golden wings.

And wheresoever our impassioned looks
Are thrown abroad, there's Picture: objects dull
To uncharmed eyes, together flow like brooks
Into the deep and world-wide Beautiful.

And Poesy no longer latent lies,
But all the air breathes her ethereal writ,
And all the hues of the diurnal skies
Are cloud-sung paeans glowing exquisite!

For from all Being, as a worn-out part,
The screen of old indifference is hurled,
And the brute Earth becomes a dreaming heart
So soon as Love is born into the world.

Self-Liberty

I would not be dependent, even for love,
   On man or woman. Nay, I would—I will
Be as the Eagles through the heavens that move
   Boundlessly free, though separate. And as still
   A torrent, dashing from its native hill,
Doth make its own best way, be't mine to groove
My individual world-path, and approve
   Its lonely fitness with a sovereign thrill!
Thus large must be my freedom, for the need
   Is in my nature and defies dispute,
Even as a bent peculiar to its breed
   Constrains yon tree to bear its proper fruit:
   And though the pliant deem me a strange brute,
What care I? being thus *myself indeed!*

James Michael

Fallen

Hearts that have lost their freshness, yearn
　In secret for those days gone by
When all the ill was yet to learn, —
　I was so young when thou wert by.
　　　　　Fallen, — ah me!

We wander'd — we two — through the wood,
　I knew no ill, and we were young;
I thought, alas! that thou wert good, —
　There was a lie upon thy tongue.
　　　　　Fallen, — ah me!

I fell — God help me! — and the tale
　So often, often true before,
How man is false if woman frail,
　Came true — too true for me — once more.
　　　　　Fallen, — ah me!

I fell: where art thou? — here I stand
　Ragged, dishonour'd, lonely, poor;
There's not for me in all the land
　One welcome at an honest door.
　　　　　Fallen, — ah me!

Hard words, hard usage, shame and scorn
　My portion, — thine an honour'd name:
Cursed be the hour that thou wert born!
　— Was not our fault at *least* the same?
　　　　　Fallen, — ah me!

Hearts that have lost their freshness, — oh!
　I was so young when thou wert by:
I cannot bear my load of woe,
　I cannot bear — but I can die.
　　　　　Fallen, — ah me!

Said the sunlight to the moonlight

Said the sunlight to the moonlight,
　When they met at the close of day
Why art thou so wan and pale,
　And I so warm and gay?

Said the moonlight to the sunlight,
 The lily is fair tho' pale,
The tulip, gaudy tho' it be,
 Perfumes no passing gale.

Said a poet, haply passing by,
 They make up the world, these two;
There is sex in all, if we knew but why, —
 And the darkness covered the blue.

Charles Thatcher

Colonial Courtship, or Love on the Diggings

A New Original Song, written and sung by Thatcher

(Air — Drops of Brandy)

What a rum lot the gals are out here,
 They jolly soon get colonized, sirs,
I twig their rum capers sometimes,
 And feel not a little surprised, sirs;
As regards love and marriage out here,
 I'm fairly licked clean off my perch, sirs,
One day they pick up a chap,
 The next day he's walked off to church, sirs.

If at home you should flirt with a girl,
 In a twinkling the old bloke, her father,
Asks what your intentions may be,
 And isn't he down on you, rather;
The mother leads you in a string,
 And sticks to you like bricks and mortar,
For she's always talking to you
 About her accomplished young daughter.

The courtship lasts some little time,
 And then of course you pop the question,
She immediately bursts into tears,
 And calls it a cruel suggestion;
She falters out 'ask my papa,'
 When you beg her to be your dear wife, sirs
And in two or three weeks from that time,
 You find that you're tied up for life, sirs.

But things are far different here,
   The girls don't consult their relations,
What's father or mother to them,
   They follow their own inclinations;
If you name the day here to a gal,
   Don't think off her perch it will lick her,
For nine out of ten will reply
   'Lor, Sammy, can't it be done quicker.'

The best of this colony is,
   The brides have no fine affectation,
In saying 'I will' they're 'all there,'
   And they don't faint upon the occasion;
A bottle lots of 'em will use,
   And it seems to come in very handy,
You might think that it's Preston salts,
   No fear! the smell tells you it's brandy.

The bride's mother, too, will be there,
   She's not overcome by emotion,
Her spirits you find she keeps up
   By old tom or some other lotion;
And sometimes her voice will grow thick,
   In her speech there's a wond'rous obstruction,
But her friends are to blame for it all,
   For they ought to allowance her suction.

Some brides upon their wedding night,
   In colonial parlance get *'tight,'* sirs,
And then in that state they evince
   A strong inclination to fight, sirs,
They've been known to take tumblers up
   And shy them in every direction,
But bless their dear hearts, we all know
   Its a proof of colonial affection.

Henry Kendall

Ulmarra

Alone—alone!
With a heart like a stone,
She maketh her moan,
At the feet of the trees,
With her face on her knees,
And her hair streaming over;
Wildly, and wildly, and wildly;
For she misses the tracks of her lover!
Do you hear her, Ulmarra?
Oh! where are the tracks of her lover?

Go by—go by!
They have told her a lie,
Who said he was nigh,
In the white-cedar glen—
In the camps of his men:
And she sitteth there weeping—
Weeping, and weeping, and weeping,
For the face of a warrior sleeping!
Do you hear her, Ulmarra?
Oh! where is her warrior sleeping?

A dream! a dream!
That they saw a bright gleam
Through the dusk boughs stream,
Where wild bees dwell,
And a tomahawk fell,
In moons which have faded;
Faded, and faded, and faded,
From woods where a chieftain lies shaded!
Do you hear her, Ulmarra?
Oh! where doth her chieftain lie shaded?

Bewail! bewail!
Who whispered a tale,
That they heard on the gale,
Through the dark and the cold,
The voice of the bold;
And a boomerang flying;
Flying, and flying, and flying?
Ah! her heart it is wasted with crying—
Do you hear her, Ulmarra?
Oh! her heart it is wasted with crying!

Campaspe

Turn from the ways of this Woman! Campaspe we call her by
    name —
She is fairer than flowers of the fire — she is brighter than
    brightness of flame.
As a song that strikes swift to the heart with the beat of the blood
    of the South,
And a light and a leap and a smart, is the play of her perilous
    mouth.
Her eyes are as splendours that break in the rain at the set of the
    sun,
But turn from the steps of Campaspe — a Woman to look at and
    shun!

Dost thou know of the cunning of Beauty? take heed to thyself
    and beware
Of the trap in the droop in the raiment — the snare in the folds of
    the hair!
She is fulgent in flashes of pearl, the breeze with her breathing is
    sweet,
But fly from the face of the girl — there is death in the fall of her
    feet!
Is she maiden or marvel or marble? O rather a tigress at wait
To pounce on thy soul for her pastime — a leopard for love or for
    hate.

Woman of shadow and furnace! she biteth her lips to restrain
Speech that springs out when she sleepeth, by the stirs and the
    starts of her pain.
As music half-shapen of sorrow, with its wants and its infinite wail,
Is the voice of Campaspe, the beauty at bay with her passion
    dead-pale.
Go out from the courts of her loving, nor tempt the fierce dance
    of desire,
Where thy life would be shrivelled like stubble in the stress and
    the fervour of fire!

I know of one, gentle as moonlight — she is sad as the shine of the
    moon,
But touching the ways of her eyes are: she comes to my soul like a
    tune —
Like a tune that is filled with faint voices of the loved and the lost
    and the lone,
Doth this stranger abide with my silence: like a tune with a
    tremulous tone.
The leopard, we call her, Campaspe! I pluck at a rose and I stir
To think of this sweet-hearted maiden — what name is too tender
    for her?

Rose Lorraine

Sweet water-moons, blown into lights
   Of flying gold on pool and creek,
And many sounds, and many sights,
   Of younger days, are back this week.
I cannot say I sought to face,
   Or greatly cared to cross again,
The subtle spirit of the place
   Whose life is mixed with Rose Lorraine.

What though her voice rings clearly through
   A nightly dream I gladly keep,
No wish have I to start anew
   Heart-fountains that have ceased to leap.
Here, face to face with different days,
   And later things that plead for love,
It would be worse than wrong to raise
   A phantom far too fain to move.

But, Rose Lorraine—ah, Rose Lorraine,
   I'll whisper now where no one hears.
If you should chance to meet again
   The man you kissed in soft dead years,
Just say for once 'he suffered much,'
   And add to this 'his fate was worst
Because of me, my voice, my touch,'—
There is no passion like the first!

If I that breathe your slow sweet name
   As one breathes low notes on a flute
Have vext your peace with word of blame,
   The phrase is dead—the lips are mute.
Yet when I turn towards the wall,
   In stormy nights, in times of rain,
I often wish you could recall
   Your tender speeches, Rose Lorraine.

Because, you see, I thought them true,
   And did not count you self-deceived,
And gave myself in all to you,
   And looked on Love as Life achieved.
Then came the bitter, sudden change,
   The fastened lips, the dumb despair;
The first few weeks were very strange,
   And long, and sad, and hard to bear.

No woman lives with power to burst
   My passion's bonds and set me free;
For Rose is last where Rose was first,
   And only Rose is fair to me.
The faintest memory of her face,
   The wilful face that hurt me so,
Is followed by a fiery trace
   That Rose Lorraine must never know.

I keep a faded ribbon string
   You used to wear about your throat;
And of this pale, this perished thing,
   I think I know the threads by rote.
Gold help such love! To touch your hand,
   To loiter where your feet might fall,
You marvellous girl, my soul would stand
   The worst of hell—its fires and all!

Emma Frances Anderson

No Room for the Dead

Hush! In the dim sad twilight of this room
The softest breath is heard, and through the gloom
Sounds like a discord in some solemn air.
Tread lightly here, it seemeth holy ground,
And all the heavy atmosphere around,
Is burdened,—burdened with unanswered prayer!
Ah, how the mother prayed as the days went by,
Each moment stealing from her little one
Some touch of life,—the bright light from the eye,
The smile, the roundness, till death's work was done!
Ah, how she prayed—'I cannot let her go,
'Spare, spare my darling one!' but God said 'No;
'She shall be Mine, and I will gently bear
'Her with Me where I go.—Would'st thou come there;
'Her little footprints see, like stars I've given
'To guide thee in thine upward path to heaven.'
And so He took her in His bosom kind,
And wrapped around the mantle of His love;
Leaving the lone ones in the mist behind,
To gaze, with watching aching eyes, above.

And they will watch and weep one lonely night,
Until the morning comes and brings the light.
Then, the glad world, released from sorrow's veil,
Will tell once more its old enchanted tale;
And with its eager hands again restore,
The joy they thought was buried evermore;
For there is no eternity of love, —
No hearts on earth that live with those above.

It was but yesterday a mother died;
   And the bereaved nurslings left behind,
Clustered together by the bed, and cried
   With a vague sorrow faint and undefined.
And for a little while they still will miss
   The gentle rocking on her soft warm breast,
The murmured singing or the 'Good-night' kiss
   That hushed them, oh so tenderly to rest.
But soon the air is full of merry laughter,
   The child-heart has forgotten all its pain: —
There is no lingering grief—no longing after
   The mother that can never come again.

'Twas only yesterday a young wife died,
Died in the midst of gladness—a sweet bride
Bound in the bands of earth's most tender tie.
A heart all full of its earthly love,
Too strong for the powers of life to move,
Living for happiness, learnt to die;
And a sad one sits in his desolate home,
And waits for a morrow that will not come,
Watches and waits till his eyes grow dim,
For his angel-bride to return for him.
But the heart must outlive its bitterest grief
And sorrow and suffering find relief;
And in after years could her spirit come,
To seek for a place in its earthly home,
With a heart brimful of the love of old,
That even the grave could not chill to cold,
Would she find a welcome waiting her there,
And outstretched arms and a vacant chair?
Could she nestle down by his side once more,
And claim the love that was hers before,
And receive it again as full and free,
Hers—all hers, to eternity?
No, — Spirit stretch upward thy quivering wing,
For thy name on earth's a forgotten thing;

The love that was thine is given away,
And there is not a whisper to bid thee stay,
From the bliss of the *present* the *past* has fled,
And our glorious world has no place for the dead!
           Yes, the earth is bright,
           And hearts are light;
           And none would know
           That years ago
           A grave was made,
           And a loved one laid
       Away from the sorrowing sight.
           For flowers have grown,
           Where tears were sown,
           And memories die
           As the years go by,
           Till the living have said,
           'No room for the dead
       'In this beautiful world of our own.
'No room for the stars in a mid-day sky,
    'No room for the grass with the garden flowers;
'No room for the tears in a joyful eye,
    'No room for the *dead* in this world of ours.'

Ada Cambridge

A Wife's Protest

1

Like a white snowdrop in the spring
    From child to girl I grew,
And thought no thought, and heard no word
    That was not pure and true.

2

And when I came to seventeen,
    And life was fair and free,
A suitor, by my father's leave,
    Was brought one day to me.

3

'Make me the happiest man on earth,'
    He whispered soft and low.
My mother told me it was right
    I was too young to know.

4
And then they twined my bridal wreath
  And placed it on my brow.
It seems like fifty years ago—
  And I am twenty now.

5
My star, that barely rose, is set;
  My day of hope is done—
My woman's life of love and joy—
  Ere it has scarce begun.

6
Hourly I die—I do not live—
  Though still so young and strong.
No dumb brute from his brother brutes
  Endures such wanton wrong.

7
A smouldering shame consumes me now—
  It poisons all my peace;
An inward torment of reproach
  That never more will cease.

8
O how my spirit shrinks and sinks
  Ere yet the light is gone!
What creeping terrors chill my blood
  As each black night draws on!

9
I lay me down upon my bed,
  A prisoner on the rack,
And suffer dumbly, as I must,
  Till the kind day comes back.

10
Listening from heavy hour to hour
  To hear the church-clock toll—
A guiltless prostitute in flesh,
  A murderess in soul.

11
Those church-bells chimed the marriage chimes
  When he was wed to me,
And they must knell a funeral knell
  Ere I again am free.

12

I did not hate him then; in faith
  I vowed the vow 'I will;'
Were I his mate, and not his slave,
  I could perform it still.

13

But, crushed in these relentless bonds
  I blindly helped to tie,
With one way only for escape,
  I pray that he may die.

14

O to possess myself once more,
  Myself so stained and maimed!
O to make pure these shuddering limbs
  That loveless lust has shamed!

15

But beauty cannot be restored
  Where such a blight has been,
And all the rivers in the world
  Can never wash me clean.

16

I go to church; I go to court;
  No breath of scandal flaws
The lustre of my fair repute;
  For I obey the laws.

17

My ragged sister of the street,
  Marked for the world's disgrace,
Scarce dares to lift her sinful eyes
  To the great lady's face.

18

She hides in shadows as I pass—
  On me the sunbeams shine;
Yet, in the sight of God, her stain
  May be less black than mine.

19

Maybe she gave her all for love,
  And did not count the cost;
If so, her crown of womanhood
  Was not ignobly lost.

20

Maybe she wears those wretched rags,
  And starves from door to door,
To keep her body for her own
  Since it may love no more.

21

If so, in spite of church and law,
  She is more pure than I;
The latchet of those broken shoes
  I am not fit to tie.

22

That hungry baby at her breast—
  Sign of her fallen state—
Nature, who would but mock at mine,
  Has made legitimate.

23

Poor little 'love-child'—spurned and scorned,
  Whom church and law disown,
Thou hadst thy birthright when the seed
  Of thy small life was sown.

24

O Nature, give no child to me,
  Whom Love must ne'er embrace!
Thou knowest I could not bear to look
  On its reproachful face.

Victor Daley

Elizabeth

'I want upon a plate of gold
  The round green Earth,' I said,
'As dark Herodias of old
  Had John the Baptist's head.

'And if to get that guerdon great
  The lack of gold debars
I'll beat the sun into a plate
  And set it round with stars.

'I take the blood of Life and write
  Upon the mask of Death,
Across the day, across the night,
  Thy name—Elizabeth.'

Lachesis

Over a slow-dying fire,
    Dreaming old dreams, I am sitting;
The flames leap up and expire;
    A woman sits opposite knitting.

I've taken a Fate to wife;
    She knits with a half-smile mocking
Me, and my dreams, and my life,
    All into a worsted stocking.

W. T. Goodge

Love and the Cycles

Bert bestrode a Bradbury,
    And Rosie rode a Rover,
Rosie she was fair to see
    And smiled as it behove her!
Away they went; it might have been
    In ancient days to Gretna Green.
'Oh, my machine's a fine machine!'
    Said Rosie on the Rover.

Rosie rode a Rover
    And Bert bestrode a Bradbury;
Rose demure was sweet and pure
    As cocoa made by Cadbury!
And not a cloud arose between
    To mar the brightness of the scene,
Till 'My machine's the best machine!'
    Said Bertie on the Bradbury.

Bertie backed the Bradbury
    To romp around the Rover,
Rosie said he'd lost his head
    And everything was over!
And so they parted, he and she,
    And both as cross as cross could be,
For Bert bestrode a Bradbury
    While Rosie rode a Rover!

George Essex Evans

From *Loraine*

PART I

There's a bend of the river on Glenbar run
Which the wild duck haunt at the set of sun,
And the song of the waters is softened so
That scarcely its current is heard to flow;
And the blackfish hide by the shady bank
'Neath the sunken logs where the reeds are rank,
And the halcyon's mail is an azure gleam
O'er the shifting shoals of the silver bream,
And the magpies chatter their idle whim,
And the wagtails flitter along the brim,
And tiny martins with breasts of snow
Keep fluttering restlessly to and fro,
And the weeping willows have framed the scene
With the trailing fall of their curtains green,
And the grass grows lush on the level leas
'Neath the low gnarled boughs of the apple-trees,
Where the drowsy cattle dream away
The noon-tide hours of the summer day.
There's a shady nook by the old tree where
The track comes winding from Bendemeer.
So faint are the marks of the bridle track,
From the old sliprails on the ridge's back,
That few can follow the lines I know —
But I ride with the shadows of long ago!
I am gaunt and grey, I am old and worn,
But my heart goes back to a radiant morn
When some one waited and watched for me
In the friendly shade of that grand old tree.
The winter of Memory brings again
The summer rapture of passionate pain,
And she comes to me with the morning grace
On her sun-gold hair and her lily face,
And her blue eyes soft with the dreamy light
She stole from the stars of the Southern night,
And her slender form like a springtide flower
That sprang from the earth in a magic hour,
With the trembling smile and the tender tone
And the welcome glance — that were mine alone.

And we sit once more as we sat of old
When the future lay in a haze of gold —
In the fairy days when the gods have lent
To our lips the silence of heart's content.
Ah! those were the days of youth's perfect spring,
When each wandering wind had a song to sing,
When the touch of care and the shade of woe
Were but empty words we could never know
As we rode 'neath the gum and the box-trees high,
And our idle laughter went floating by,
As we rode o'er the leagues of the billowy plain
Where the grass grew green 'neath the summer rain,
And over the hills in the range's heart
To the fern-decked glen where the waters dart,
And we railed at time and the laggard year
Ere a bride would be mistress of Bendemeer.

Now the old-time feud that was first begun
When the Gordons settled on Glenbar run,
It had passed away, it was buried deep
In the quiet graves where our fathers sleep,
And sweet Mary Gordon was left alone
In the quaint old station of rough-hewn stone,
The maiden whom lovers sought near and far —
The stately lily of old Glenbar.
Our kinsfolk had hated, from year to year,
Since the first Loraine came to Bendemeer:
They have passed where none can cavil and strive;
How could she and I keep the feud alive!
I, James Loraine, who were better dead
Than harm one hair of her gentle head!
So we made the bond that would bind, one day,
Glenbar and Bendemeer for aye.

For at last, though it left me with saddened face,
I was master of all in my father's place.
Of the grey old dwelling, rambling and wide,
With the homestead paddocks on either side,
And the deep verandahs and porches tall
Where the vine climbs high on the trellised wall,
Where the pine and cypress their dark crowns rear
O'er the garden — the glory of Bendemeer —
From whence you can dream o'er the tranquil scene
Of the scattered sheep on the lucerne green,
And the mighty plain in the sunlight spread,

With the brown hawk motionless overhead,
And the stockmen's cottages clustering still
On the gentle slope of the station hill,
And the woolshed grey on the swelling rise
Where the creek winds blue 'neath the bluer skies.
And here in the days when our hearts were light
We lived life joyously day and night.
For the friend of my soul, who was dear to me
As no friend hath been or again can be,
Was Oliver Douglas. In cloud or shine
My heart was his and his heart was mine,
And we lived like brothers from year to year,
And toiled for the honour of Bendemeer,
And my life moved on thro' a golden haze—
The splendid glamour of fortunate days.
What more to a man can the high God send
Than the fairest maid and the firmest friend!
I have read in some poet how Friendship may
Stand strong as a tower in the darkest day,
When the lips of Love that were quick to vow
Have failed 'neath the frown upon Fortune's brow.
What a friend was he, without fear or guile,
With his careless ways and his ready smile,
With the voice to cheer, and the eye to praise,
And the heart to toil through the hardest days!
How he won all hearts, were they high or low,
By the easy charm that I envied so!
For they say in jest I am true to race—
The dark Loraines of the haughty face—
Awkward, and shy, and unbending when
I am full of love for my fellow-men.
But I caught at the sunshine he flung about—
The man to whom all my heart went out.
Ah! how oft at dusk 'neath the evening star
Have we reined our horses at old Glenbar,
And sat in the quaint familiar room
Made sweet with the scent of the jasmine bloom,
Where my soul first saw in her dreamy eyes
The lights of the gateways of Paradise!
How we lingered over our hopes and fears
As we planned the course of the coming years!
Whilst Oliver chatted with easy flow
To Margaret Bruce with the hair of snow—
The proud old dame of a proud old race
Who lived for the child with her sister's face.

O the joyous days! O the morning air!
When the blood was young and the world was fair!
When from Tara and Westmere and Boradaile,
And from Snowdon Hills and from Lilyvale,
And from Tallaran and the plains of Scar
All sent down their horses to old Glenbar.
From many a station for miles away
Came the happy faces on racing day,
Came the big bush buggies fast rolling in
With the four-in-hands and the merry din.
And if strife was keen in those days of old
'Twas for love of sport, not for lust of gold;
For then each man rode as a man should ride
With his honour at stake and the station's pride,
When every racehorse was sent to race
And each run had a crack for the steeplechase.
And I see the last timber loom big and bare
As we held the field with a length to spare,
And Douglas crashed past me on Charioteer,
The big grey gelding from Bendemeer.
But I rode the bay with the tiny star
That had carried the Lily of old Glenbar.
And I rode for all that I cared for most
And I collared the grey ere he passed the post.
Ah! how gaily and lightly our pulses beat
As the night went out to the trip of feet!
And though all men sought her with hope and praise
It was *I* she loved—with my awkward ways—
It was *I* she loved in the golden days!

Mary Gilmore

In Poverty and Toil

I—ANGER

Git up an' out, you lazy lump,
    I'll give y' late a-bed!—
The fire to make, the cows to milk,
    The chickens to be fed;

The children waiting to be dressed,
   The table to be laid;
The floor to sweep, the beds to air,
   The breakfast to be made;

The bread to mix, the clothes to sort,
   The churn to scald and scour—
An' I've to come an' call you,
   Though it's daylight near an' hour!

II—CONTRITION

Be up an' out of bed, my girl,
   As quick as you can be;
There ain't no morning rest, my girl,
   For such as you an' me.

It's workin' early, workin' late,
   Year in, year out, the same;
Until we seem but work-machines,
   An' women but in name.

Life grinds the sweetness out of us,
   Life makes us hard an' cold;
We kiss shame-faced, an' grow uncouth;
   Unlovely—young and old.

Kind speaking dies for lack of use,
   Soft ways mean only grief;
And in the lash of biting words
   We find a half relief.

So up, and out to work, my girl,
   We have no time to waste,
Our lot, the bitter bread of life,
   We eat in bitter haste.

Down by the Sea

The sea has soddened the baby clothes,
   The flannel, the shirt, the band;
The rats have bitten the baby face,
   And eaten the baby hand.

It lay at my breast and cried all night
    As through the day it had done;
I held it tight and rose with stealth
    When the day and the night were one.

And on through the city streets I crept—
    (But the hand of fear is strong!)
And they mocked my steps with echoing,
    They mouthed as I went along—

Past houses, where mothers like me slept warm,
    And babies like mine were born;
Where it was not sin to have loved as I,
    And motherhood meant not scorn.

And they drove me fast, those leering streets;
    They took up my baby's cry,
And tossed it about, and flung it up
    Till it seemed to go God-high.

But the cry came back to the mother-heart,
    Knowing that it would hear;
I gathered my baby close and close—
    What was it I seemed to fear?

And down by the sea the sun crept up—
    Did you hear a baby cry?
I know where one lies beside the quay,
    But I will not tell—not I!

And down by the sea the sun crept up—
    There's a child's cry seems to come
From the darkness, there, beyond the wall—
    But I know the dead are dumb!

And down by the sea the sun crept up . . .

Eve-Song

I span and Eve span
A thread to bind the heart of man;
But the heart of man was a wandering thing
That came and went with little to bring:
Nothing he minded what we made,
As here he loitered, and there he stayed.

I span and Eve span
A thread to bind the heart of man;
But the more we span the more we found
It wasn't his heart but ours we bound.
For children gathered about our knees:
The thread was a chain that stole our ease.
And one of us learned in our children's eyes
That more than man was love and prize.
But deep in the heart of one of us lay
A root of loss and hidden dismay.

He said he was strong. He had no strength
But that which comes of breadth and length.
He said he was fond. But his fondness proved
The flame of an hour when he was moved.
He said he was true. His truth was but
A door that winds could open and shut.

And yet, and yet, as he came back,
Wandering in from the outward track,
We held our arms, and gave him our breast,
As a pillowing place for his head to rest.
I span and Eve span,
A thread to bind the heart of man!

From the Spanish

In hell once met four ghosts,
Who, for a little space,
Stood while each asked of each
What brought them to that place.

'I from a high bridge sprang—
Sped like a stone to hell.'
'I from a tower.' 'So I.'
Then she, 'I only fell.'

In Life's Sad School

She grew, but he remained where he began,
And so, as eager fancy hungry ran,
She turned to dreams, imagining a mind
That burned to vision where the less are blind,
That held firm hands whose strong reserves lay still,

Or leaned upon indomitable will,
Which, self-contained, could haste, or pause, or wait.
Nor lose the fullness of its high estate.
Yet ever on the background of her thought
Waited the narrow forehead of the fool
Who called her his. I saw her tear-marked face,
I saw her deep eyes' baffled look, which sought
To know what was it that, in life's sad school,
Matched the swift-footed to the dullard's race.

William Gay

Love's Menu

POMMES DE TERRE FRITES

(Lines to a picture)

Fried potatoes is a dish
Good as any one could wish:
Cheap it is, and appetizing;
Turn a saint to gormandizing:
Good and cheap and tasty too,
Just the thing for Love's Menu.
Love is dainty, and his food,
Even though common, must be good:
Love hath little to disburse,
So his fare must fit his purse:
Love hath fickle appetite,
We his palate must invite:
Crisp and hot, the price a sou,
Fried potatoes, Love's Menu.

Inez Hyland

Jilted

Jilted—yes, 'tis an ugly word;
   Yet even so it is better
Than the sickening sense of hope deferred,
   Waiting each day for a letter—

Waiting in fear lest any should see
  That weary and anxious air.
He said, 'Let our love a secret be,'
  And I, 'Do you think I would care

'To tell of our love to anyone?
  Ah, no! I will keep it hidden;
I only fear that its light, like the sun,
  Will shine on my face unbidden.'

But he wrote not a word; yet day by day
  My foolish heart was so strong
That I laughed my doubting fears away—
  He would not, he could not stay long.

How shall I tell you, oh, trusting heart!
  That he who vowed love could not die,
Was only mocking a lover's part—
  Had always been acting a lie.

The silent love we so fondly hid
  Together, my heart, you and I,
I do not know any harm it did—
  I only know it must die.

It was not a little wanton thing,
  To suggest and quicken desire;
It had not the cunning hand to fling
  Passion's flame on a fading fire.

If cherished now it would steal away
  The nerve of our body and brain;
It would woo us out of life's battle fray
  To dreams of peace that are vain.

Lay down our love in its grave, my heart,
  Its head on its girl-mother's breast;
A woman now from those dead must part,
  Believing what is is best.

Barcroft Boake

A Wayside Queen

She was born in the season of fire,
    When a mantle of murkiness lay
On the front of the crimson Destroyer:
And none knew the name of her sire
    But the woman; and she, ashen grey,
    In the fierce pangs of motherhood lay.

The skies were aflame at her coming
    With a marvellous message of ill;
And fear-stricken pinions were drumming
The hot, heavy air, whence the humming
    Of insects rose, sudden and shrill,
    As they fled from that hell-begirt hill.

Then the smoke-serpent writhed in her tresses:
    The flame kissed her hard on the lips:
She smiled at their ardent caresses
As the wanton who smiles, but represses
    A lover's hot haste, and so slips
    From the arm that would girdle her hips.

Such the time of her coming and fashion:
    How long ere her day shall be sped,
And she goes to rekindle past passion
With languorous glances that flash on
    The long-straightened limbs of the dead,
    Where they lie in a winter-wet bed?

Where the wide waves of evergreen carry
    The song sad and soft of the surge
To feathered battalions that harry
The wizen-armed bloodwoods that tarry
    For ever, chained down on the verge
    Of a river that mutters a dirge.

'Tis a dirge for the dead men it mutters—
    Those weed-entwined strangers who lie
With the drift in the whirlpools and gutters—
Swoll'n hand or a garment that flutters
    Wan shreds as the waters rush by,
    And the flotsam, froth-freckled, rides high.

Is it there that she buries her lovers,
  This woman in scarlet and black?
Those swart *caballeros*, the drovers —
What sovranty set they above hers?
  Riding in by a drought-beset track
  To a fate which is worse than the rack.

A queen, no insignia she weareth
  Save the dark, lustrous crown of her hair:
Her beauty the sceptre she beareth:
For men and their miseries careth
  As little as tigresses care
  For the quivering flesh that they tear.

She is sweet as white peppermint flowers,
  And harsh as red gum when it drips
From the heart of a hardwood that towers
Straight up: she hath marvellous powers
  To draw a man's soul through his lips
  With a kiss like the stinging of whips.

Warm nights, weighted down with wild laughter,
  When sex is unsexed and uncouth:
In the chorus that climbs to the rafter
No thought of the days to come after:
  She has little regret and less ruth
  As she tempts men to murder their youth.

Is she marked down as yet by the flaming
  Great eye of the Righter of Wrong?
How long ere the Dreaded One, claiming
His due, shall make end of our shaming?
  'How long, Mighty Father, how long?'
  Is our wearisome burden of song.

Bernard O'Dowd

Lust

I

A shuddering deluge whelmed your wake of yore:
  You razed the halls of fatal Paris' sire:
  Loaded the dice of Actium: lit the fire
Changing pale Magian to the Scarlet Whore,

Who Phrygian swine and Messalina bore,
    And sterile spouses of the modern mire:
    Your undertone jangles the lyric choir:
Your furtive fingers smear the lover's lore.

Mandrake, disgorged by grave of murdered shame,
    Clinging to dozing trust with vampire lips,
        Oily with fetid Sodom, or the wan
Gomorrah-sin the ages dare not name!
    Seductive wrecker of immortal ships!
        Serpent of Eden! Brothel toad! Begone!

II

Tho' flaming swords unfit intruders warn,
    I am the Tree of Life in Paradise:
    I mould the savage clay to Helen, Bice:
Valkyr of souls, the chooser of the born,
I sieve the virile races from the worn:
    And hermit satyrs from their caves entice
    To parenthood and high self-sacrifice:
Virtue I am, though monk or eunuch scorn!

On atom, world, my Living Creatures' breath
Active is wheeling Life, lethargic, Death:
Yea, when upon my noonday shrine ye can
    Your sweet oblations frank and faithful burn,
The veil that darkens God shall lift from man,
    Sin shall depart, the Golden Age return!

Henry Lawson

The Watch on the Kerb

Night-lights are falling;
    Girl of the street,
Go to your calling
    If you would eat.
Lamplight and starlight
    And moonlight superb,
Bright hope is a farlight,
    So watch on the kerb.

Watch on the kerb,
Watch on the kerb;
Hope is a farlight; then watch on the kerb.

Comes a man: call him —
Gone! he is vext;
Curses befall him;
Wait for the next!
Fair world and bright world,
Life still is sweet —
Girl of the night-world,
Watch on the street.

Dreary the watch is:
Moon sinks from sight,
Gas only blotches
Darkness with light;
Never, O never
Let courage go down;
Keep from the river,
O Girl of the Town!

He's Gone to England for a Wife

He's gone to England for a wife
Among the ladies there;
And yet I know a lass he deemed
The rarest of the rare.
He's gone to England for a wife;
And rich and proud is he.
But he was poor and toiled for bread
When first he courted me.

He said I was the best on earth;
He said I was 'his life';
And now he thinks of noble birth,
And seeks a lady wife!
He said for me alone he'd toil
To win an honest fame;
But now no lass on southern soil
Is worthy of his name!

I think I see his lady bride,
A fair and faultless face,
And nothing in her heart beside
The empty pride of race.

And she will grace his gilded home,
  The wife his gold shall buy;
But will she ever dream of him,
  Or love as well as I?

Taking His Chance

They stood by the door of the Inn on the Rise;
May Carney looked up in the bushranger's eyes:
'O why did you come?—it was mad of you, Jack;
You know that the troopers are out on your track.'
A laugh and a shake of his obstinate head—
'I wanted a dance, and I'll chance it,' he said.

Some twenty-odd bushmen had come to the Ball,
But Jack from his youth had been known to them all,
And bushmen are soft where a woman is fair;
So the love of May Carney protected him there;
And all the short evening—it seems like romance—
She danced with a bushranger taking his chance.

'Twas midnight—the dancers stood suddenly still,
For hoofs had been heard on the side of the hill!
Ben Duggan, the drover, along the hillside
Came riding as only a bushman can ride.
He sprang from his horse, to the shanty he sped—
'The troopers are down in the gully!' he said.

Quite close to the homestead the troopers were seen.
'Clear out and ride hard for the ranges, Jack Dean!
Be quick!' said May Carney—her hand on her heart—
'We'll bluff them awhile, and 'twill give you a start.'
He lingered a moment—to kiss her, of course—
Then ran to the trees where he'd hobbled his horse.

She ran to the gate, and the troopers were there—
The jingle of hobbles came faint on the air—
Then loudly she screamed: it was only to drown
The treacherous clatter of slip-rails let down.
But troopers are sharp, and she saw at a glance
That someone was taking a desperate chance.

They chased, and they shouted, 'Surrender, Jack Dean!'
They called him three times in the name of the Queen.
Then came from the darkness the clicking of locks;
The crack of the rifles was heard in the rocks!
A shriek and a shout and a rush of pale men—
And there lay the bushranger, chancing it then.

The sergeant dismounted and knelt on the sod—
'Your bushranging's over—make peace, Jack, with God!'
The bushranger laughed—not a word he replied,
But turned to the girl who knelt down by his side.
He gazed in her eyes as she lifted his head:
'Just kiss me—my girl—and—I'll—chance it,' he said.

The Sliprails and the Spur

The colours of the setting sun
    Withdrew across the Western land—
He raised the sliprails, one by one,
    And shot them home with trembling hand;
Her brown hands clung—her face grew pale—
    Ah! quivering chin and eyes that brim!—
One quick, fierce kiss across the rail,
    And, 'Good-bye, Mary!' 'Good-bye, Jim!'

        O he rides hard to race the pain
            Who rides from love, who rides from home;
        But he rides slowly home again,
            Whose heart has learnt to love and roam.

A hand upon the horse's mane,
    And one foot in the stirrup set,
And, stooping back to kiss again,
    With 'Good-bye, Mary! don't you fret!
When I come back'—he laughed for her—
    'We do not know how soon 'twill be;
I'll whistle as I round the spur—
    You let the sliprails down for me.'

She gasped for sudden loss of hope,
    As, with a backward wave to her,
He cantered down the grassy slope
    And swiftly round the dark'ning spur.

Black-pencilled panels standing high,
  And darkness fading into stars,
And blurring fast against the sky,
  A faint white form beside the bars.

And often at the set of sun,
  In winter bleak and summer brown,
She'd steal across the little run,
  And shyly let the sliprails down,
And listen there when darkness shut
  The nearer spur in silence deep;
And when they called her from the hut
  Steal home and cry herself to sleep.

A great white gate where sliprails were,
  A brick house 'neath the mountain brow,
The 'mad girl' buried by the spur
  So long ago, forgotten now.

      And he rides hard to dull the pain
        Who rides from one that loves him best;
      And he rides slowly back again
        Whose restless heart must rove for rest.

The Shearer's Dream

'O I dreamt I shore in a shearin' shed, and it was a dream of joy,
For every one of the rouseabouts was a girl dressed up as a boy—
Dressed up like a page in a pantomime, and the prettiest ever
  seen—
They had flaxen hair, they had coal-black hair—and every shade
  between.'

  'There was short, plump girls, there was tall, slim girls, and
    the handsomest ever seen—
  They was four-foot-five, they was six-foot high, and every size
    between.'

'The shed was cooled by electric fans that was over every shoot;
The pens was of polished ma-ho-gany, and ev'rything else to suit;
The huts was fixed with spring-mattresses, and the tucker was
  simply grand,
And every night by the biller-bong we darnced to a German band.

'Our pay was the wool on the jumbuck's backs, so we shore till all
    was blue—
The sheep was washed afore they was shore (and the rams was
    scented too);
And we all of us cried when the shed cut out, in spite of the long,
    hot days,
For every hour them girls waltzed in with whisky and beer on
    tr-a-a-a-ys!

'There was three of them girls to every chap, and as jealous as they
    could be—
There was three of them girls to every chap, and six of 'em picked
    on me;
We was draftin' 'em out for the homeward track and sharin' 'em
    round like steam,
When I woke with my head in the blazin' sun to find 'twas a
    shearer's dream.'

    'They had kind grey eyes, they had coal-black eyes, and the
        grandest ever seen—
    They had plump pink hands, they had slim, white hands, and
        every shape be-tw-e-e-n.'

'E'

(Mary E. Fullerton)

The Selector's Wife

The quick compunction cannot serve;
She saw the flash,
Ere he had bent with busy hand
And drooping lash.

She saw him mark for the first time,
With critic eye,
What five years' heavy toil had done
'Neath roof and sky.

And always now so sensitive
Her poor heart is,
That moment will push in between
His kindest kiss.

The moment when he realised
Her girlhood done—
The truth her glass had long revealed
Of beauty gone.

Until some future gracious flash
Shall let each know
That that which drew and holds him yet
Shall never go.

Travellers

The human heart is a traveller.

I knew a heart that went
Far from the land of love,
Armed with a shield and spear,
Into the land of hate.

Also I knew a heart
That without scrip or staff
Took the more perilous journey
Away from the land of hate
Into the land of love.

The human heart is a bold traveller.

Lovers

To be unloved brings sweet relief:
The strong adoring eyes
Play the eternal thief
With the soul's fit disguise.

He will not sleep, and let be drawn
The screen of thy soul's ark;
They keep, those lidless eyes,
Thy sanctuary stark.

God, when he made each separate
Unfashioned his own act,
Giving the lover eyes,
So his love's soul be sacked.

To be unloved gives sweet relief;
The one integrity
Of soul is to be lone,
Inviolate, and free.

Christopher Brennan

From *Towards the Source*

2

We sat entwined an hour or two together
(how long I know not) underneath pine-trees
that rustled ever in the soft spring weather
stirr'd by the sole suggestion of the breeze:

we sat and dreamt that strange hour out together
fill'd with the sundering silence of the seas:
the trees moan'd for us in the tender weather
we found no word to speak beneath those trees

but listen'd wondering to their dreamy dirges
sunder'd even then in voiceless misery;
heard in their boughs the murmur of the surges
saw the far sky as curv'd above the sea.

That noon seem'd some forgotten afternoon,
cast out from Life, where Time might scarcely be:
our old love was but remember'd as some swoon;
Sweet, I scarce thought of you nor you of me

but, lost in the vast, we watched the minutes hasting
into the deep that sunders friend from friend;
spake not nor stirr'd but heard the murmurs wasting
into the silent distance without end:

so, whelm'd in that silence, seem'd to us as one
our hearts and all their desolate reverie,
the irresistible melancholy of the sun,
the irresistible sadness of the sea.

From *Lilith*

XII

She is the night: all horror is of her
heap'd, shapeless, on the unclaim'd chaotic marsh
or huddled on the looming sepulchre
where the incult and scanty herb is harsh.

She is the night: all terror is of her
when the distemper'd dark begins to boil
with wavering face of larve and oily blur
of pallor on her suffocating coil.

Or majesty is hers, when marble gloom
supports her, calm, with glittering signs severe
and grandeur of metallic roof of doom,
far in the windows of our broken sphere.

Or she can be all pale, under no moon
or star, with veiling of the glamour cloud,
all pale, as were the fainting secret soon
to be exhaled, bride-robed in clinging shroud.

For she is night, and knows each wooing mood:
and her warm breasts are near in the charm'd air
of summer eve, and lovingly delude
the aching brow that craves their tender care.

The wooing night: all nuptials are of her;
and she the musky golden cloud that hangs
on maiden blood that burns, a boding stir
shot thro' with flashes of alluring pangs,

far off, in creeks that slept unvisited
or moved so smoothly that no ripple creas'd
their mirror'd slip of blue, till that sweet dread
melted the air and soft sighs stole, releas'd;

and she the shame of brides, veiling the white
of bosoms that for sharp fulfilment yearn;
she is the obscure centre of delight
and steals the kiss, the kiss she would return

deepen'd with all the abysm that under speech
moves shudderingly, or as that gulf is known
to set the astonied spouses each from each
across the futile sea of sighs, alone.

All mystery, and all love, beyond our ken,
she woos us, mournful till we find her fair:
and gods and stars and songs and souls of men
are the sparse jewels in her scatter'd hair.

It is so long ago!

It is so long ago!
How shall the man I now am know
the man I was before you came?
    I have forgot his name
    It was so long ago —
    How shall I know?

    It is so long ago
the time when life was faint and low
the time that was not love, you came,
    And call'd me by my name:
    It is so long ago —
    A month or so!

'Sydney Partrige'

(Kate Margaret Stone)

The Lonely Man

She put him on a pedestal,
A carven marble pedestal
    (The only man loved she).

She praised him for his godly ways,
His goodly, goodly, godly ways
    (A sinner cruel was he).

And when he wished to sin again,
And when he ached to sin again
    (So innocent was she)—

She held him with her eyes of blue,
Her eyes of truest, bluest blue
    (That only him did see).

And by her little mouth so red,
By rote he knew her mouth so red
    (That would not let him be).

He could have crushed her in his grasp,
So dainty small within his grasp
    (But nothing wotted she).

That only bowed her heart to him,
Adoring tender heart to him
    (The while her weird did dree).

Apotheosis was to him
A suffocating thing to him,
    Grim visions did he see

Of long and lonely years go by,
The long, long years that passed him by
    (He panted to be free).

And direful things spake in his ear;
They whispered, whispered in his ear
    (They whispered hatefully).

And up he rose and raised his knife,
His shining, slender, servile knife
    (And dreadfully smote he).

She gave one little gurgling sigh
A little moaning, passing sigh
    (Then quiet — quiet — she).

O God, that lonely, lonely man,
He thought he was the only man
    (That Hell did ever see).

He thought he was the only man,
That wretched, wretched lonely man
    (That Heav'n must ever flee).

John Shaw Neilson

You, and Yellow Air

I dream of an old kissing-time
    And the flowered follies there;
In the dim place of cherry-trees
    Of you, and yellow air.

It was an age of babbling,
    When the players would play
Mad with the wine and miracles
    Of a charmed holiday.

Bewildered was the warm earth
    With whistling and sighs,
And a young foal spoke all his heart
    With diamonds for eyes.

You were of Love's own colour
    In eyes and heart and hair;
In the dim place of cherry-trees
    Ridden by yellow air.

It was the time when red lovers
    With the red fevers burn;
A time of bells and silver seeds
    And cherries on the turn.

Children looked into tall trees
    And old eyes looked behind;
God in His glad October
    No sullen man could find.

Out of your eyes a magic
    Fell lazily as dew,
And every lad with lad's eyes
    Made summer love to you.

It was a reign of roses,
    Of blue flowers for the eye,
And the rustling of green girls
    Under a white sky.

I dream of an old kissing-time
    And the flowered follies there,
In the dim place of cherry-trees,
    Of you, and yellow air.

Love's Coming

Quietly as rosebuds,
    Talk to the thin air,
Love came so lightly
    I knew not he was there.

Quietly as lovers
    Creep at the middle moon,
Softly as players tremble
    In the tears of a tune;

Quietly as lilies
    Their faint vows declare
Came the shy pilgrim:
    I knew not he was there.

Quietly as tears fall
    On a warm sin,
Softly as griefs call
    In a violin;

Without hail or tempest,
    Blue sword of flame,
Love came so lightly
    I knew not that he came.

Song be Delicate

Let your song be delicate.
    The skies declare
No war—the eyes of lovers
    Wake everywhere.

Let your voice be delicate.
    How faint a thing
Is Love, little Love crying
    Under the Spring.

Let your song be delicate.
    The flowers can hear:
Too well they know the tremble,
    Of the hollow year.

Let your voice be delicate.
    The bees are home:
All their day's love is sunken
    Safe in the comb.

Let your song be delicate.
    Sing no loud hymn:
Death is abroad . . . oh, the black season!
    The deep—the dim!

The Worshipper

What should I know of God he lives so far
In that uncanny country called the blue
Sweetheart I cannot worship moon or star
I worship you.

I shall have miracles of light above
My church will be an acre of green spring
And while I pray I'll see the world you love
Still blossoming.
I shall be lifted with the scent of air
And the strong sun will wash my doubts away
You will be near me when I go to prayer
To hear me pray.

C. J. Dennis

A Spring Song

The world 'as got me snouted jist a treat;
    Crool Forchin's dirty left 'as smote me soul;
An' all them joys o' life I 'eld so sweet
    Is up the pole.
Fer, as the poit sez, me 'eart 'as got
The pip wiv yearnin' fer—I dunno wot.

I'm crook; me name is Mud; I've done me dash;
    Me flamin' spirit's got the flamin' 'ump!
I'm longin' to let loose on somethin' rash . . .
    Aw, I'm a chump!
I know it; but this blimed ole Springtime craze
Fair outs me, on these dilly, silly days.

The young green leaves is shootin' on the trees,
    The air is like a long, cool swig o' beer,
The bonzer smell o' flow'rs is on the breeze,
    An' 'ere's me, 'ere,
Jist moochin' round like some pore, barmy coot,
Of 'ope, an' joy, an' forchin destichoot.

I've lorst me former joy in gettin' shick,
　　Or 'eadin' browns; I 'aven't got the 'eart
To word a tom; an', square an' all, I'm sick
　　Of that cheap tart
'Oo chucks 'er carkis at a feller's 'ead
An' mauls 'im . . . Ar! I wish't that I wus dead! . . .

Ther's little breezes stirrin' in the leaves,
　　An' sparrers chirpin' 'igh the 'ole day long;
An' on the air a sad, sweet music breaves
　　A bonzer song—
A mournful sorter choon thet gits a bloke
Fair in the brisket 'ere, an' makes 'im choke . . .

What *is* the matter wiv me? . . . I dunno.
　　I got a sorter yearnin' 'ere inside,
A dead-crook sorter thing that won't let go
　　Or be denied—
A feelin' like I want to do a break,
An' stoush creation for some woman's sake.

The little birds is chirpin' in the nest,
　　The parks an' gardings is a bosker sight,
Where smilin' tarts walks up an' down, all dressed
　　In clobber white.
An', as their snowy forms goes steppin' by,
It seems I'm seekin' somethin' on the sly.

Somethin' or someone—I don't rightly know;
　　But, seems to me, I'm kind er lookin' for
A tart I knoo a 'undred years ago,
　　Or, maybe, more.
Wot's this I've 'eard them call that thing? . . .
　　　　Geewhizz!
Me ideel bit o' skirt! That's wot it is!

Me ideel tart! . . . An', bli'me, look at me!
　　Jist take a squiz at this, an' tell me can
Some square an' honist tom take this to be
　　'Er own true man?
Aw, Gawd! I'd be as true to 'er, I would—
As straight an' stiddy as . . . Ar, wot's the good?

Me, that 'as done me stretch fer stoushin' Johns,
　　An' spen's me leisure gittin' on the shick,
An' 'arf me nights down there, in Little Lons.,
　　Wiv Ginger Mick,
Jist 'eadin' 'em, an' doing in me gilt.
Tough luck! I s'pose it's 'ow a man is built.

It's 'ow Gawd builds a bloke; but don't it 'urt
  When 'e gits yearnin's fer this 'igher life,
On these Spring mornin's, watchin' some sweet
      skirt—
  Some fucher wife—
Go sailin' by, an' turnin' on his phiz
The glarssy eye—fer bein' wot 'e is.

I've watched 'em walkin' in the gardings 'ere—
  Cliners from orfices an' shops an' such;
The sorter skirts I dursn't come too near,
  Or dare to touch.
An' when I see the kind er looks they carst . . .
Gorstrooth! Wot is the *use* o' me, I arst?

Wot wus I slung 'ere for? An' wot's the good
  Of yearnin' after any ideel tart? . . .
Ar, if a bloke wus only understood!
  'E's got a 'eart:
'E's got a soul inside 'im, poor or rich.
But wot's the use, when 'Eaven's crool'd 'is pitch?

I tells meself some day I'll take a pull
  An' look eround fer some good, stiddy job,
An' cut the push fer good an' all; I'm full
  Of that crook mob!
An', in some Spring the fucher 'olds in store,
I'll cop me prize an' long in vain no more.

The little winds is stirrin' in the trees,
  Where little birds is chantin' lovers' lays;
The music of the sorft an' barmy breeze . . .
  Aw, spare me days!
If this 'ere dilly feelin' doesn't stop
I'll lose me block an' stoush some flamin' cop!

Hugh McCrae

Song of the Rain

Night,
And the yellow pleasure of candle-light . . .
Old brown books and the kind fine face of
      the clock
Fogged in the veils of the fire—its cuddling
      tock.

The cat,
Greening her eyes on the flame-litten mat;
Wickedly wakeful she yawns at the rain
Bending the roses over the pane,
And a bird in my heart begins to sing
Over and over the same sweet thing —

Safe in the house with my boyhood's love,
And our children asleep in the attic above.

Gallows Marriage

The king lay a-bed with his queen one night,
And a snow-white dove came on to the sill:
'I am the lass,' said the bird, 'whom your might
Made the poor plaything one day of your will.

'You left me a corse on the road to Dee,
Where the poplars grow and the two ways part;
But a lang-syne gift ye bestowed on me —
The little wee knife they found in my heart.'

'Ye lie!' said the king — but the queen turned
          pale
And her tears fell down like rain from the
          sky —
'May God be my judge if ever this tale
Have aught in it else save the sound of a lie!'

He sprang from his bed to catch at the dove,
When a bow-string sang to the stars without,
And he fell like a knave to a mailéd glove,
With his eyes fast shut, as the world went out.

But the dove sailed down to her own true lad,
Who stood in the shade of the Southgate Tree:
'Johnnie,' she whimpered, 'my good is your
          bad;
The gallows will marry you back to me.'

Names

Long ago, when I was young,
I had trolled upon my tongue
Words like white or golden wine,
Names of ladies fair and fine;
That my loved one might be glad
To be called so by her lad.

All through Monday she would be
Darling Helena to me;
Tuesday found her Christabel;
Every day that we could tell
Brought another silver sound
To ring her pretty presence round.

Unaware, came surly Time,
Dried our blood, and spoiled our prime,
Drew the gallant sunlight down,
Shoved it in his ugly gown;
Stole our bread and cheese and kisses—
'Christabel's' now—just 'The Missus'!

'Furnley Maurice'

(Frank Wilmot)

Praise

'I will praise her sweet gentleness,' I said
And wandered out toward the approaching moon;
I wandered out remembering how red
The sunset was, how sweltering the noon.

A soft grey slip of bush track turned between
Two lonely houses and a sawyer's shed
Into a clump of beech I knew was green
And, rising, lost itself at the spurhead.

'It is her gentleness,' I said aloud—
Or thought sounds noisy in a buried day—
The groaning summer hills screened in a cloud
Of cooling showers had hidden the moon away.

Like leaves in sunlight, rustled words in thought
Trembling upon disclosure. Her sweet worth
Eluded every lead. The slow wind brought
An odour of rain that sunk in the parched earth

'Her goodness!' Why in vanity pursue
That baulk? . . . But I remember to this day
The thirsty ranges fading from my view
In showers and a slim track lost in grey.

'Brian Vrepont'

(B. A. Trubridge)

Night

I watched the pale moon slowly slip,
Inch by inch, till gone;
Shrink like a friend's face on a ship,
Die like a song.

And what was left was emptiness,
And a wind sighing,
The magic and the wistfulness
Of a bird's flying.

The negro night lay woman-still
And fixed her eyes on me,
Casting her ancient secret will
On man and tree.

I felt her supple black hands reach
And finger-tip my eyes;
Her nakedness clung like a leech
About my thighs.

She smothered me with soft, wide lips;
She held me with her stare;
My limbs grew numb beneath her hips;
I breathed her hair.

Cold mists rose ghostly from her breath;
Her hands were clammy-dead;
She sighed; it had the lisp of death;
She raised her head.

She rose, and tiptoed secret back
With a finger on her mouth;
She left a shadow in her track
For lovers' drouth.

Thin leaves stood up and felt the sun,
An earthy, moulding tang
Unbent, a trembling cobweb hung,
And a bird sang.

Ethel Anderson

Doubtful Lover

'Sarsaparilla false has gone
    Where a naughty flower must go,
To that region now has won
    Clematis' pretended snow;
        'Ring-a-ding' the Bell-birds cry,
        'Ting-ling' Christmas knells reply,
        None is sad but I.

'Prinking out the grass with puce
Trigger-flowers trap flies and beat them,
Art, they say, must come with use,
    You have charms, let truth complete them;
        Are those joys which, honey-sweet,
        So entice my eager feet,
        Tell me, are they, too, a cheat?'

Orchard Secret

The dumping plum thumps O! thumps O!
    The apple blushes red.
(Her guilty thoughts have stained her so
    Since Eve was brought to bed.)

The careless fig cares not who past,
    What lovers went her way;
The peach-tree grows with leaves aghast
    At what her boughs might say.

'William Baylebridge'

(William Blocksidge)

From *Love Redeemed*

XXXIX

'All love stands by its sacrament,' they said.
'And, ere this seals it, let no rebel touch!'
Who barter beauty for that piece of bread
Methinks are wise and righteous overmuch.

Ah! this sweet, this, life's myriad sours redeeming,
This grace of the gods, shall priest or statute tell?
Even as a flower is culled for its fair seeming
Blithe love is, springing where and when it will.

Let the world choke! Though all its envy rail,
Our love, found stronger, it shall not prevent.
Nor priest may there nor statute blind prevail;
For love its own law hath and sacrament. —

His right my foe in law took, I in love;
Doth his, or mine, more just and valid prove?

From *Life's Testament*

III

I worshipped, when my veins were fresh,
A glorious fabric of this flesh,
Where all her skill in living lines
And colour (that its form enshrines)
Nature had lavished: in that guess
She had gathered up all loveliness.
All beauty of flesh, and blood, and bone
I saw there; ay, by impulse known,
All the miracle, the power,
Of being had come there to flower.
Each part was perfect in the whole;
The body one was with the soul;
And heedful not, nor having art,
To see them in a several part,
I fell before the flesh, and knew
All spirit in terms of that flesh too.

But blood must wither like the rose:
'Tis wasting as the minute goes;
And flesh, whose shows were wonders high,
Looks piteous when it puts them by.
The shape I had so oft embraced
Was sealed up, and in earth was placed—
And yet not so; for, hovering free,
Some wraith of it remained with me:
Some subtle influence that brings
A new breath to all beauteous things,
Some sense that in my marrow stirs
To make things mute its ministers.
I fall before the spirit so,
And flesh in terms of spirit know—
The Holy Ghost, the truth that stands
When turned to dust are lips and hands.

'Anna Wickham'

(Edith Hepburn)

The Man with a Hammer

My Dear was a mason
And I was his stone.
And quick did he fashion
A house of his own.

As fish in the waters,
As birds in a tree,
So natural and blithe lives
His spirit in me.

The Resource

When I gave you honest speech
You were annoyed,
When I gave you honest love
Your taste was cloyed.
And now I give you silence,
And a smile you take for chaste.
In these things I am less worthy than a harlot,
And your pride has worked this waste.

Song of Ophelia the Survivor

There is no smirch of sin in you only its fires,
You are a man burned white with merciless desires,
A restless heat consumes you, and your brain
Tortured to torturing craves for ugly pain.

Beauty still lives in you and from her seat
Controls your glances and directs your feet,
One look from you taught me so much of love,
I have all pleasure just to watch you move.

That look was like a wet blue mist of flowers
Which held compelling loveliness and sleepy powers.
I dreamed of calling pipes down a warm glade,
By the transposed music of your soul was I betrayed.

Pipe for me, my dear lover. I will come
And your sick soul shall find in me a home,
I will be your house clean, high and strong
And you shall live in me all winter long.

As you are fevered, I will be a pool
Full of green shadows level, silent, cool,
You shall bathe in me, in my being move;
I will put out your fires with my strong love.

A thousand changes shall my love reveal
And all its changes shall have power to heal,
And in the end we'll be as we began:
I will be simple woman, you my man.

Dorothea Mackellar

The Heart of a Bird

What does the bird-seller know of the heart of a bird?

There was a bird in a cage of gold, a small red bird in a cage of
    gold.
The sun shone through the bars of the cage, out of the wide
    heaven.
The depths of the sky were soft and blue, greatly to be longed-for.

The bird sang for desire of the sky, and her feathers shone redder
    for sorrow:
And many passed in the street below, and they said one to another:
'Ah, that we had hearts as light as a bird's!'

But what does the passer-by know of the heart of a bird?

What does the bird-seller know of the heart of a bird?

'I have given grain for you to eat, and water that you may bathe.'
Shall not this bird be content? is there need to clip her wings?
No, for the cage is very strong, the golden bars are set close.
Yet the real bird has flown away, very far away over the rice-fields.
There is only the shadow-body in the cage.

What does the bird-seller care for the heart of a bird?

Riding Rhyme

Mount, mount in the morning dew;
A man loved me when the world was new.

Ride, ride while the dawn is cool:
I was angry and he was a fool.

Ride, ride through the shadows grey:
I told him to go and he went away.

        Ride, ride through the sun's first gold;
        I go alone now the world is old.

        Ride, ride, for your horse is good;
        He never came to me or understood.

        Ride, ride, and you'll travel far;
        I tore my heart out and hid the scar.

        Ride with a man at your bridle-rein—
        My man never will come again.

                Ride, ride, for the sun is strong:
                O but a lonely road can be long!

                Ride, ride, for the light grows dim:
                What of the others? I wanted him.

                Home, home, for the tale is told:
                I was young and now I am old.

The Other Woman's Word

Did you suppose, who are so rich
  In all Love's lovely imagery,
I should not mark the one name which
  You yet have kept from me?

Your love-words clothed me like a queen,
  Dress after shimmering splendid dress
Of flame and flower and jewel-sheen,
  Desire or tenderness.

Around me like a flock of birds,
  So many, only one I missed,
Lighted or flew your coloured words,
  Nestled and sang and kissed.

Wild praise quivered hovering
  About this ordinary head:
Most sweet, most proud, most lovely thing—
  'Dearest' you never said.

Most wonderful and darlingest
  You've called me: those are not the same,
Would you believe I love you best
  For holding back that name?

Not all your jests at law and life,
  Nor all your hot heart's pulse and stir
Could make you rob your cheated wife
  Of what you'd given her.

'Adultery is trivial,
  And faith—ah, what's a word?' you said.
Beloved and most illogical,
  Words are *your* daily bread.

Your bread, your wine. And I, so cold
  So miserly of love, at least
Have given you words that you may hold
  In drought-time, for a feast!

Once When She Thought Aloud

I've had all of the apple, she said,
  Except the core.
All that many a woman desires—
  All and more.

Children, husband, and comfort enough
   And a little over.
Hungry Alice and bitter Anne
   Say I'm in clover.

I've had all of the apple, she said.
   —All that's good.
Whiles I feel I'd throw it away,
   The wholesome food,
Crisp sweet flesh snowy-cool, and skin
   Painted bright—
To have a man that I couldn't bear
   Out of my sight.

J. Alex Allan

The Bride Wakes

Nothing except the knocking of my heart
And your slow breathing, in this room apart,
Faint sounds, like steps on velvet, come and go,
Strange shadows crowd within the portico,
And you lie sleeping close to me, your bride
Half-risen from the pillow at your side.
You, who a handsbreadth from me lie so still,
Why should my heart cry out, who have my will,
Or mourn because you came, though late, to me
Whose love had sought you long and fixédly?
Why should I loose the fountain of my tears
For your past loves and many-pleasured years?
What gain to probe and pry, and find, perchance,
The knowledge that is worse than ignorance?
Yet, if but one dear name of all your store
You had not said to any love before,
Or if I knew that any one caress
Had not been spent on some strange loveliness
Of other time—if I might only own
One phrase or title for myself alone,
I should sleep happier, nor clasp again
These taloned thoughts that tear my heart in twain!

Could you not keep the fresh first love for me
Whom, then, you had not met—your bride to be?
A many loves, they tell me, you have known—
What would my love not give to have been thrown
First of all loves across your path?—and yet
Would I love truer, if I could forget,
Or if your manhood, raw and wondering,
Came to my arms a white unsullied thing?
I love you, knowing all! Is it not, so,
Better than if I loved and *did not know?*
Are you not, now, all mine—the short brown hair
Thinning a little at the temples (where,
Staining the tan, one small blue vein appears)
The thin, strong face, full throat, and close-set ears,
The steady eyes beneath the lids' eclipse.
The little laughter-lines about your lips,
One careless arm the covers thrust among,
Its fellow on the pillow loosely flung—
The hand palm upward—and the straight limbs' length,
The shoulders and the firm, lithe body's strength—
Close-knit, yet as a woman's white and fair—
That I have clothed with kisses everywhere,
The breath that lifts the light hair at my brow . . .
All that is you—I hold and have you now!

O heart of mine, beating so nearly still
For fear to waken him—you have your will
As I have mine: we hold him, you and I,
Heart, and shall hold him, so, until we die!
Naught may unmake the past—'tis better so . . .
And yet, if only, heart, I did not know!

Zora Cross

My Muse

My muse is a minx with a spell for a smile.
   She gallops a waggon of whims through
      the skies,
And teasings capricious and pranks all the while
   She pours upon me who would sing to her eyes.

She coaxes me on like a siren at play,
　　Then leaves me alone with a shadow to doze.
As faithless as Venus, she flits with a fay,
　　Or marries her moods to the rim of a rose.

I went to her house and I opened the door
　　To peep at the exquisite corridors there,
And thousands of dreams that were strewing the
　　　　floor
　　Cried: 'Constancy only can win the most fair.'

And so on her lily-white doorstep I wait,
　　Or wander away with my lover in glee.
Now faithful, now fickle, I toy with my Fate,
　　For I am a maiden as wilful as she.

Thou Shalt Not

Woman, pausing on the marble stair,
　　Come down one . . . come down two;
Death is creaking through the doors of air,
　　And a red, red knife for you.

Woman, lying on the gleaming floor,
　　Warm the blade . . . cold your skin;
Love's a madman when he loves no more,
　　And a heart is hot with sin.

Night-Ride

Faster speed we through the bracken,
Catch me closer to your heart!
Clench the reins before they slacken
Lest the frightened filly start!
Oh, the blazing pennons whirling
Ruby jewels on the grass
And the burnished blossoms curling
Into phantoms as we pass!

Down the slender tongue of tracking
Let her fly, she cannot trip!
Back of us we hear the cracking
Of the scarlet stockman's whip.
He is rounding up his cattle—
Fiery steers and steeds of gold,
Crimson stallions—hear them rattle
Through the forest, fold on fold!

He is groaning with his plunder.
Turn her quickly to the creek!
Though his feet be swift as thunder
We shall hear his angry shriek
As we gallop, helter-skelter,
Through the cool and plashing tide,
To the land of peace and shelter
On the safe and southern side.

On he follows. Nearer, nearer
Ring his brumby's brazen feet.
Clipping-clopping, clearer, clearer—
Death's the fire we must defeat.
Keep your lips on mine, my darling,
Let the flame-flowers lick my hair;
Love can brook the angry snarling
Of their passionate despair.

Cross the creek—he cannot follow!
Love will ever conquer all.
Down we canter through the hollow
Safe at last from scathe and fall.

Thus I fancied we were speeding
All night long, with Love's control,
From our Passion and its pleading
To the safety of our soul.

Nina Murdoch

Warbride

There has been wrong done since the world began,
   That young men should go out and die in war,
And lie face down in the dust for a brief span,
   And be not good to look at any more.

It is the old men with their crafty eyes
   And greedy fingers and their feeble lungs,
Make mischief in the world and are called wise,
   And bring war on us with their garrulous tongues.

It is the old men hid in secret rooms,
   Feign wisdom while they sign our peace away,
And turn fair meadows into reeking tombs,
   And passionate bridegrooms into bloodied clay.

It is the old men should be sent to fight!
   The old men grown so wise they have forgot
The touch of mouth on mouth in the still night,
   The tenderness that wedded lovers wot;

The dreams that dwell in the eyes of a young bride;
   The secret beauty of things said and done;
The hope of children coming, and the pride
   Of little homes and gardens in the sun.

It is the old men that have nought to lose,
   And nought to pray for but their gasping breath,
Should bear this ill of the world, and so choose
   Out of their beds to meet their master, Death.

This is the bitterest wrong the world wide,
   That young men on the battlefield should rot,
And I be widowed who was scarce a bride,
   While prattling old men sit at ease and plot.

Lesbia Harford

I can't feel the sunshine

I can't feel the sunshine
Or see the stars aright
For thinking of her beauty
And her kisses bright.

She would let me kiss her
Once and not again.
Deeming soul essential,
Sense doth she disdain.

If I should once kiss her,
I would never rest
Till I had lain hour long
Pillowed on her breast.

Lying so, I'd tell her
Many a secret thing
God has whispered to me
When my soul took wing.

Would that I were Sappho,
Greece my land, not this!
There the noblest women,
When they loved, would kiss.

The Folk I Love

I do hate the folk I love,
They hurt so.
Their least word and act may be
Source of woe.

'Won't you come to tea with me?'
'Not today.
I'm so tired, I've been to church.'
Such folk say.

All the dreary afternoon
I must clutch
At the strength to love like them,
Not too much.

A Bad Snap

HE   That isn't you.
SHE   It's me, in my blue skirt
And scarlet coat and little golden shoes.
HE   Not good enough.
SHE   Well, burn it if you choose
And take myself.
HE   Yourself like skies and days
To praise and live in, worship and abuse.

I'm like all lovers

I'm like all lovers, wanting love to be
A very mighty thing for you and me.

In certain moods your love should be a fire
That burnt your very life up in desire.

The only kind of love then to my mind
Would make you kiss my shadow on the blind

And walk seven miles each night to see it there,
Myself within, serene and unaware.

But you're as bad. You'd have me watch the clock
And count your coming while I mend your sock.

You'd have my mind devoted day and night
To you and care for you and your delight.

Poor fools, who each would have the other give
What spirit must withhold if it would live.

You're not my slave, I wish you not to be.
I love yourself and not your love for me,

The self that goes ten thousand miles away
And loses thought of me for many a day.

And you loved me for loving much beside
But now you want a woman for your bride.

Oh, make no woman of me, you who can,
Or I will make a husband of a man.

By my unwomanly love that sets you free
Love all myself, but least the woman in me.

Grotesque

My
Man
Says
I weigh about four ounces,
Says I must have hollow legs.
And then say I,
'Yes,
I've hollow legs and a hollow soul and body.
There is nothing left of me.
You've burnt me dry.

You
Have
Run
Through all my veins in fever,
Through my soul in fever for
An endless time.
Why,
This small body is like an empty snail shell,
All the living soul of it
Burnt out in lime.'

You want a lily

You want a lily
And you plead with me
'Give me my lily back.'

I went to see
A friend last night and on her mantelshelf
I saw some lilies,
Image of myself,
And most unlike your dream of purity.

They had been small green lilies, never white
For man's delight
In their most blissful hours.
But now the flowers
Had shrivelled and instead
Shone spikes of seeds,
Burned spikes of seeds,
Burned red
As love and death and fierce futurity.

There's this much of the lily left in me.

Elsie Cole

The Slayers

When we loved, between us two
How the cloudy glamour grew!—
Thoughts unspoken, rainbow tears,
Sweet reserves and darling fears,
Exquisite imaginings
Shyly preening untried wings—
All in one dim radiance blent.
Could we not have been content?

But we judged too daringly
Naught must stand 'twixt You and Me.
Reticence, and secret pride,
What were they but mists that hide?
Break the sundering barrier frail!
Rend the rosy-golden veil!
So we laboured, till at last
Eye to eye we stood, aghast.

The veil was riven shred from shred
All for love . . . and love lay dead.

Leonard Mann

Girls and Soldiers Singing

Young people in the bus began to sing
Popular songs of this war and the last.
Strange that the sentimental words could wring
My older heart! A bus-load in the past
Of such young people I heard sing again
Songs that were hopes of peace; and all in vain
Or else these now had not begun to sing.

But loudly yet the girls and soldiers sang.
They had been picking wild heath then in flower
And their full laps were bowers of the spring.
So from harsh Time they plucked the singing hour.
The bus became a mass of song in flight
Down the road tunnelled through the bush at night
While now of love the girls and soldiers sang.

E. M. England

Incompatibility

Of what avail is this crass bickering?
Our words, like savage shafts in poison dipped,
Cleave each proud heart and come away flesh-tipped,
And still lives on this deep, insidious Thing —
This Love-turned-Hate!
                    Confessions shyly given,
Small acts read wrongly, thoughts misunderstood,
Are now paraded, as of old men would
Bring out their dungeon-food, that it be riven

By the ravening crowd! Love, once insouciant, gay,
And reckless even, is at the driven stake
Bound, stripped; and round it break
Our hates, as flames licked in an older day!
. . . . . Is there no mossy stone of Memory
That, once upturned, might yield the wildest clue
To the sweet primrose-paths that once we knew
—Down which, of old, Romance led you and me.

Bush Girl

If I had been born a dragon-fly in a little, quiet stream,
And drifted into the hot, gold world on the summit of a dream,
If I had been born a bluebell with the high grass quivering round
   me,
And danced there to the magpie's song, and nobody had found
   me . . .

I would have been no happier then. I, too, have the grass for cover.
I, too, have the sun upon my back, and the cloud-ships sailing
   over.
More! there is my shining colt to ride, and I have a tall brown
   lover!

Jack Lindsay

From *Clue of Darkness*

Release

I

And now the gay girl of my body and I
walk the straight streets of our open vows,
turn casual corners, and ever come closer
the enclosed heart of the maze.

Her face in the mirror of my kiss
and her face at the stranger's window are one.
Our dream-dumb words and the words of our mouths
go different ways, but we walk in the sun,

hand in hand, with a marrying smile
through the open streets of our busy days:
and one with the plan of the builded town
is the storm at the heart of the maze.

II

Love is the sweet bird in the nest of our hands.
We are patient and will not wake him before the roses

Outside our door a genuine angel stands,
touching his cap, as the door opens or closes.

III

We shall go out and climb the rungs of fury
and ride the purple horses home to stable.
     and put it in a song
     no bitter noise can wrong.
Bore through the granite mountains with a wishbone,
and count the freckles on a seaside virgin.
     And put it in a tune
     we'll grave upon the moon.
Knock out a star's tooth with a rusty nail
and then outsing the sulky nightingale.
     And put it in a play
     no deaths can blur away.

Mate on our wilful mattress oak and daisy
and raise the towers of Troy from a crackt teacup.
   And put it in a picture,
   a pure abiding rapture.
There is nothing now we cannot do, nothing,
inside the kiss, the accepted wound, the triumph.
   Nothing at all is past
   the nets which we can cast.

Kenneth Slessor

Earth-Visitors

(To N. L.)

There were strange riders once, came gusting down
Cloaked in dark furs, with faces grave and sweet,
And white as air. None knew them, they were strangers—
Princes gone feasting, barons with gipsy eyes
And names that rang like viols—perchance, who knows,
Kings of old Tartary, forgotten, swept from Asia,
Blown on raven chargers across the world,
For ever smiling sadly in their beards
 And stamping abruptly into courtyards at midnight.

Post-boys would run, lanterns hang frostily, horses fume,
The strangers wake the Inn. Men, staring outside
Past watery glass, thick panes, could watch them eat,
Dyed with gold vapours in the candleflame,
Clapping their gloves, and stuck with crusted stones,
Their garments foreign, their talk a strange tongue,
 But sweet as pineapple—it was Archdukes, they must be.

In daylight, nothing; only their prints remained
Bitten in snow. They'd gone, no one knew where,
Or when, or by what road—no one could guess—
None but some sleepy girls, half tangled in dreams,
Mixing up miracle and desire; laughing, at first,
Then staring with bright eyes at their beds, opening their lips,
Plucking a crushed gold feather in their fingers,
And laughing again, eyes closed. But one remembered,
Between strange kisses and cambric, in the dark,
That unearthly beard had lifted . . . 'Your name, child?'
'Sophia, sir—and what to call your Grace?'
 Like a bubble of gilt, he had laughed 'Mercury!'

It is long now since great daemons walked on earth,
Staining with wild radiance a country bed,
And leaving only a confusion of sharp dreams
To vex a farm-girl—that, and perhaps a feather,
Some thread of the Cloth of Gold, a scale of metal,
Caught in her hair. The unpastured Gods have gone,
They are above those fiery-coasted clouds
Floating like fins of stone in the burnt air,
And earth is only a troubled thought to them
That sometimes drifts like wind across the bodies
    Of the sky's women.

There is one yet comes knocking in the night,
The drums of sweet conspiracy on the pane,
When darkness has arched his hands over the bush
And Springwood steams with dew, and the stars look down
On that one lonely chamber . . .
She is there suddenly, lit by no torch or moon,
But by the shining of her naked body.
Her breasts are berries broken in snow; her hair
Blows in a gold rain over and over them.
She flings her kisses like warm guineas of love,
    And when she walks, the stars walk with her above.

She knocks. The door swings open, shuts again.
'Your name, child?'
    A thousand birds cry 'Venus!'

Polarities

Sometimes she is like sherry, like the sun through a vessel of glass,
Like light through an oriel window in a room of yellow wood;
Sometimes she is the colour of lions, of sand in the fire of noon,
Sometimes as bruised with shadows as the afternoon.

Sometimes she moves like rivers, sometimes like trees;
Or tranced and fixed like South Pole silences;
Sometimes she is beauty, sometimes fury, sometimes neither,
Sometimes nothing, drained of meaning, null as water.

Sometimes, when she makes pea-soup or plays me Schumann,
I love her one way; sometimes I love her another
More disturbing way when she opens her mouth in the dark;
Sometimes I like her with camellias, sometimes with a
    parsley-stalk,
Sometimes I like her swimming in a mirror on the wall;
Sometimes I don't like her at all.

R. D. Fitzgerald

Her Hands

When their dumb wings assault the night
with strokes as soft as a caress
dark-haunting birds in secret flight
have not so much of gentleness
as have the movements that are made
by those incomparable hands
with the brown fingers, smooth as jade,
wherethrough my life-thoughts slip like sands.

Remembering how claws and beak
ravage the tenderest night-borne things,
how there's no mercy for the weak
in downy silence, quiet wings,
sorely I dread that those hands dart,
cruel as hunters, toward my dream;
I fear her fingers at my heart
lest they be harder than they seem.

Of Some Country

Though he has loved you and been glad,
his world re-built, his stars made new,
take note of how that fidget-lad
turns to the door, away from you.
He will be split apart and frayed
by sharp distress of shorn farewell;
but you must hear his footsteps fade
down a blown track where none can tell
what bend he took or say what morning
brings back the unlooked-for fugitive,
his arms about you without warning,
and no course left you but forgive.

Oh, girl, you have taken to your side
one as unresting as torn flame,
not of your people, who abide,
but of some country with no name
which rules by shadow of its laws,
flung far yet round him from of old,

till he is fretful for no cause
and leaves you, with his love half told,
to tread burnt roads of sand and gravel
or roads not rational which thrust
where only those would choose to travel
whose thoughts are grittier thirst than dust.

From *Moonlight Acre*

IX

Envy goes groping for the kisses
others have had of your mouth's red;
gropes in morass, and thereby misses
these, flowerlike, which have sprung instead—

these which are ageless and not vexed
by ancient jealousy, old grime,
but span this instant and the next,
trembling upon the edge of time,

hawks hung in the wind above that verge
where all falls bottomless and is nought,
whence the tomorrows shall emerge
which yet are cloudy and unwrought.

Poised at time's focus on strong wings,
like birds turned sharply into the gust,
your kisses have linked me to wise things
saner than envy or distrust:

Space for this moment is not more
than a swollen raindrop, which could burst
here at my lips and spill its store
of riches on my clamouring thirst;

and Now, holding its breath, reveals
how each new summer like saved wine
treasures old summer, and conceals
springs yet ungathered, and all mine.

The Waterfall

We never went back. Doubtless all that we knew
is gone now. Water over the fall
in terms of atoms, molecules, drops, eddies,
is not that water, the same leaping silver;
the trees have tried new leaves year after year;
and we cannot tread twice on the same earth.
Even the grey rocks are not as we saw them,
since light has rushed somewhere out in space
which made them rocks for eyes hardly these eyes.
We might perhaps touch again rough surfaces,
but not with changed hands declare them unchanged.

Nor is it enough to say: 'The mind keeps
days, places, happenings; nothing is lost.'
I would not dispute the mind's vision as truth
or deny its vast permanence; but there is more
to take into account than preserved moments.

For water breaks from the cliff always; and breaks
while we recall it thus breaking long since,
whether or not other eyes watch it now.
Therefore it must be said places endure
more than just in our minds, here, elsewhere,
or at some saved instant; that under change
the changeless breathes air with no taste of time,
apart from men breathing or places breathing
which yet are caught in it—caught in their own shadow
breathing, like moon-shadow that breathes the moon.

A self clings to the changed place, and is
its life still; as the heart knows, perceiving
how what the fall is, is the old thought
of water becoming mist, melting in mist,
of green dripping scrub little more solid
than green mist would be, and of free void
disguised as rock, dropping to final mist.
It is a drift, then a quickening of waters
towards the gay leap to justify being—
a thing surely of spirit, not atoms, molecules;
and so it survives, though we never went back
pushing our way through stiff tea-tree, nor back
to youth and the first days of love—threaded
with beads that mist put in your dress and hair.

Mary Finnin

As You Like It

Swinging the liripipe of an older jest,
Anne's Will, remembering
The running of the deer,
The Lucy keepers in the Charlecote woods,
Ladies that laughed along the terraced walks,
The horny-handed crofters coming home
To alehouse clamour with redundant thirst,
Firelight and broken heads and young men's songs,
Made mirth a touchstone for the spring of life,
Love its high summer,
Death a wintering tree
Grown garrulous.

For a Picture of Lovers in Stained Glass

You have caged light within your long embrace,
Ruby and emerald and sapphire burn—
Brittle, unfading flowers for risen sun
Become a dancing glory.

And worshippers within this cave of stone
Bear your bright image as they pass through light
Into deep peace of shadowed blessedness.
The colours waste like torches, travelling
Through a light beam from window to the floor,
And with them beauty, travelling
Through the fierce rage of passion
To love's large tenderness.

When voices darken, and the eyes that speak
Passionate imaginings are dumb for death,
The fatal stillness of a farewell look
Stands warden 'gainst the fears that stifle breath,
May your bright image steel my heart from storm—
The moment's desolation—vanquish harm:
Love's colour slant translucent through the gloom,
Love's virtue crowd time to a little room.

Approach

Delicate and lovely are the winds
Riding the western roads on throbbing wire,
Threading the organ pines for their own dirge,
Fretting pale water with their unseen hands.

They cannot hear; their own song meshes them
In a great web of sound, impenetrant;
I wait for silence like a wide snowfall
Blotting out tempest in a space of calm.

So shall I hear, each in its silence set,
Footfall of bird, or ragged cry of bat
Quickening the ear, and flood-tide's mastery
Of crabs that edge through shingle to the sea,
Red petal dropping dim, and gentle last—
Your coming in a little wind of haste.

A. D. Hope

The Wandering Islands

You cannot build bridges between the wandering islands;
The Mind has no neighbours, and the unteachable heart
Announces its armistice time after time, but spends
Its love to draw them closer and closer apart.

They are not on the chart; they turn indifferent shoulders
On the island-hunters; they are not afraid
Of Cook or De Quiros, nor of the empire-builders;
By missionary bishops and the tourist trade

They are not annexed; they claim no fixed position;
They take no pride in a favoured latitude;
The committee of atolls inspires in them no devotion
And the earthquake belt no special attitude.

A refuge only for the shipwrecked sailor;
He sits on the shore and sullenly masturbates,
Dreaming of rescue, the pubs in the ports of call or
The big-hipped harlots at the dockyard gates.

But the wandering islands drift on their own business,
Incurious whether the whales swim round or under,
Investing no fear in ultimate forgiveness.
If they clap together, it is only casual thunder

And yet they are hurt—for the social polyps never
Girdle their bare shores with a moral reef;
When the icebergs grind them they know both beauty and terror;
They are not exempt from ordinary grief;

And the sudden ravages of love surprise
Them like acts of God—its irresistible function
They have never treated with convenient lies
As a part of geography or an institution.

An instant of fury, a bursting mountain of spray,
They rush together, their promontories lock,
An instant the castaway hails the castaway,
But the sounds perish in that earthquake shock.

And then, in the crash of ruined cliffs, the smother
And swirl of foam, the wandering islands part.
But all that one mind ever knows of another,
Or breaks the long isolation of the heart,

Was in that instant. The shipwrecked sailor senses
His own despair in a retreating face.
Around him he hears in the huge monotonous voices
Of wave and wind: 'The Rescue will not take place.'

An Epistle

Edward Sackville to Venetia Digby

Ainsi, bruyante abeille, au retour du matin,
Je vois changer en miel les délices du thym.

First, last and always dearest, closest, best,
    Source of my travail and my rest,
The letter which I shall not send, I write
    To cheer my more than arctic night.
Sole day and all my summer in that year
    Of darkness, you were here,
Were here but yesterday, and still I go
    Rapt in its golden afterglow.

Caught in the webs of memory and desire,
  The cooling and the kindling fire,
Through all this house, from room to room I pace:
  Here at the stair we met; this place
You sat in; still I see you sitting there,
  As though some trace the printless air
Retained; a tremulous hush, as though you spoke,
  Enchants its silence; here your cloak
I held for you and here you looked farewell
  And went, but did not break the spell,
By which I feel you here yet know you gone—
  So men, who winking see the sun
And turn into the dark, awhile descry
  His image on the dazzled eye.
But like a tale I tell it all again
  And gloss it with a scholar's pen,
For so Love, though he harvest all his store,
  Gleans in bare fields to make it more.
Now like the garner ant when frosts begin,
  I have my harvest heaped within:
Abundance for my year to come, a feast
  Still cherished, still increased;
For all it spends from its ripe yesterday
  The heart shall copiously repay:
Words, glances, motions, all that I rehearse
  My joy transfigures, as great verse
From music may have a perfection lent
  More than the poet knew or meant;
And as the cunning craftsman can prolong
  Through cadences and shifts of song,
And make what was by nature beautiful,
  By art more dulcet, keen and full,
So from one day, one meeting, I prepare
  Music to last me out the year.

Yet I cannot recall it as I should;
  Too much surprised by joy I stood,
A child who finds his long expected treat,
  Coming, too sudden and too sweet—
Or greedily I gulped it like a beast
  And missed the true, the lasting taste.

'Poor beast,' I say, 'poor beast indeed, who comes
  To be content with scraps and crumbs!
Poor heart, poor Lazarus, overjoyed to wait
  The scrapings of another's plate!'

For, though I could restore, vivid and strong,
　　That late, pure, breathless trance of song,
I know myself but a dumb listener, where
　　I have sung bourdon to her air.

I that was rich, now at the treasury door
　　May only glimpse that golden store
Piled in fantastic heaps; the jewelled shrine
　　Worship, not touch, no longer mine;
At most, a starveling Tantalus, must see
　　The shadow crop upon my tree
Slide through the hand and from my gaping lip
　　The mocking naiad glide and slip.

Or rather—for in similes of woe
　　I lose my way—full well I know
The food was real: 'Twas I who could not eat
　　The spirit's insubstantial meat,
Pleasure of angels, such as flesh and blood
　　Taste not, though all may take their food.
I, who have held you in my human arms,
　　Must gaze as if on ghostly charms,
Or on the painting of a mistress dead—
　　Yet we both breathe and might to bed.
To bed! At the mere thought I feel arise
　　That rebel in the flesh, who cries:
'It was no picture we saw yesterday,
　　But she, in all the living play
Of light on restless body, limbs, hair, breast,
　　Eyes, hands—what need to tell the rest?'
What need? But, ah, what sure recourse of joy!
　　This nothing can or shall destroy,
Custom deny nor honour stand between,
　　Nor your own change of heart demean.
He whose you are, your husband and my friend
　　—I do not grudge it, but commend—
Took, when he took you hence, your picture too
　　Lest I should keep some part in you.

What should I care, who had my gallery lined,
　　Crowded with pictures of the mind?
What care for silk or lute string who possess
　　The splendour of your nakedness,
The lily, the jet, the coral and the rose
　　Varied in pleasure and repose?
Three years we lived as blessed angels do
　　Who to each other show the true

Bareness of spirit and, only when they would
   Travel abroad, wear flesh and blood.
So clothed we met the world: at set of sun,
   Our foolish, needful business done,
Home we would turn, eager to taste at even
   Our native and our naked heaven.
So now by heart each single grace and all
   Their glowing postures I recall.
Absent, you come unbidden; present, you
   Walk naked to my naked view;
Dead, I could resurrect you from your dust;
   So exquisite, individual, just
The bare, bright flesh, I swear my eyes could tell
   You by throat, thighs or breast as well,
Or any least part almost, as your face.

   Alas, as courtiers out of place
Speak of the court, I boast and dream the rest.
   In exile now and dispossessed
I think of how we used, so long ago,
   In that tremendous overthrow
Of our first worlds, when first we loved, first knew
   No world except these selves, this Two,
How we would laugh to see that Last World pass
   For real beyond our Wall of Glass;
And we untouched, untouchable, serene,
   Plighted within our magic screen,
Would pity those without, whose curious eyes
   Could see, could judge, could recognise,
Know with the mind, but coldly and in part,
   Not with the comprehending heart.
This was our game; and, with the growth of love,
   We said, these walls of glass remove;
We re-embody those shadows by our joy;
   The frontiers of desire deploy
Until our latitudes of grace extend
   Round the great globe and bend
Back on themselves, to end where we begin
   Love's wars that take the whole world in.
So little states, rich in great men and sound
   In arts and virtues, gather ground
And grow to empires mighty in their day.
   And we, we said, more blest than they,
Shall not decline as Persian kingdoms do
   Or those the Tartar overthrew.

Who lives outside our universal state?
  And all within ourselves create.
Will angels fall twice, or the moon breed Turks?
  Or dread we our own works?—
But even while the architects designed
  The finials, their towers were mined.
He, your child-lover, twice reported dead,
  Once false—but all was false—some said
He died at Pont-de-Cé, and some said not
  But on rough alps his bones might rot—
For whom, though your heart grieved, it grieved as for
  Childhood itself that comes no more,
Yet came, and not as ghosts come from the grave,
  But as strong spirits come to save,
And claimed the love we buried long ago.
  I watched it rise and live. I know,
Alas, I know, though I believed it not,
  The spell he casts who breaks the knot;
And this you told me once and bade me learn
  Even before his strange return.

Now it is I outside our Wall. I stand
  And once a year may kiss that hand
Which once with my whole body of man made free—
  O, my twice-lost Eurydice,
Twice must I make my journey down to Hell,
  Twice its grim gods by prayer compel,
And twice, to win you only for a day,
  The spirit's bitter reckoning pay,
Yet for my first default their just decree
  Grants me to hear you now and see,
As deserts know peace, as barren waters calms,
  Only forbidding me your arms.
Why, since my case is hopeless, do I still
  Exacerbate this wrench of will
Against the force of reason, honour, rest
  And all that is in manhood best?
Is not this second Orpheus worse than he
  Who perished in his misery,
Torn by the drunken women in their chase
  Among the echoing hills of Thrace?
To cherish and prolong the state I loathe
  Am I not drunk or mad or both?

Not so! These torments mind and heart approve,
   And are the sacrifice of love.
The soul sitting apart sees what I do,
   Who win powers more than Orpheus knew,
Though he tamed tigers and enchanted trees
   And broached the chthonic mysteries.
The gate beyond the gate that I found fast
   Has opened to your touch at last.
Nothing is lost for those who pass this door:
   They contemplate their world before
And in the carcass of the lion come
   Upon the unguessed honeycomb.
There are no words for this new happiness,
   But such as fables may express.
Fabling I tell it then as best I can:
   That pre-diluvian age of man
Most like had mighty poets, even as ours,
   Or grant them nobler themes and powers.
When Nature fashioned giants in the dew
   Surely the morning Muses too
Created genius in an ampler mould
   To celebrate her Age of Gold.
Yet think, for lack of letters all was lost,
   Think Homer's *Iliads* to our cost
Gone like those epics from before the Flood
   As, but for Cadmus, sure they would.

Books now preserve for us the boasts of time;
   But what preserved them in the Prime?
Where did they live, those royal poems then,
   But in the hearts and mouths of men,
Men of no special genius, talents, parts,
   Patience their sole gift, all their arts
Memory, the nurse, not mother, of ancient songs;
   No seraph from God's fire with tongs
Took the live coal and laid it on their lips;
   And yet, until their last eclipse,
Age after age, those giant harmonies
   Lodged in such brains, as birds in trees.
The music of the spheres, which no man's wit
   Conceives, once heard, he may transmit:
Love was that music, and by love indeed
   We serve the greater nature's need.
As on the rough back of some stream in flood
   Whose current is by rocks withstood,

We see in all that ruin and rush endure
    A form miraculously pure;
A standing wave through which the waters race
    Yet keeps its crystal shape and place,
So shapes and creatures of eternity
    We form or bear. Though more than we,
Their substance and their being we sustain
    Awhile, though they, not we, remain.
And, still, while we have part in them, we can
    Surpass the single reach of man,
Put on strange powers and vision we knew not of—
    And thus it has been with my love.
Fresh modes of being, unguessed forms of bliss
    Have been, are mine: But more than this,
Our bodies, aching in their blind embrace,
    Once thought they touched the pitch of grace.
Made for that end alone, in their delight,
    They thought that single act and rite
Paid nature's debt and heaven's. Even so
    There was a thing they could not know:
Nature, who makes each member to one end,
    May give it powers which transcend
Its first and fruitful purpose. When she made
    The Tongue for taste, who in the shade
Of summer vines, what speechless manlike brute,
    Biting sharp rind or sweeter fruit,
Could have conceived the improbable tale, the long
    Strange fable of the Speaking Tongue?
So Love, which Nature's craft at first designed
    For comfort and increase of kind,
Puts on another nature, grows to be
    The language of the mystery;
The heart resolves its chaos then, the soul
    Lucidly contemplates the whole
Just order of the random world; and through
    That dance she moves, and dances too.

Eve Langley

Among Wild Swine in the Woods

But when you fast, come, break the fast with me
In gardens of jewel and ruined fantasy.
Above and far beyond, the great walls pour
Their magic eyes afar, and ever more
The heavens reply, and evermore the seas,
And the lips turn, and the heart no more at ease,
Tastes, wastes and to its ancient rites returns.
Break fast with me before the soft food burns.
The fountain in the lonely place you see,
Was once as you . . . water and ecstasy
Clotted with purple. And his peacock eyes
Filled me with love. That love I now despise.
All things I loved stay with me, but the sweet
And raging storm they nurtured with their heat
Has gone, has vanished. Still my ancient life exhales
The mist of their being, veil on lifted veils.
I am the tree. And love, my long lost leaf,
Rots at my feet in autumns wet with grief.
Behold the years, the images, the men
Thronged on my wall. But is this peace? And then
Behold the war of movement that they wage.
Above within my galleries, the sage
And softly echoed colors of a dream
Rise to my call, and the musics stream
Across my arms, and in the fantasy
Ships are possessed, and bring the cargo, Sea.
Come, break the fast. Put forth your hand and take
The sleeping wine before it rolls awake.
I am busy with enchantments, unashamed.
Sitting white faced, in some lost land, unnamed.
The gift of life was placed upon my palm,
So heavy with loneliness that it brought my arm
Down to the earth, to lie so idle there,
That death may come, and still I shall not care.
Turn not away from me, weary with my pain.
I give the musics and the foods again . . .
The apple and the mother of the soil,
The silken meats, the trodden wine, the spoil
Of all my forests, all myself, and all
That feeds upon the earth within a pall.

Ronald McCuaig

Sydney, A Fine Town

Sydney is a fine town
  And that's quite true,
And I love Sydney
  Because I love you;

I love the long, crooked streets
  The city through;
I've walked them all, side by side,
  At all times, with you;

I love all the ferry-boats
  That dance on the blue,
For I've gone a-voyaging
  In ferries with you;

I love all the theatres
  And picture-shows, too;
You've kissed me in most of them
  When I've kissed you;

But I don't love Shakespeare's
  Bronze statue;
It was there that you left me
  And I left you;

But I do love the alleyway
  Where, in the 'Loo,
We both felt sorry,
  As often we do.

The Hungry Moths

Poor hungry white moths
That eat my love's clothing,
Who says very soon
Ye'll leave her with nothing,
Here under the moon
I make bold to persuade ye,
Ye may eat all her clothes
So ye leave me milady,
Poor
      hungry
            white
                  moths.

Elizabeth Riddell

The Letter

I take my pen in hand
                    there was a meadow
Beside a field of oats, beside a wood,
Beside a road, beside a day spread out
Green at the edges, yellow at the heart.
The dust lifted a little, a finger's breadth,
The word of the wood pigeon travelled slow,
A slow half pace behind the tick of time.

To tell you I am well, and thinking of you
And of the walk through the meadow, and of another walk
Along the neat piled ruin of the town
Under a pale heaven, empty of all but death
And rain beginning. The river ran beside.

It has been a long time since I wrote. I have no news.
I put my head between my hands and hope
My heart will choke me. I put out my hand
To touch you and touch air. I turn to sleep
And find a nightmare, hollowness and fear.

And by the way, I have had no letter now
For eight weeks, it must be
                    a long eight weeks,
Because you have nothing to say, nothing at all,
Not even to record your emptiness
Or guess what's to become of you, without love.

I know that you have cares,
Ashes to shovel, broken glass to mend
And many a cloth to patch before the sunset.

Write to me soon, and tell me how you are.
If you still tremble, sweat and glower, still stretch
A hand for me at dusk, play me the tune
Show me the leaves and towers, the lamb, the rose.

Because I always wish to hear of you
And feel my heart swell, and the blood run out
At the ungraceful syllable of your name
Said through the scent of stocks, the little snore of fire,
The shoreless waves of symphony, the murmuring night.

I will end this letter now. I am yours with love.
Always with love, with love.

Here Lies

*'Weep, if ever you have wept, for this beautiful youth . . . he was on
his way to a café when a prostitute shot him.'* — Inscription on a
tomb on an island in the Aegean Sea.

The lies they set on tombstones live and lie
Forever in cold stone. The way they tell it
He was pure gold, perfect flower of men
Who, wearing his second-best suit and carrying figs
To stop his hunger, went to drink some wine
And play backgammon with other village heroes
Outside the café, in the cypressed dusk.

And was shot. Astonished, he turned then
And offered his hand to the girl
With the gun, and stumbled and died.

What a tragedy, said the gossips
Into their black kerchiefs.
But the stonepines and the swifts
Tell another story.
'She was a good and lovely girl and he betrayed her,
The cockerel, with promises.
So this poor girl (no whore)
Shot him to avenge her honour,
And for all thin girls with big eyes
Who have been robbed of laughter
(For it has happened before).'

Finally she was invited in marriage
By the man who kept the café,
And lived happily ever after
Though avoiding the graveyard
When she walked out at sunset.

The most terrible of all lies
Are those set out with love
Under the weeping angel, the cross and the crouched dove,
On cold stone.

'Autobiography'

Not in the book. She would have thought
to be in the book. Not in the index,
nothing of consequence but honoured by
a footnote or identifying asterisk.

Not in the book the afternoons
in rented rooms when she brought flowers
for the fun of it, for playing at playing house,
to parody the furious surge of love.

There were rooms five stories over the street
or a staircase down, a basement where
through glass, cement and brick
the traffic hissed.

Not in the book the week of snow
near Lincoln, or the other snow
that slowed a train rolling over Minnesota
on Christmas morning, smoke streaking snow,
black claw mark on the snow,
above the snow a frozen sun.

Not in the book the lies, denials and public tears
or how they would separately leave such rooms
in the city's innocent evening,
defaulters, with the crowd of good intent.

Not in the book where his life's displayed,
arranged, accounted for.

Still she looks for clues, and finds one.
He has smuggled her into a line of print
as once across a frontier. She can close the book.

Walter Adamson

For Non-Swimmers

A lyric-minded eskimo
sat quietly at his deskimo
and put on paper white as snow
'o eskima I love you so'.

An answer came into his igloo
which tickled him and made him giggloo
and melted all the snow around
until the loving poet drowned.

They dug for him a little hole
and buried him quite near the pole.
His epitaph was short and grim:
'To all the poets: Learn to swim!'

Hector Monro

From *Don Juan in Australia*

XXI

And yet she was the very incarnation
    Of all men's daydreams: lovely, languorous,
Her bare existence was a stimulation
    For passions which, though fierce and clangorous,
Yet have as their surprising culmination
    That dreamy peace where none can anger us.
She was (what else would Fate beget her for?)
Libido's animated metaphor.

XXII

Her glance spoke volumes, each one rated X,
    Her walk was the whole Kama-sutra potted,
Her slightest gesture coyly murmured: Sex!
    Her smile would make an anchorite besotted.
An actress, she was not one to perplex
    Her fans in dramas intricately plotted
But roused dark passions, clamorous and urgent,
In television ads for some detergent.

XXIII

Her looks were stimulating, but that word
    Would not, you'd think, describe her conversation,
And yet I doubt if that had once occurred
    To any man as worth consideration
For, when they talked to her, she always heard
    Their chatter with small gasps of admiration.
What was there left to find remiss in her
Who'd made herself the perfect listener?

XXIV

Juan with her found undissembling bliss
    Unsicklied by the palest cast of thought.
No anti-masculine hypothesis
    Intruded on the joys Amanda brought.
Life seemed to him one never-ending kiss
    For which eternity would be too short
Until one day (perhaps the gods were jealous?)
It struck him that her men friends were too zealous.

John Bray

Lust and Love

Lust's an honest robber,
Bludgeoning for sex.
Love's a whining con-man,
Passing phony cheques.

Lust is intermittent,
Sups his fill and sleeps.
Love from dawn to sunrise
Castigates or creeps.

Lust is standard issue—
Men or pigs or geese.
Love's a visitation
From some god's caprice.

Lust can be diverted
Towards another goal.
Love is monomanic,
Compass to the pole.

Yet some say the prize piece
Life's mint ever coined
Comes when by some chance freak
Lust and love are joined.

Margaret Diesendorf

Modigliani Nude

So awkwardly you wrote your name
    into the upper left corner,
as if looking too long at her loved body
    had sapped all your strength,
this counting of the red roses there—
    desires your brush meant to
        conceal . . .

For years now, you have both been dead,
    your sense's fire sealed in ash,
but the red roses burn in her canvas lap.

Selections from *Holding the Golden Apple*

Morning,
    my feet ache with the need of loving
you.
    I have a dancer's feet,
narrow, arched & spirited:
    they urge for the corporal dance,
to feel you, stroke you . . . &
    sometimes threaten
to trample you
        with pony hooves.
    There's more tenderness
in my feet
    than in the hands
of a hundred wives.

●

She puts Juno in the shade,
like the red rose in summer
she exudes her own light.

Unnoticed, in the leafwork
of the garden, *I* stand nude
holding the golden apple.

●

Yesterday I took off all my rings:
    the ones that bound me to the dead,
the one that bound me to the living
    (so I thought)
but my bare hands
        do not make me feel free . . .
    besides, I miss the glitter of the gems,
the lights of the blue opal
        above all.
    But then: the one to whom we all remain bound
needs no symbols
        & if he did
    they would be as dark as the starless night,
at best as heliotrope or black jasper.
    He will claim his right,
            rings or not.
The bond is absolute.

Love has occupied the den of my heart.
Now she sits at the mouth & howls night &
day at the moon & the sun.
                                She has etched
your wolf-face into its unbreachable
walls with fire & brimstone & drives away
all her rivals with a fierce flick of paw;
& sits there, long after, fletching her teeth.

Barbara Giles

Eve Rejects Apple

In serene sixties strolling in the Louvre,
I am accosted, and being old enough,
I answer, to have him take my arm.
'Voulez-vous vous promener? I am Michel,
I come from the South. Are you alone in Paris?
Now you have a friend.' Stating a preference for pictures,
like an old player I elude his grasp.
The swarthy hunter is hot after the quarry, renewing
his clutch on my arm, and dangling the ultimate bait.
'I want to sleep with you. I much prefer
an older woman. The young are acid, raw.
You are alone. No one will know what you do.
Here is your chance to live!' My unkind laughter
releases me to enquire of a ripened lady, who kindly
points me the way to the Dürer, and I go
happy in that I have repelled seduction
entirely in French.

In the Park, Looking

I'm not too old to like the shape of a man,
his walk, the set of his head on his shoulders,
the strong legs, well fleshed, and that bright,
dark-browed glance. There's a nose that I like,
admiring blank-faced. If you should
see me looking, if you saw me at all,
you'd think I'm reminded of someone,
husband, son, grandson, not that I look at you
as a woman looks at a man who stirs her.

The heart lifts, it's good to see a fine man,
to think — there goes a man I could love.
I'm looking at you, not remembering.
But as I well know, you don't see me,
old women are almost invisible. If I do catch your eye,
likely enough you'll be thinking, 'She has a look of my
    mother.'

Oh I will cut him up on little stars . . . (Juliet)

She married less for love than loving:
Candle against the dark.
How hard to refuse the hot rejoicing flesh,
those grown-up-children's games a glance could spark.

Such joys poured in their laps, such romps,
such innocent frolics, such discoveries,
all without fee, fun-cornucopia, without
one cerebral stir, tussle of wills or jealousies.

Oh, those came later, when she found she'd married
her father. These were his terms, as read —
sweeties and toys, for kisses from a pliant darling.
The stage machinery creaks. Scene 1. The bed.

And 2. The mismatched pair, selfish, ambitious,
sharp-tongued and obstinate, quarreling at their dinner.
He's found new comforters, she success and praise.
Scene 3. The bed. He's run to fat, she's thinner,

their tumblings now routine, a conscious anodyne.
Scene 4. You've guessed. No need to be explicit.
Informed, fatigued, unlinked, they fall apart.
Rudely he snatches at his walking ticket.

Roland Robinson

The Water-Lubra

Nalul came out of the desert,
out of the red sand glare,
down to a deep green water
came Nalul with long bound hair.

He heard, in a noon of silence,
when only the deep shade is cool
voices and splashings and laughter
that came from a reeded pool.

He passed over sunlight and shadow
and saw where the stirred water shone.
He caused the tall reeds to tremble.
The splashings and laughter were gone.

He came where a water was flowing
suddenly out of the ground,
and heard, as he paused in drinking,
a voice like the water's sound.

He moved as a passing shadow
and saw, on the river sand there,
the water-lubra who sang as
she shook out her streaming hair.

He moved as the eagle stooping,
and caught at her flying feet,
and wound her hair on his forearm
for her gleaming teeth to meet.

He bound her at wrists and ankles,
she cowered in his fire's smoke.
He touched her shrinking shoulders,
and a word for her name he spoke.

She followed him into the desert.
They passed over sand and stone,
and scooped at the soaks for water
where the desert-oak stands alone.

They came to the spear stone ranges,
and crossed where his hunting led,
and they came to a lilied water
left in a river-bed.

She pleaded to drink where the slender
white egret rose in flight.
She waded between the lilies,
then dived and swam from his sight.

And Nalul camped in the white sand
moaning his love songs there,
but never rose out of the water
his lubra with streaming hair.

Gymea

She rips up his past. Lacerated,
he smashes on her parquet floor
the hand painted plaque of glazed
camellias he gave her; swears he'll
smash seven years of slashing cat,
murder throated dog; no communication
but one.
　　　　　She's planted in her garden,
before he came, a 'bush-lily'. He saw
the shock of long bladed leaves, spat
'Gymea', in contempt. Then, after
seven years, it shot up its fifteen
feet spear. Its dark red bud burst—
a shock of long buds. Split, they sprang
out into fleshy, orchid like flowers—
branched, pollen green stamens standing
out of centres filled with thick
semen nectar.
　　　　　Solitary, savage, his
lust thrust through to her at last—
a barbaric phallus, burst,
burning in her cultivated garden.

John Blight

Conversation

Talking about life instead of
living is part of life I liked
with Lucille Love who kept a pet
tongue she let outside the cage of
her white smiling teeth for laughter.

I have been with her when she has
shut that cage on my finger, with
peals of laughter outside and,
oh,
how we laughed together inside.

Then she would talk on longer like an
old spinster, until there would
arrive the moment of silence,
then the action of life's renewal.

Afterwards, was there the hint
of death for a while?

We would lie, silent — so silent
that only bees toiling in
the white flowering clover would
remind us that we were two people
lost without life's conversation.

Flexmore Hudson

Waiting for a Letter

Though I could hardly bear
the pain, I still was thinking
of the silence you have kept since parting-day.
So when a round gold moon came rolling
up the long white road on the skyline
and the sullen cloud near hovering
swooped and smothered it with gray,
such bitter wistfulness was mine,
I didn't care, I didn't care.

The Sorrow of Earth

Deserts my love had turned
to pastures where waters pour,
the sorrow of others has burned
to deserts once more.

This is the germ that poisons
action, and starves our blood;
the drought that degrades swift visions
to stagnant mud.

Tears, all the deaf world through,
cry must there always be war,
the poor go shamed, the Jew
homeless evermore?

Cry, while my blood runs hot
burning your body's kiss,
why everywhere Time is not
always like this?

The Kiss

(For Bronnie Norman)

Because my lips construed her cheek
as lorikeet light on a wattle creek,

today I learnt that soursobs meant
distant thrushes by their scent,

while cicada chirrs, to my listening eyes,
were a rippling heat-haze in disguise.

And since her laughter shook again
almond blossom down the rain,

the gannet stitching the silver swell
rang on my tongue a muscat bell,

while the purr of the reef where the surf broke
was a kitten wind my hand could stroke.

A Sleep of Grief

Because we two that love must lie alone,
because my tears are aching to be born
and the blue day a vast and hateful eye,
sleep sends me climbing a winter mountain worn
by rain as passionate as your heart is shy,
until I scale a peak of naked stone
where the wind savaging the wounded sky
is a tiger fanged and cruel as our pain.
And there at last I weep, secure from scorn
of stars or sun, for tears don't show in the rain.

Joyce Lee

Double Wedding

My aunt, youngest of eleven
sent to light the church, remembers
people in the dark, waiting
for a festival. Running
breathless she warned the family,
'By eight there'll be no room.'

My grandfather, trailing bridesmaids
and flower girls, a cream silk bride
on each arm, in his proudest moment,
a small man floating through the crush,
surrendered his loves
to ranked bridegrooms and best men.

On Sunday, in his blossoming garden,
photographers arranged Murtoa's
fashion peak, long-trained brides,
maids all mauve, beribboned
shepherd crooks and lampshade hats.

One of twenty pictures survives.

At the Melbourne train, a bride
soft in travelling grey,
kissed a new cousin rapturous goodbye.
'Isn't it wonderful.
I'm going away, *alone*, with Harold.'

Kenneth Mackenzie

How Full Kate is . . .

How full Kate is, of me and her and a soul!
How she does writhe, about the belly, in sleep!
And how I love her swollen, genial bole
that in its trunky vastness scarce can keep
the kicking limbs and contours of the child
whom she and I begot, giving love for love,
embrace for embrace, orgasm on orgasm piled
like heaps of molten gold poured out above

the sardine, purblind flesh! How dare I know
less rich, more fainting actions, when we two
have engineered a third estate, that'll grow
like us, in pain, and as we in pleasure grew—
    each having a heart, strong loins, good mind, and breath;
    each born in love, in striving, and in death.

Tripoli

'They're bombing Tripoli,' she said
    as she passed by the sealing door,
and there upon the tumbled bed
    and here upon the kindly floor
we sat and laughed about the dead
    as we had never laughed before.

What trembling madness of the blood,
    hysteria of the flesh, the bone,
behind that door of painted wood
    possessed us? We were not alone,
for through the transom's open hood
    came souls of soldiers, one by one.

Jealous of life, they watched us both
    lean close together, laughing still
as, hand to hand and mouth to mouth,
    we argued out desire and will.
Who were more noble and uncouth,
    we or the dead men? Who can tell!

The Moonlit Doorway

The peacock-eye of the half-moon long since up;
the peacock-blue of the iridescent sky
moonlit to starless pallor; the scream of peacocks
across the bay from here mock night together
outside my windows—a wild, gritty scorn,
a jeer at memory, a blue-lit laughter
at man and me.
    Once, though, there was a doorway
set full of night and this same genial pallor
of moon-made sky-magic. Memory
does not give jeer for jeer. Memory's faithful
and so am I to memory—even tonight

when the imperial birds across the bay
scream out their scornful warning through the light
of blue darkness. 'She was white and golden
in that dark room the moonlight entered no more.
She was a pale woman lying there
whom you have never seen, whom you have known
well at night only—never well by day.'
And that mad scream through the doorway of my windows,
though less with distance, still cries out 'Beware.'
Beware of you, it says, your man's fallibility
in keeping faith. Beware of moons and midnights
lest the white body of the beloved suffer
a sad sky-change, and through that moonlit doorway
pass headlong into the hell of discontent,
the double hell of conscience and of scorn,
the final hell of hate. Beware, beware . . .
    Of what I say. Of my heart? Of my mind?
Of the dark entry of this blood and flesh
into that younger and more innocent
flesh and blood, when the night was not far worn?
And I say, this was my fortune and delight,
and my long dreamed yet long withheld desire—
but more yet: my momentary destiny
that dream should harden into softest flesh
which, melting to the tongue, almost returns
to dream. This was my fortune, that her breasts
should stand upright and for an hour or more
tell me this body warmed and tensed and turned
with love to mine. This was my fine reward
for nothing more than kisses and caresses—
that in some hour or two there should have been
utter forgetfulness of me and life
in the profundity of face-to-face
against a doorway full of the moonlit sky,
silence, solitude, and she and I
alone and together.
    Against the moonlit doorway is a tree,
flowered with a sparse but vigorous red by day
and black as a groping hand's lean skeleton
at night, when the moon's high. As I lay looking
I thought you had flown into it like a bird,
my child, my darling, silent and solitary
and watchful of the peacock treachery
of night, like a wary bird above the pool
of green lawn and new coming-together,
green knowledge and new understanding,
question, request, confession, answer, silence

as still as water. Then you were there again
with laughter in your mouth (I could not see
your clear eyes laughing in that silken darkness)
and in your hands a sudden secret cunning
as the desire and the will were mixed into
the slow and speechless deed itself. The tree
clawed kindly at the opal of the sky
with its red talons, and your own hands
are a mile away from you in space; and you
are a mile away from me, in space and time
and in intention. I, the servitor,
the bolder yet more humble of us two
who so astonishingly lie together,
am here no longer; I am in your body,
and, as the tree grown out of earth is earth,
so am I you, and you are my protection
against the tempests of the hated surface.
And into you I shall dissolve at last
with a great falling crash and sigh, contented.
    With your cool graveness of a painted angel,
what do you think of, child, bedded in darkness
with your feet towards the peacock-coloured panel
of the open door? Just that the game is over?
Just that the night is cold and I am warm?
(This is what we were made for.) Just that the doorway
is beautiful in its silky moonlit splendour
slashed once with the dagger-sounds of a dog's barking
and once again with the unholy cry
of the royal birds impassioned by the night?
Tell me now — so long afterwards but so soon —
what you think lazily about, stretched here at ease
across my arm and shoulder and my heart.
Or yet — these are your own words — why should you speak?
I speak enough for both. My tongue's uncaged,
the padlock opened by a key of passion,
the door sprung wide, the wooing moon of love
luring it out and on, across the lawns,
down through the trees of your own silences
into the valley of your quiet body,
into the shadow of your lidded eyes,
between the moonlike mountains of your bosom,
through the whole world that's you, until it falls
silent, and with a sigh we almost sleep.

Through the tall moonlit doorway night looks in,
and once again the peacocks cry at us.

In this pain-enchanted place . . .

In this pain-enchanted place
quiet beats the heart,
quiet turns the passing face,
of pain a part.
Still the step and stayed the hand
stretched to aid
Pain alone can understand
and be glad.

Thought lies down in my white bed:
I embrace it here.
Every fear I ever had
is no more fear:
every shame I ever earned
shame no more,
starved and purged and dried, turned
into a star.

Let no love come near me now
nor its slave desire:
I am where all light is low
till pain shall tire
and let its engine throb to death
in my hand.
Waiting, the quiet heart and breath
understand.

Douglas Stewart

As the Crow Flies

It's not so far as the crow flies
Lady from me to you;
But it's far and it's far for the little cock wren
With his head and his ruff of blue;
And over the mountains it's miles to go
For the lazy wings of the crane
Who screamed for love like a ship on the rocks
Then dropped to his fishing again.

Straight he would go that shrewd old crow
Like a blacktracker over the sky;
But the ducklings would run for the reeds my dear
When they saw his shadow go by;
The bold red lory may fly through the gums
But fiery and brief he flashes,
And the bald old coot with his twitching tail
Can hardly clear the rushes.

'I squeak and I twitch,' said the silly old coot,
'But the best of love is its laughter;
Wait, I am coming, my chick, my feather,'
Then he fell on his head in the water.
'I'll bring you a frog,' said the lazy crane,
'A tadpole, a trout or a perch;
I'll fish for another hour and then——'
And the bride she waits at the church.

The gay blue wren he longed to shine
On a lady's hand or breast;
He flew and he flew till his wings fell off
And the red ants got the rest.
Crimson and bold from his mountain home
The lory came in his glory,
But the flash of his wings set the sky on fire,
You wouldn't like the story.

It's not so far as the crow flies,
But soft are your lips my dear;
How would you like that beak at your mouth,
The sound of that voice at your ear?
Sighing and cawing and croaking and tolling
Of bushfire ages ago—
Oh, what would you do with a crow, my love,
What would you do with a crow?

J. M. Couper

Selections from
Letters to Aunt Welch in the Year of Her Death

Drunk with the sight of life, fair drenched with living I was,
my cronies the sun and the sea, and we raked that length of shore,
clean believed it was us that the Crawton was for,
reached out, and near drew ón, the sleeves of the braes

green and blue and gold like football jerseys.
My, but yon passionate summers lasted the whack of the year.
Kept quick hold on the night, too: attics yawning the air.
Then, on the heels of the whole of that heaven, the lasses.

Shallow picnics of flesh we soon took on.
Oh, but what a fasherie at that green growth!
It was only the dooking: it was tennis: the telegraph time of youth:
me and my body starving in great admiration.

Lord, but I led a thankful life as a lad
in the sacraments and great rampages we did.

fasherie = fuss
dooking = bathing

●

You used to tell me how the Elizabethans
shot off sonnets as if their mistresses,
that fired them into passionate utterance,
were bullets, and their poets blunderbusses.

We served out writs of critical Habeas Corpus
wandering disappointed among the trim
cemeteries of their sequences
filled with many a feminine empty tomb.

Never spied the skerrick of living woman.
Strangulated goddesses they made.
The necrophilic victim: Beauty's totem
put in smooth pentameter to bed.

So turn in your chair, Aunt Welch, cry the rest of them ben.
Grim Scotsmen ken the quick of any feeling needs live women.

●

Be pleased to hear about this. There came a lass
and looked about the house, and took to its ways
as though she had some bidding about the place
and nipped about it naked in her pyjamas.

Fine do I hear your spiering, Was it wise?
and if you would take my answer: Well, it was,
for love was her credential and she was a part of us.
Possessions, the lad and she were hers and his.

It was just that the years were credited with their lives,
a sport of book-keeping generous and feminine,
my wife away at her daughter's lying-in

of a daughter, and then this next among the wives.
In the mightiful feck of its women, and women-to-be,
my, but the family endures its immortality.

spiering = asking
feck = crowd

Patrick Hore-Ruthven

In Palestine

Where does my lover lie?
Under what blinding sky
Dead, or prepared to die?
Where lies my lover?

Does the soul swiftly fly,
Soaring exultantly?
Or like a butterfly
Hesitant hover?

Or as the peregrine
Stoops to the hardly seen
Prey, strikes the unforeseen
Death to my lover?

What stone in Palestine
Pillows what once was mine?
Bloody now lies the fine
Head of my lover!

And does the spark divine
In his black eyes still shine
Or has the spirit fine
Bravely passed over?

Would that my breast could hold
That which now lies so cold;
God! Give me back the bold
Head of my lover!

Dorothy Auchterlonie

A Problem of Language

How praise a man? She cannot vow
His lips are red, his brow is snow,
Nor celebrate a smooth white breast
While gazing on his hairy chest;
And though a well-turned leg might please,
More often he has knobbly knees;
His hair excites no rapt attention—
If there's enough of it to mention.
She cannot praise his damask skin,
Still less the suit he's wrapped it in;
And even if he's like Apollo
To gaze upon, it does not follow
That she may specify the features
That mark him off from other creatures.
No rime can hymn her great occasion
But by a process of evasion;
And so she gives the problem over,
Describes her love, but not her lover,
Despairs of words to tell us that
Her heart sings his magnificat.

Present Tense

'Nothing can ever come of it', he said.
—Outside the window, the white rose waved its head,
A late bird sang, insouciant, in the tree,
The sunset stained the river red.

'There is no future, none at all', he said.
—She stretched her arms up from the tumbled bed:
'What future has the river or the rose?' said she,
'The bird's song is, and nothing comes of red.'

He held her as the river holds the red
Stain of sunset; as, when the bird has fled,
The tree holds the song. 'Listen,' said she,
'Bird, rose and sunlit water sing from this bed.'

'The Hollow Years'

It is a bitter thing to love
When the womb is dry,
Without the Chagall homunculus
In the mind's eye.

It is a bitter thing to love
When the womb is dry,
And the spiral promise sinks
To a lipless cry.

It is a bitter thing to give
As proof of the heart
The fruit of the mind's womb
In a work of art

And watch the begetter
Set it aside
Like a disowned child
On a cold hillside.

What shall she do now
To leave for a sign
That perfection blessed once
Her solitary vine?

David Campbell

Come Live with Me

HE   Come live with me and we'll be drovers;
When stars are lambing in the rivers,
By couples we will count the sheep
Yet kiss before we go to sleep.

All summer down the Lachlan-side
We'll sing like Clancy as we ride
Till hawks hang charmed above the plain
And shearing-time comes in again.

For love of you I'll ring the shed,
And we'll have breakfast served in bed
By slattern maids in cotton caps,
And go to work at noon perhaps.

SHE   And in a basket I will keep
      The skirtings of the finest sheep
      For spinning tights for ballet-girls
      With combs and cutters in their curls;

      And they will dance at each smoke-oh
      For your delight upon the toe
      And bring you beer and violets
      In garlands for your gallon hats.

      With mistletoe I'll crown my hair
      And sing most sweetly to the air,
      'Since Time's a shearer, where's the sin
      In kissing in the super-bin?'

We Took the Storms to Bed

We took the storms to bed at night
When first we loved. A spark
Sprang outward from our loins to light
Like genesis the dark.

On other things our minds were bent,
We did not hear the Word,
But locked like Sarah in her tent
The listening belly heard.

And though we wept, she laughed aloud
And fattened on her mirth:
As strange as creatures from a cloud
Our children walk the earth.

Lovers' Words

Like swallows, no, like hawks they live
And take the minute on the wing
And pick it bare. Love is a thing
They seek to prove or else disprove.
Selfish, unstable, on the move,
They die unless an eagle sing,
While we have time for hovering,
To brood a season on our love.

O lovers' words are mostly lies,
Their cross-my-heart and I-love-you
Are lessons learned to win a prize,
Extorted, or for payment due.
How sweet it is with open eyes
To say, I love, when it is true.

From *Two Songs with Spanish Burdens*

I   A Grey Singlet

I was washing my lover's grey shearing singlet
When a squatter drew rein beside our quince tree
On a red impatient horse, with me at the copper:
And 'How much do you want for that stinking shirt?'
    says he.

Though his singlet is grey, his skin is a lily.

'A semi-trailer load of trade wethers would not buy it,
Nor a pen of prime lambs sappy from their mothers,
Nor a yarding of vealers with a leg in each corner,
Nor a mob of springing heifers with the dew on their
    nostrils.'

Though his singlet is grey, his skin is a lily.

'Not for a white homestead with a verandah all around it
And in vine-shade a waterbag of cool well water,
Thyme crushed on stone paths and bruised plums in
    the orchard,
Would I sell my lover's singlet to a show-off on horse-
    back.'

Though his singlet is grey, his skin is a lily.

John Manifold

The Griesly Wife

'Lie still, my newly married wife,
    Lie easy as you can.
You're young and ill accustomed yet
    To sleeping with a man.'

The snow lay thick, the moon was full
  And shone across the floor.
The young wife went with never a word
  Barefooted to the door.

He up and followed sure and fast,
  The moon shone clear and white.
But before his coat was on his back
  His wife was out of sight.

He trod the trail wherever it turned
  By many a mound and scree,
And still the barefoot track led on
  And an angry man was he.

He followed fast, he followed slow,
  And still he called her name,
But only the dingoes of the hills
  Yowled back at him again.

His hair stood up along his neck,
  His angry mind was gone,
For the track of the two bare feet gave out
  And a four-foot track went on.

Her nightgown lay upon the snow
  As it might upon the sheet,
But the track that led on from where it lay
  Was never of human feet.

His heart turned over in his chest,
  He looked from side to side,
And he thought more of his gumwood fire
  Than he did of his griesly bride.

And first he started walking back
  And then began to run
And his quarry wheeled at the end of her track
  And hunted him in turn.

Oh, long the fire may burn for him
  And open stand the door,
And long the bed may wait empty:
  He'll not be back any more.

Song

My dark-headed Käthchen, my spit-kitten darling,
You stick in my mind like an arrow of barley;
You stick in my mind like a burr on a bear,
And you drive me distracted by not being here.

I think of you singing when dullards are talking,
I think of you fighting when fools are provoking;
To think of you now makes me faint on my feet,
And you tear me to pieces by being so sweet.

The heart in my chest like a colt in a noose
Goes plunging and straining, but it's no bloody use;
It's no bloody use, but you stick in my mind,
And you tear me to pieces by being so kind.

David Martin

Geometry

To drink a glass of wine is good
But to drink two is better.
To love two women is like loving
Christ and the Devil together.

To make a song of love is sweet
But to make love is sweeter.
Who loves two women finds his song
Grow inward and turn bitter.

Who seeks to make the circle square
Shall see his reason vanish,
But who would square the triangle
Venus will blind and punish.

Judith Wright

Woman to Man

The eyeless labourer in the night,
the selfless, shapeless seed I hold,
builds for its resurrection day—
silent and swift and deep from sight
foresees the unimagined light.

This is no child with a child's face;
this has no name to name it by:
yet you and I have known it well.
This is our hunter and our chase,
the third who lay in our embrace.

This is the strength that your arm knows,
the arc of flesh that is my breast,
the precise crystals of our eyes.
This is the blood's wild tree that grows
the intricate and folded rose.

This is the maker and the made;
this is the question and reply;
the blind head butting at the dark,
the blaze of light along the blade.
Oh hold me, for I am afraid.

From *The Blind Man*

II   Country Dance

The dance in the township hall is nearly over.
Hours ago the stiff-handed wood-cheeked women
got up from the benches round the walls
and took home their aching eyes and weary children.
Mrs McLarty with twenty cows to milk
before dawn, went with the music stinging
like sixty wasps under her best dress.
Eva Callaghan whose boy died in the army
sat under the streamers like a house to let
and went alone, a black pot brimming with tears.

'Once my body was a white cedar, my breasts the buds on the
    quince-tree,
that now are fallen and grey like logs on a cleared hill.
Then why is my blood not quiet? what is the good
of the whips of music stinging along my blood?'

The dance in the township hall is nearly over.
Outside in the yard the fire like a great red city
eats back into the log, its noisy flames fallen.
Jimmy Dunn has forgotten his camp in the hills
and sleeps like a heap of rags beside a bottle.
The young boys sit and stare at the heart of the city
thinking of the neon lights and the girls at the corners
with lips like coals and thighs as silver as florins.
Jock Hamilton thinks of the bally cow gone sick
and the cockatoos in the corn and the corn ready to pick
and the wires in the thirty-acre broken.
Oh, what rats nibble at the cords of our nerves?
When will the wires break, the ploughed paddocks lie open,
the bow of the fiddle saw through the breast-bone,
the dream be done, and we waken?

Streamers and boughs are falling, the dance grows faster.
Only the lovers and the young are dancing
now at the end of the dance, in a trance or singing.
Say the lovers locked together and crowned with coloured paper:
'The bit of black glass I picked up out of the campfire
is the light that the moon puts on your hair.'
'The green pool I swam in under the willows
is the drowning depth, the summer night of your eyes.'
'You are the death I move to.' 'O burning weapon,
you are the pain I long for.'

Stars, leaves and streamers fall in the dark dust
and the blind man lies alone in his sphere of night.

Oh, I,
red centre of a dark and burning sky,
fit my words to music, my crippled words to music,
and sing to the fire with the voice of the fire.
Go sleep with your grief, go sleep with your desire,
go deep into the core of night and silence.
But I hold all of it, your hate and sorrow,
your passion and your fear; I am the breath
that holds you from your death.
I am the voice of music and the ended dance.

The Man Beneath the Tree

Nothing is so far as truth;
nothing is so plain to see.
Look where light has married earth
through the green leaves on the tree.

Nothing is so hard as love—
love for which the wisest weep;
yet the child who never looked
found it easily as his sleep.

Nothing is as strange as love—
love is like a foreign land.
Yet its natives find their way
natural as hand-in-hand.

Nothing is so bare as truth—
that lean geometry of thought;
but round its poles there congregate
all foliage, flowers and fruits of earth.

Oh, love and truth and I should meet,
sighed the man beneath the tree;
but where should our acquaintance be?
Between your hat and the soles of your feet,
sang the bird on top of the tree.

'Dove–Love'

The dove purrs—over and over the dove
purrs its declaration. The wind's tone
changes from tree to tree, the creek on stone
alters its sob and fall, but still the dove
goes insistently on, telling its love
          'I could eat you.'

And in captivity, they say, doves do.
Gentle, methodical, starting with the feet
(the ham-pink succulent toes
on their thin stems of rose),
baring feather by feather the wincing meat:
          'I could eat you.'

That neat suburban head, that suit of grey,
watchful conventional eye and manicured claw—
these also rhyme with us. The doves play
on one repetitive note that plucks the raw
helpless nerve, their soft 'I do. I do.
                    I could eat you.'

Eve Scolds

Still so entrepreneurial, vulgarly moreish,
plunging on and exploring where there's nothing
left to explore, exhausting the last of our flesh.
Poor Natura; poor Eve.
Sungods are parvenu. I never could believe
that old rib-story you told.
You, to come first? It was Night, Water,
Earth, Love, I.
You Adam, son of the Sun—
you thought his maleness chose
you out of the unshaped clay
(his huge masculine beard, his dictator-hand
giving you strength). But I—
I *was* the clay. Little boys
have to invent such tales.
It's insecurity—always your trouble. You say
I nag you, hag of the night
drawing attention to your weaknesses.

But my trouble was love—
wanting to share my apples. You
called that temptation, put us both in with Him.
Not fair; I should have run home to Mother.
Now, it's too late. I could never decide to leave.
Wholly bewizarded,
bullied, used as you use us, I rather liked it—
asked for it, no doubt.

But you and I, at heart, never got on.
Each of us wants to own—
you, to own me, but even more, the world;
I, to own you.

Lover, we've made, between us,
one hell of a world. And yet—
still at your touch I melt. How can there be
any way out of this?
As always, I go overboard for you,
here at the world's last edge.

Ravage us still; the very last green's our kiss.

From *Four Poems from New Zealand*

IV   The Beach at Hokitika

A narrow shelf below the southern alps,
a slate-grey beach scattered with drifted wood
darkens the sullen jade
of Tasman's breakers. Blackbacked gulls
hunt the green turn of waves.

One girl with Maori eyes
gathers up driftwood for a winter fire.
But for her smile, the beach is bare.
I am a one-day stranger here,

not knowing even the gulls' language.
I hawk their beach too, looking for momentos
(as the souvenir shops wisely spell it.)
A coppery log, a Maori twine of roots—
can't carry that.

Behind me, the sky's paled
by a swoop of mountains, scope of snow
northward and southward. Jags, saw-teeth, blades of light
nobody could inhabit. Not my country.
I go back to my loves, my proper winter.

Here in the chant of sea-edge, grind of shingle,
I choose one stone,
a slate-grey oval scrawled with quartz
like a foam-edge, an edge of mountains
white as my hair.

I take you this for love, for being alone;
for being, itself. Being that's ground by glaciers,
seas and time. Out of the sea's teeth
I chose it for you, for another country,
loving you, loving another country.

James McAuley

When Shall the Fair

When shall the fair
Hair on the thin scalp spilled
(Wherein the summer lies distilled)
Suffice? A stare

Is more than eyes;
A smile appears on lips
(Like sunrise gleam on spars of ships)
But is more, and dies.

Love so is
Despair, being spirit too.
Hair and eyes in love can do
Lips can kiss;

Five senses build
A pentagon of pleasure:
But mind, exceeding common measure,
Is unfulfilled.

Canticle

Stillness and splendour of the night,
When, after slow moonrise,
Swans beat their wings into the height,
Seeking the brilliant eyes
Of water, where the ponds and lakes
Look upward as the landscape wakes.

The loved one, turning to her lover,
Splendid, awake, and still,
Receives as the wild swans go over
The deep pulse of love's will.
She dies in her delight, and then
Renews her tender love again.

Where fragrant irises disclose
A kingdom to the sense,
The ceremony of pleasure goes
With stately precedence;
Like rich brocade it gleams and glooms
Through the heart's dim presence-rooms.

The wagtail in the myrtle-tree
Who cannot sleep for love
Sings all night long insistently
As if his song could prove
What wisdom whispered from the start,
That only love can fill the heart.

He sang under the boughs of youth,
Through twisted shadowed years;
He sings in this clear night of truth,
And now my spirit hears;
And sees, when beating wings have gone,
The lucid outline of the Swan.

One Thing at Least

One thing at least I understood
Practically from the start,
That loving must be learnt by heart
If it's to be any good.

It isn't in the flash of thunder,
But in the silent power to give—
A habit into which we live
Ourselves, and grow to be a wonder.

Some like me are slow to learn:
What's plain can be mysterious still.
Feelings alter, fade, return,

But love stands constant in the will:
It's not alone the touching, seeing,
It's how to mean the other's being.

Father, Mother, Son

From the domed head the defeated eyes peer out,
Furtive with unsaid things of a lifetime, that now
Cannot be said by that stiff half-stricken mouth
Whose words come hoarse and slurred, though the mind is sound.

To have to be washed, and fed by hand, and turned
This way and that way by the cheerful nurses,
Who joke, and are sorry for him, and tired of him:
All that is not the worst paralysis.

For fifty years this one thread—he has held
One gold thread of the vesture: he has said
Hail, holy Queen, slightly wrong, each night in secret.
But his wife, and now a lifetime, stand between:

She guards him from his peace. Her love asks only
That in the end he must not seem to disown
Their terms of plighted troth. So he will make
For ever the same choice that he has made—

Unless that gold thread hold, invisibly.
I stand at the bed's foot, helpless like him;
Thinking of legendary Seth who made
A journey back to Paradise, to gain

The oil of mercy for his dying father.
But here three people smile, and, locked apart,
Prove by relatedness that cannot touch
Our sad geometry of family love.

Jack Davis

Tribal Girl

You laughed, head flung back,
Hair wafting in the wind,
Bare feet
Sensuous on the flat rock,
And desire
Closed around me.
Your fingers long, brown,
Removed strips of bark from the witchety-tree.
I knew,
But the joy was in your telling me.
I whispered of green grass,
Rainy places.
You looked askance with trembling lips,
We knew
Of tribal law between us,
And what could not be.
I screamed my anger—at her—
Gin, barefoot black gin,
Keep your red earth and your wurley,
I can walk my own path,
In the sun or in the dark,
And find my own affinity.

Anne Elder

At Amalfi

She climbed slowly in her black worn
not for mourning but as a custom, garb
to cover scars, inadequacies, repel
strangers and wipe hands. In the high square
the moorish cupola of a toy cathedral
winked gold and verdigris. With diffident
deliberation she approached the table and chair
of the town scribe.

        'I wish a letter written.
        With delicacy . . .' and she faltered
        and then, quick and low
        because she was poor:
        'What is the cost?'

        'A letter from the heart, Signora?
        The cost is high and no bargaining.
        Take it or leave it. Mille lire.'

        'I will take it,' she said,
        'when it is written and read
        to my satisfaction.'

For a moment their eyes met
in a clash of respect. She sat
and watched his hand as he wrote
dashingly the stock effusion
and read it to her with great
propriety. Mille lire
passed between them. She left
the letter on the table for him, a thing
as pale and fluttering and lovelorn
as a womanish glance.
By nature courteous he waited
until she was out of sight
to have to smile.

Italy. Where the tongue is easy
in plausible flower towards a reluctant caesura;
where the belvederes of the crumbling villas
hang over haze over turquoise enamel
of bays over emerald caverns: and where

the old gods of broken stone
recline discourteously in their grottoes
and do not smile. In a certain light
their pitted eyeballs roll
deploringly as though they had foreseen
through the wreaths of time
no laughing matter.

Nancy Gordon

The Lady and the Pheasant

A pheasant—
then where is the gamekeeper
leather leggings and smelling of the earth,
to lead her down into the hollow
lay her under the bushes
thrust into her
skin against skin against earth.
Then smoothing her hair
he whispers hush
   the honeyeater is feeding her young
   hear their tiny throats shriek their hunger.

Rosemary Dobson

The Rape of Europa

Beautiful Europa, while the billy boils
Underneath the she-oaks, underneath the willows,
Underneath the sky like a bent bow of silver,
Like the arms of a god embracing a mortal—
Beautiful Europa has set out a picnic.

All her father's paddocks that slope to the water
Are singing with runnels and freshets of crystal
And the voice of the river is loud as it plunges
By boulders of granite and shouldering basalt—
On a spit of white sand she is boiling the billy.

The cattle come down to the sand by the river,
Europa is plaiting green willows and buttercups,
Daisies and water-weeds: mocking, she crowns them
With wreaths and festoons, with dripping green garlands,
And climbs to the back of the dark one, the leader.

Europa, Europa, the billy is boiling,
Down from the woolsheds your brothers come riding.
There's a splash in the shallows, a swirl, a commotion,
He has leapt, he is swept in the rush of the current,
And the riders draw rein on the hillside, astounded.

Oh wave to Europa for far she is faring
Past farmyard and homestead, past township and jetty,
And many will say that they saw them go riding,
The girl and the bull on the back of the river
Down to the harbour and over the ocean.

And distant indeed are the coasts of that country
Where the god was revealed in splendour and ardour.
Europa, Europa, as you lay quiet
In sunshine and shadow, under a plane-tree,
Did you remember the river, the she-oaks?

Gwen Harwood

The Wine is Drunk

The wine is drunk, the woman known.
Someone in generous darkness dries
unmanly tears for what's not found
in flesh, or anywhere. He lies
beside his love, and still alone.

Pride is a lie. His finger follows
eye, nostril, outline of the cheek.
Mortal fatigue has humbled his
exulting flesh, and all he'd seek
in a loved body's gulfs and hollows

changes to otherness: he'll never
ravish the secret of its grace.

    I must be absent from myself,
    must learn to praise love's waking face,
    raise this unleavened heart, and sever

from my true life this ignorant sorrow.
I must in this gross darkness cherish
more than all plenitude the hunger
that drives the spirit. Flesh must perish
yet still, tomorrow and tomorrow

be faithful to the last, an old
blind dog that knows the stairs, and stays
obedient as it climbs and suffers.
My love, the light we'll wake to praise
beats darkness to a dust of gold.

Carpe Diem

'Carpe diem.' Your voice attests
this charity of solitude,
ours as we like to use or waste.
You wait for me. The moment rests
like a dry wafer on my tongue.
It is my future that I taste.

Still between kiss and eyelid fall
there's time to change, to turn this day
into unrealized regret.
Tasted and known you will be all,
an everlasting hunger in
this body that will not forget.

Half-drunken with *at last*, the mind
performs fantastic pantomimes
of thought, conjures away tomorrow,
hunts through its bag of tricks to find
illusion's water-into-wine,
dissolves in smoke all future sorrow

and prompts my sober tongue to try
words unrehearsed, as if in cool
mastery of intended pleasure:
'*Carpe diem*, my dear one, lie
light in my arms and on my life.'
Far beyond memory or measure

stretches the time of grief that I
still, this one moment, might escape,
while my true tongue that has not learned
lying, and will not learn to lie,
steadfast and dumb waits on my word.
I give my body to be burned.

Fever

Kröte lies feverish and sick
in hospital where sterile gleams
of chrome pluck at his aching head.
Pain wrings his hands, a phantom double
out of control. Some fever-trick
beguiles a desolate hour: he dreams
a host of friends come to his bed
with fruit and wine. But who would trouble

to flesh the unstaged reality
of Kröte's dreams? Someone. He wakes
to see one of his pupils standing
close to him, a thin child whose plain
features, unformed as yet, could be
ugly or beautiful. She makes
no secret of her undemanding
worship, is happy to remain

awkwardly, in school uniform,
ignorant of her inmost hunger,
thinking of love as a child may—
gentle kisses and sweets. 'I've brought
a gift.' As Kröte takes the warm
packet, his chill hand feels a younger
quick-fingered grasp; she tears away
the wrappings. Gift. *Vergiftet*. Caught

between two languages his mind
falters. *Gift*. Poison. Fever wears
his flesh. His sickness raps upon
facades beyond which Nothing grins.
Demons and near-men howl behind
his headache, but the young girl stares
transfixed as if a great light shone
from Kröte's face. A nurse begins

her rounds: sees on his bed the box
of sweets. 'You can't have those.' His hands
close on the box. A ludicrous
struggle ensues as Kröte holds
harder, frowns like Beethoven, locks
fingers of power. His pupil stands
giggling, while Kröte, furious,
triumphant, glares at the nurse, who scolds

her patient as she would a child,
and, thinking that his pupil is
his daughter, leaves the two alone.
Kröte leans on his pillow breathing
as if asleep. It seems the wild
mane of his hair is touched. A kiss
light as a wafer? Or his own
imagining? He sleeps. A seething

darkness finds where his life is laid.
Maps of an empty continent,
himself, are drawn in bleeding scrawls.
Keep me, his spirit prays, from ill.
By its own scope the heart's betrayed
to monstrous dreams, and throbs assent:
'I'll make the creature mine.' He falls
through a black void, himself, and still

falling wakes into darkness, crying
'Poison!' A tired sister lays
her book aside and jabs his arm.
Rest shall be given where rest is wanted.
Elsewhere this night a child is lying
restless, sure-hearted as she prays
innocently for undreamed-of harm,
then sleeps, certain her prayer is granted.

Carnal Knowledge I

Roll back, you fabulous animal
be human, sleep. I'll call you up
from water's dazzle, wheat-blond hills,
clear light and open-hearted roses,
this day's extravagance of blue
stored like a pulsebeat in the skull.

Content to be your love, your fool,
your creature tender and obscene
I'll bite sleep's innocence away
and wake the flesh my fingers cup
to build a world from what's to hand,
new energies of light and space

wings for blue distance, fins to sweep
the obscure caverns of your heart,
a tongue to lift your sweetness close
leaf-speech against the window-glass
a memory of chaos weeping
mute forces hammering for shape

sea-strip and sky-strip held apart
for earth to form its hills and roses
its landscape from our blind caresses,
blue air, horizon, water-flow,
bone to my bone I grasp the world.
But what you are I do not know.

Iris

Three years with our three sons you worked to build her,
   named for the rainbow, late and lively child
whom the sea fondles. A fresh breeze has filled her.
   Tension and buoyant ease are reconciled

as she puts off the heavy yoke of land
   and takes the wind's light burden in her sails.
Ship-shape; an even keel: we understand
   old clichés truly—sixty pounds of nails

gripping her ribs, six hundredweight of lead
   flourishing water's frail cascading lace.
Age after age the same, still tenanted
   with earth's first creatures, water bears no trace

of time or history on its shining skin.
   Far from the shore where small crabs trim the rotten
scraps from a city's fringes, we begin
   (husband and wife so long we have forgotten

all singularity), our day of rest
   above that element where none sit hand
in hand, salt glitter tossed from crest to crest
   lights nothing of those gulfs where none can stand

upright; here nothing smiles; pity's unknown.
   A crippled gull I found helplessly dying
used its last life to stab me to the bone.
   Some old, lost self strikes from time's shallows, crying

'Beyond habit, household, children, I am I.
  Who knows my original estate, my name?
Give me my atmosphere, or let me die.'
— Give me your hand. The same pure wind, the same

light-cradling sea shall comfort us, who have
  built our ark faithfully. In fugitive
rainbows of spray she lifts, wave after wave,
  her promise: those the waters bear shall live.

Meditation on Wyatt II

'Forget not yet, forget not this'
    We are what darkness has become:
    two bodies bathed in saffron light
    disarmed by sudden distances
    pitched on the singing heights of time
    our skin aflame with eastern airs,
    changed beyond reason, but not rhyme.

'The which so long hath thee so loved'
    counting the pulsebeats   foot to foot
    our splendid metres   limb to limb
    sweet assonance of tongue and tongue
    figures of speech to speech   bemused
    with metaphors as unimproved
    as the crooked roads of genius

    but our hearts' rhymes are absolute.

John Millett

From *Tail Arse Charlie*

VII

On disembarcation leave
in a strange country   a girl
tasting of sailors

took me to headlands and islands —
huge bays   ruins
a road too steep for age to follow us

archangels   weddings
fear hiding a wing
and the shadow of one broken trailing away

I am afraid for my own body
tongue stiff with salt and the gull
that same first sound or scream without sea

I remember the lights in her skin
huge walls   spinnifex   starfire—
grim delicate lovemaking

a sea-move
and a sea-mane
looping marvellous wind forms over us.

Oodgeroo
from the tribe Noonuccal

(formerly Kath Walker)

The Young Girl Wanda

Crooning her own girl thoughts and dreams
The young girl Wanda,
Grinding nardoo with the women
Softly chanted her simple song
Of all she hated.

'I hate death and the going away,
All sad endings.
I hate things that have no joy,'
Said the young girl Wanda.
'I hate sunset bringing the dark
That is full of secrets,
I hate silence of desolate places,
Swamp-oaks sighing by lonely waters,
And tree graves,'
Said the young girl Wanda.
'I hate old men's rules and laws,
Old wrinkled faces,
The elders who no longer know
What the young know,'
Said the young girl Wanda.

'All time too much hate, you,'
Said the old gin Onah.
'Tell us what you love.'

'I love joy of life,
I love arms around me,
I love life and love,'
Said the young girl Wanda.
'I love all young things,
The young dawn, not the grey day dying,
The white of daybreak on awaking waters.
I love happy things,'
Said the young girl Wanda.

'High eagles, the light in eyes we love,
The camp crying for joy when one returns.
I love colour, berries yellow and red,
The grass when it is green,
The blue that is on the kingfisher,
And a bright flower for my black hair,'
Said the young girl Wanda,
'But most of all my strong lover I love,
And his arms under me.'

Gifts

'I will bring you love,' said the young lover,
'A glad light to dance in your dark eye.
Pendants I will bring of the white bone,
And gay parrot feathers to deck your hair.'

But she only shook her head.

'I will put a child in your arms,' he said,
'Will be a great headman, great rain-maker.
I will make remembered songs about you
That all the tribes in all the wandering camps
Will sing for ever.'

But she was not impressed.

'I will bring you the still moonlight on the lagoon,
And steal for you the singing of all the birds;
I will bring down the stars of heaven to you,
And put the bright rainbow into your hand.'

'No,' she said, 'bring me tree-grubs.'

My Love

Possess me? No, I cannot give
    The love that others know,
For I am wedded to a cause:
    The rest I must forgo.

You claim me as your very own,
    My body, soul and mind;
My love is my own people first,
    And after that, mankind.

The social part, the personal
    I have renounced of old;
Mine is a dedicated life,
    No man's to have and hold.

Old white intolerance hems me round,
    Insult and scorn assail;
I must be free, I must be strong
    To fight and not to fail.

For there are ancient wrongs to right,
    Men's malice to endure;
A long road and a lonely road,
    But oh, the goal is sure.

Lex Banning

Moment in Time

The roses were yellow, my darling,
and in that imprisoning Tuscany the cypress
and the poplar stood in formal patterns.
And from a bush a bird called, sharply,
Eros! Eros! Eros!

The wheel turned,
and the mountains fell into the sea.

Alas, poor bird,
you should have cried hereafter,
there might have been a time,
and place, for such a word.

But the wheel turned,
and the mountains fell into the sea.

What matters now the bird, or the bird's song,
or the formal Tuscan cypresses and poplars?
The past moment cannot reintegrate itself
in the moving present, or cause its own repetition.
And what matters now the roses; or you, my darling?
All these are gone: and all that can be said of the
      moment
is that it formed a unique juxtaposition of factors.

Touts les Chats sont Gris

But, Darling
I don't love you that way,
but, yet, I do love you.

The white leopard sits on its haunches,
demurely curling its tail around its paws,
and trying to look
as if it had not just swallowed
a whole aviaryfull of canaries.

Of course, I know that Plato
was really a perverted old man,
but

The green eyes widen,

I thought we had so much in common,
so much to give each other,
just being together.

the velvet nostrils expand,
the round ears sleek down,

and now, I feel that,
somehow,
it's all spoilt.

and the white leopard yawns,
delicately curling its pink tongue.

Myself, I prefer purple crocodiles.

Alister Kershaw

The Gift

Because you touched me, I moved in a sleep
That was deeper than any sleep; I began
To remember vehement seasons, to forget
That I was day's exile and a dead man.

Because you were naked, because your mouth and hands
Shaped sudden perils and claimed my blood's praise,
You remain the loved betrayal, you are still
My night's victor, challenger of my days.

Because you have gone, this zodiac of nerves
Reels in an anguished noon; darkness lies
Contorted around me, the fusion of memory
Cripples my heart, jeers at my blinded eyes.

Because you were gentle, because you loved—
If only for the space of a caught breath—
Be generous now, make me a bitter gift—
Go, loved and triumphant, but give me back my death.

Nan McDonald

The Mountain Road: Crete, 1941

(For Bill)

The roads of all your life closed in that night
To the one road through the mountains to the sea;
And that one night was all your travelling time
Lest by the brutal daybreak you should be
Trapped on that narrow ledge for sacrifice
And all your bitter striving thrown away;
And as the steep miles and black hours wore on,
Around the next bend, straining hope would say,
The rocks must part, the way must turn downhill—
But ever the dark road wound upward still.

You had come a long march since you watched the sun
Crawl slow and murderous down a glare of sky,
While the swooping terror that had hunted you
Across the open ground shot screaming by,
Spattered your covering leaves to deathly foam,
Seeking you all those loud mad hours of light;
And dusk had fallen like the shade of God,
But thickened soon to this hot, moonless night;
And the dark's desperate need was swift to kill
Its fragile peace — and the way toiled upward still.

Beyond that black wall lay the brave grey ships
And the vast shining freedom of the sea —
The sea that breaks on endless alien coasts
With the old, loved voice of childhood memory;
So that its tides rise in the heart like tears
And but to wind it on the freshening gale
Is to come home, be done with wars and wounds —
But all this seemed some far-off fairytale.
Men so betrayed trust only what is ill
And that the road for ever winds uphill.

Nor any more remembering that stream,
Snow-cold beyond the blazing village, brought
Its blissful chill to seared throats, sweated skins,
All that returned was the flames' fury caught
In eyes dried with long waking, so their stare
Smeared on the eastward mirk its red and made
An angry dawn yet earlier than its hour —
At best, too early — and the heart, dismayed,
Had cried defeat but for the flogging will
As the road swung, and turned once more uphill.

And all along men fell and slept, more lost,
More piteous as they drew their shallow breath,
Than the still dead, who would not wake too late
To see the bright sky scarred with shrieking death.
But in the end all these things dropped away
As one huge labour gripped the darkening brain —
How each dull, weighted boot must be moved on,
The swaying body thrust — and yet in pain
At every turn the unwanted hope surged still,
And the sick ebb, and the road once more uphill.

This was a tale once wildly strange to me —
That you should go such ways, and I not there —
But I have come to know that deadly road,

The windings of that black snake of despair;
And you around the last turn met the sky,
The sudden, sweet drop downward to the shore,
And, feeling the deck lift to the long swell,
You smiled, and fell asleep, and feared no more;
But I in the dark pass, with heart struck chill,
See the east pale—and the way goes upward still.

Dimitris Tsaloumas

Girl Riding

I think of you, a stranger in my life, because
this is the end of the season and all my guests

have left. Your returns are past the drift
of the trivial year. You inhabit secret maps,

the imperfections in the calendar, the unrecorded
days of miracles, where I saw you cross my path

Girl on Proud Horse and therefore lovely
beyond forgetting. Thus you come riding again

across the border lands between the river
and burning summer, and raucous birds break forth

over the silos, above noon-perfect vineyards,
to smash the windshield air to myriad granules

that crash on lonely roads and roofs. Cicada-still,
I see you halt; hear the crunch of restive hooves.

Geoffrey Dutton

Love Song

When bottlebrush grows in wreckers' yards
And black crows scorn red meat,
When mothers-in-law give up playing cards
And a swaggy sleeps in a sheet,
    Then will my love come back to me.

When haystacks hide not a single mouse
And lizards love the cold,
When politicians whisper in the House
And I myself strike gold,
    Then will my love come back to me.

When the countryside is free of tins
And bottles are never broken,
When mannequins have hair on their chins
Then I'll take her word as token
    That she will come back to me.

From *A Body of Words*

2
Constant/Consistent

'I am not constant' she said,
'I mean, consistent.'
Those slips of the tongue! They might not stop at words,
One night she might slip her tongue
Into a strange lover's mouth.

This is because she has the deepest fears
That 'steadfast, faithful, true 1400'
Could turn into 'Of things: Invariable,
Fixed, unchanging, uniform 1549.'

The horror of waking to a winding, a humming, a ticking,
And finding she has become a thing
—That living doll longed for by all hairy men.

No, she meant 'consistent', never to be
'Marked by consistency; constantly adhering
To the same principles of thought and action.'

She knows about stagnant ponds,
She has seen middle-aged women in black,
Eyes quarried from quartz, mouths like a fault in granite.

Oh no, each day is a dance, but the steps not the same.
Maybe she knew too well what she was saying.
Of 'Constant', Sense 8 is 'Consistent 1580.'

3
Greediness

She is far too slim to be accused of being greedy,
Though of course it is not a question of food.
What a legacy of sin those guzzling monks left us!
They would lift their cassocks watching her fingers
Working in a hot chicken carcase.

That soft-spoken woman in a French market was right:
'Madame, to be a good cook it is necessary to be greedy.'

And so to be a good lover.
Her tongue could never have enough of him.

It is no use pursuing her with clubs and muck-tins.
'The greedinesse of the Wolfe 1641.'
'Two gredy sowes. Langland.'
'Running headlong after greedy spoils. Marlowe.'

Headlong, necklong, her hair as she runs
Flows above her slim wrists and ankles,
Spoils, trophies, golden apples do not halt her,
There is no one prize, always more for the catching.

And if she is a victim
Of 'excessive longing or desire in general 1553',
That is because desire is always excessive,
And the general, like the eye of a fly,
A million particulars.

8
Happy

Happiness is a persecuted word,
Not safe for a moment from the advertising man
Glueing it with 'is' to something sticky,
Nor from the politician with his teargas
Spraying the greatest number and calling it good.

But just right for lovers, who never bought each other,
Whose secret votes are counted on their fingers,
And who never need to ask
'Has it been said before?'
Any more than the earth questions the spring rain.

Lovers crush happiness till it bleeds
Like a strawberry eaten mouth to mouth.
There are also easier implications of gaiety,
As when he eats a strawberry from her navel
Or somewhere else, joy beyond skin,
Ecstacy deeper than love, and pleasure,
Simply, the pleasure of your company.
This is the time, without lifting a cork,
When 'happy' means '*colloq. (joq.)*. Slightly drunk 1770.'

Lovers and children are happy because they praise,
They say so, with their lips and eyes,
Knowing and unknowing, for children are on parole
And lovers are all escaped prisoners,
'Wanted', 'Reward', by those who claim to need them.

She opens no dictionary to know
That for six or seven hundred years
'Happy' is 'having good hap',
And that 'hap' is 'chance or fortune (good or bad);
Luck, lot; often, an unfortunate event, mishap.'

That is why they give thanks (to that kind goddess
Who pitches her shrine in any old bed)
To the luck that out of millions
Brought them together.

And when he draws the sunlight of her face
From the tent of her hair
The shadows are still there, mishap, bad luck,
But at this moment having no power at all,
The persecuted, in each others' arms
Having become '2. b. Blessed, beatified.'

9

Body

She threw the dictionary out the window
Cursing him for a semantic, pedantic
Man of words, words, and it was spring,
A chalice of scent the red rose of her navel
Honeysuckle hiding behind her earlobes
The gold iris waking to the tan of summer
Pink nipples lifting from the caps of gumblossom
Her feet lost in the simplicities of daisies
Her hands twining columns with wistaria

The brown earth succouring red radishes
Everything fermenting, every bubble of the champagne air
Bursting against the frothing clouds
And the land throwing scarlet and green fountains
Of whirring parrots into the infinite blue.

Defying words, she reinterpreted
The illiterate spring by the pure vowels
Of birdsong and the consonants of bees.

When they were together as an arum lily
No one wanted a history of the spring.
They were silent as the sun through the rise and fall of day.

Yet words shake out of the past
From roots, on stems, with leaves and flowers.

Their bodies are the bearers of all those messages
And finally, when they wake from the trance
They open each other like letters, being lovers
Words are their sap and their electricity.

Definitions are a game of absence,
Like old ladies behind lace curtains
Playing patience, the dictionary is solitaire.

As soon as she moves, she has redefined all words.

BODY. 'The word has died out of German, its place being taken by *leib*,
orig. 'life', and *körper* from Latin: but, in English, *body* remains a great
and important word.'

O.E.D.

Dorothy Hewett

Country Idyll

A glittering girl went out one day
On a dappled horse through the meadow hay,
And the quail rose clumsily, freckled brown,
In the morning light he rose up high
              and then dropped down.
And 'Sweet, sweet, we all must die'
Sang the glittering girl on the louring sky.

O she rode down to the gliding river
And the water covered her face forever,
And she prayed on horseback all of the way,

Crying, 'This is the judge of all the days,
                    this is the master day.'
And the sun rose up in a dusty haze,
And the plover sank in his song of praise.

O the girl went out on the gladsome water,
And the farmer searched for that whore, his daughter.
He smashed the haycocks, rattled the barn.
He said he'd find where the slut was laid
                    if he wrecked the farm.
While her lovers squatted in dust and played
Two-up under the peppermint shade.

And the river hid that she'd never been married,
And the river hid the child she carried
From the tea-cup tongues of the town.
It hid her breasts and her round high belly
                    as she floated down.
But her lovers never came out to see,
Playing two-up under the peppermint tree.

Psyche's Husband

*He is the Monster-husband who comes
to Psyche in the darkness of her wish-palace.*
Robert Duncan: The Truth & Life of Myth

In the darkness of the myth-palace I sit waiting
the feast is laid the tapers lit   the musak plays
the crow sharpens & taps a beak on the iron cradle
along the marble halls I can hear paws dragging
a giant shadow falls
the baby cries with the wind in its christening robes
& the beast is upon me
the stink from its snout   its sad pig eyes
its fur ripples along my skin
kiss me   it sobs   melodious-voiced   *kiss me*

I run shrieking through the palace
as I snatch up the child the crow pecks at my wrists
the carpet lifts with the draughts under the doors
the air-conditioner   humming   is set up high
I look back only once
there is a toad with a horned head

sadly plopping down the stairs behind me
kiss me   it croaks   *kiss me*
the crow drinks my blood on the doormat
that spells   WELCOME

now I live in the woodcutter's cottage
nodding in the peaceful kingdom
sometimes I hear the crow squawking
as it scans the canopy of leaves above my head
the toad squats & snaps in the marshes
the glamorous roar of the beast hums under my feet

my son with the beast's snout   the toad's horn
& the crow's claw snuffles for acorns
along the floor of the rain-forest
kiss me   he snorts   *kiss me.*

From *Alice in Wormland*

10

In the Dream Girl's Garden
there were dolls & rocking horses
gilt hornets built clay houses on the verandah
tom-tits swung dry grass nests in almond trees.

This was Eden   perfect   circular
the candid temples of her innocence
the homestead in the clearing
ringed with hills
the paddocks pollened deep in dandelions
the magic forest dark & beckoning

Giants & marvels would she ever go there?
Alice ringed   her hair & wrists with chains
He loves me   loves me not
what did it mean?

There was some point
where picture books dissolved
& prophecy was rampant
the shearing shed giddy as blown glass
teetered on the edge of the known world
blue-heelered swaggies shellshocked
mocked and blind

fell down the tunnel of this nothingness
horned toads & dugites hid in hollyhocks
the spotted snake spoke as she leaned to listen
his hooded world-sick eyes instructed her
Alice was driven howling from the garden.

21

Alice rose up
& went looking for love
but didn't find it
she tried
the Lecturer in Zoology
who'd once played the lead
in   *Waiting for Lefty*

the Associate Professor of History
who'd led the party split
in Melbourne
the thermometer
under her tongue
recorded her first hot flush

the marbles fell   for Vietnam
& spared her son
the buddists   burned
in pillars of wildfire
Alice fought
the dictatorship of the proletariat
abandoned socialist realism
(her lectures on Blake were famous)
tried to put democracy
back into centralism
the Russian tanks
rumbled through Czechoslovakia
she stood on the platform
in tears   resigning
The Jewish Party Secretary
with a wattled neck
stared out the window
a veteran called her
the lady with the sob story.

38

Alice came to Camelot
it was sad there   the peacock screamed
the guelder roses dreamed in moonlight
dripped cold petals in her hand
When we inhabited this mythic land
I loved you & your swagger
not more than life but like my life
she watched him passing by her with his wife
all she'd prophesised had come to pass
she saw quite clearly
what she'd never seen   he glanced at her
                              & turned aside

Stay with me always   the tide begins to flow
do not forsake me   never let me go
the willows arch   *we cannot live apart*
but nothing answered her   *Go crack my heart!*

Adios!   she cried
& wondered down   what corridor she'd find
dried petals   arching back   the drip of rain
she loosed the boat on the broad stream
she would not come to Camelot again.

Nancy Keesing

Sydney Domain

I   LADY AND COCKATOO

One Saturday afternoon I saw her walking
Across the grass with a dead branch over her shoulder
And perched on it, by her ear, the sulphur-crested
Garrulous bird—but she was mostly talking,
Speaking to him in intimate whispers. He,
Head cocked, bent low and attentive, brushing her cheek;
And, so content with each other they were, the world,
The grass, the trees might well have ceased to be.

And what would a woman say to a handsome bird
Or he to her? Perhaps what Leda said
To other white dazzling feathers. The parrot preening—
Replies or questions? They could not be overheard.
He muttered and croaked. If cockatoos do not sing
One could not doubt that his pebbly desert voice
To her was sound like the fine songs of a dream . . .
He had eaten her heart and left her one beating wing.

Sailor and Lady

'Listen,' said the sailor to the lady beneath the street-lamp,
'I've been thinking of you
Every day and night since we sailed from this town!'
The lady said, 'It's true
That every nice girl loves a sailor
But we don't believe a word
Of any such foolishness. Yours is the fiftieth
Spiel like this I've heard.'

'See,' said the sailor, 'if you don't believe me
Here is what I bring.'
On the salty palm of his sinewy hand
Winked a wedding ring.
The lady said, 'That's all very fine,
But I'll bet in every port
You've a girl imprisoned in a golden hoop,
For you look the marrying sort.'

'I can tell,' said the sailor, 'you've been misled
By wicked old men of the sea.'
He looked very sadly at the lady, crying,
'I'm young—be kind to me.'
'Now,' said the lady, 'what a fool am I,
But your words win my belief,
It goes straight to my woman's heart
To hear such steadfast grief.'

When his ship returned to that quiet harbour
He did not climb her stair.
Heavily the lady wandered the dockside
Seeking him everywhere.
He was talking to a yellow-haired lass beneath a street-lamp,
Bitterly she turned her head.
'I don't believe a word,' came the girl's clear voice
And 'See!' the sailor said.

Eric Rolls

Akun

Akun was seen
Sitting astride the thighs of her lover.
She panted as she rocked with him
And her breath warmed his face.
Her breath belongs to her husband, Nghala.

The webs of the long orb-weaving spiders
Can catch grasshoppers and cicadas,
Beetles and brown moths.
Can the breath of Akun
Thrash harder than a two-inch beetle?

When a square of plaited web
Is thrown over her nose and mouth
Akun's breath is as silent as a moth
But the web jerks
As though an owl was enmeshed.

When it is finally removed
It is grasped so that nothing can escape.
Then it is taken quickly to Nghala
Who ties the top with a cord of his own hair.
His property has been restored.
He has got back the breath of Akun.

David Rowbotham

Like a Gnome of Grimm

Wanting to be with someone all the time—
I think that's love,
And the problem.
I wish everyone in the world
Solution.
'Hush, you fool,
Or reshuffle your pack of wilful rhyme.
Think of me—the world—
My want, and time.'
Now there's our wilful world!

Pretty, isn't it?—
Like a gnome of Grimm
With an undermining presumptuous hump
Of toadish tricks—Tarot, Tar-O!
A solution is—
If ever solution exists—
To round on the howling fairy-tale
That runs in packs like wolves
And howl till its howl's hushed.
Love could devour the world if it wished.
But what's the best: to be hunted
Or have nothing to turn against?
We are greedy because we are wanted
By the wolf in the gnome in the world of time.

Vincent Buckley

From *Late Winter Child*

I

hardest to talk about,
your skin: the intent colour
that flows towards your eyes
under the room's pressure

sound of water splashing: apricot
light in the window
growing knots of wood
your eyes curving

I shiver
with the pleasure
of earliness

II

(Gently rounded as your hips
in the yellow kaftan)
we'll hear him, some time,
whistling and changing in your body,

your flesh and blood. Sweet william
with candytuft in the one bowl
I brought you. Stationed here,
we'll wait as he strains into

his clinging tent of waters,
waiting for fins,
for eyes bulbing, for breath
itching at the dance-like morning.

Before the phone shrills there is
a ticking in the wood beside it

gardens rise level as platforms
pressing their smell through every leaf

we spent our summers
preparing
a late-winter child

VIII

Once more, the hair raised on your nape,
you sit, legs akimbo
under the stretched red dress,
'privacy the mark
of true love', and you are
foreign as you were
in the old days,
with the smell of new life on us.

Points of passage   the landscape
flushed as a dream,
your heart trip-hammering, and your hands
at the burden of your dress
tracing the ellipse
of your whole life, a hissing movement
sheets of light fill the horizon,
the thunder comes in
clean as a cat.

Mouth and womb open together;
the eye, too, seeking birth.
Sometimes, I can hardly breathe
for the smell of pregnancy: a tiny
bud-creature altering the hormones
so that I smell the change in your limbs
in your hair-parting,
a second lust.

XXV

1
Standing, naked, feet apart,
you are an athlete in triumph
and in the bed's proposed light
the grain of your skin tells me
what it was like in the old days
when all night we'd lie,
limbs twined in each other's smell,
loved, and betraying no-one.

2
Then, gradually, the years of part love
when you learned, as you grew desolate,
how the language runs out like milk
to waste and dry along your body.
The soul wears out. And the eyes.
Another skin drifts in the mirror.
Alarmed, you call out your name
hesitantly to the blurred bones.

3
Worst of all, because we expected them
so humbly, the years of nothingness
when, separate, more and more slowly,
we both fought against age
with childless poems, dance classes,
images of cities built on journeys,
counting as triumphs every chance
of laughter, each fresh nuance of dress.

4
We kept one power, the shared pulse
across gaps and continents, version
of the dolphin's whistle. If we lost that
our skins would dry out like bark,
and if I rang you, it would be
a no-face pressed to the phone,
struggling to believe one cadence
of your voice floating with static.

5
It was so tempting to construct
an angry, taut 'I', spinning out
lifetimes of poems. My passivity saved me.
Your touch (was) the heat that upheld me.

Believing nothing, I could hope
to see, not a god, but a child,
a place: sunrise: a whistle: bird on stem:
a low sky, downy with rednesses.

I have you poised in the mind

I have you poised in the mind
Like an unbreaking wave

You, separate in your air,
Sitting always by the window,
Your colour changed, day by day,
But a flush leading down the cheekbones.
Your eyes dry, used to patience.

Seen always leaving rooms
With a small twist of the knee
As the door closes, and a linen
Freshness left across the air.

Water starts in my mouth
As if a spring there
Came from something spurting under my heart.
In the day, a great head of blossom.

Laurence Collinson

The Lover, on Returning from the Wars

The girl I had the night before I left
told me I had a body like a tree:
a sapling gum, she said, her fingers deft
as she tugged and tickled the hairy bark of me.
My flesh was toned just like that gum—the one
that stretched itself, she said, in her backyard—
white, with just a smiling sweep of sun,
and not by time, or man, or weather marred.
That was before the war they said was mine . . .
and pocked my skin, and turned my green to grey,
and lopped my twig of sex, and seared my spine,
and stifled my song of manhood—in just a day.
Frail now, stunted, I joke each time I fall;
and girls have nothing to say to me at all.

The Room

I always dreamed I'd own a room
in which, unfearing, I'd consume
lovers innumerable and new
and old and faithful and untrue;
lovers in leisure and in haste;
lovers to fit my ample taste;
lovers who want to *this* or *that*
in the bed or on the mat,
upright or horizontally
(the angle is all the same to me);
lovers to kiss, to clasp, to crush;
lovers austere or lovers lush;
lovers who whisper or who roar;
lovers who tease (but none to bore);
lovers shy or rough; above
all other lovers those who *love*.

And here I am in my perfect room
with bed and mat and cleansing broom,
docile colours and blending drape,
bread and wine and hanging grape
and books and prints and light and air:
fair setting for a game so fair;
a lamp to hush the atmosphere;
a door to lock when love is near;
walls so thick that who can pry?
a secret place where who can spy?
and here my every lover thrives . . .

but O! on waking, none arrives.

Jill Hellyer

The Puzzle

We sat night-through positioning the pieces:
It was simple enough to reset the broken pledges
And build a general picture of our lives
Pressed neatly into shape at all four edges.

Carefully we reassembled truth with truth
Above the flowers of an incongruous border,
Groping through the uneasy hours of morning
In the agony of setting our world in order.

But when the final segment had been placed
And each apportioned a just share of blame,
We saw by the red wound of dawn that not one
Painstaking detail had remained the same.

Joan Mas

A Death

When he died
that evening in the half light,
everything became fluid
like water moving away from me.
Trees melted in the garden
and substance seemed not to be
in anything . . . anywhere . . . anymore.
Flesh became transparent—suddenly.

It never looked like that before.

The Water Pool

O do not leave me. I love you—said the water pool.
Feel me. I yield to you. Softly and gently now.
Listen to me. My voice is in the stream which
replenishes me. My voice is under the ledges of
the rocks. My voice is like two hands whispering
against your body. O do not leave me. See, I curl
against you in such talkative desire.

Haiku: Love

A mystery. From the charred
Earth of myself—that flower,
Still growing . . .

Grace Perry

The tulip

The tulip
masculine
rising
swanneck stem
evening tremor
morning revelation

the sheath torn back
the blood cups
         everywhere

Eros in Moss Vale

At least that tame bull knows where he is going
stepping past houses
taking the right turn
to join the whitefaced females
sure of himself
     his destination
     accepting the bridle
     boy on his neck
     with gentle humour
the emanation is around him now
the children will soon give up
go away
heifers hardly moving
lick him
lick one another
nuzzle and mount
the bull calls softly
lunging at empty bellied cows
inching into the few unbroken
those out of season
not understanding
suffer the hammering of heated sisters
one by one he soothes them
     rocking them
     gunshot sunshine
          in the dark places

Bruce Beaver

From *Death's Directives*

XI

Death, how could I fail to celebrate her?
You'd have me eat and drink no more sooner
than stifle my sighs and hurrahs due to
and in honour of her. I have loved
this and that one or those together—
love comes to me easier than the devotion
she has almost taught me to emulate, her
beautiful vocation.

              I am the obsessional
maker and unmaker of friendships, alliances
even the no less exciting acquaintanceships—
the once in a lifetime glimpse or glancing word
that echoes and scatters meanings over a moment's
barest recognition—

                  Yes, it was these partial
encounters and congenial passings by
that stayed in memory and refreshed
more than the lover in me.

                    Yet with her
it is always a meeting for the first right time.
And the best times together come back at moments
that catch me up in the embrace of a rare
music that at the time of making we must have
overlooked and failed to overhear
because of the noise of our hearts and our spontaneous cries.

Or simply companionable, that rarer
than love relationship, the pause in foraging
nuzzle of the mated animal, the angelic
instant of belonging wherever one is
with another like no other known or unknown.
How did one live before? goes the cliché, and further
how may one live on after? comes its antiphon.
Another did, another may or may not.
Celebrations cannot admit such negatives.

And yet, says death, *there have been occasions*
even when together when the first and last
of loss cut through content and let the life blood
out. Beneath those trees there, it recalls,
along that road at such and such an hour
early or late and in the poignant ambience
of whatever flowerings, blossomings, or leafage
a chill came in the sun or a flush of shock
in coolest air and you were unmanned and she
already fading to the eyes and fingers,
to the tongue's petitioning and tasting
and the cinnamon scent gone under
the immortal tides of transient flowerings.

No elegizing now, I vowed, and with the next
breath stammered sadly to myself
until death interposed with the slightest
gesture of something like annoyance.
At what?

       It said: *I merely indicated*
imbalances that none could afford
to live with, over-expenditures
of what you choose to call positives
and an accrual of implosive negatives.

But I gave no damn for its rationale.
It is, after all, barely personal.
I'd not be caught talking to it through myself
again, unless I forgot. I will forget
of course. But she must move and be
a moment even in such company
as trips one into chilly or heated truisms.

There was a tree, there was a road,
there was a woman with me. And for once
there was forever in an instant
so that I picked a fallen leaf from out
the scruffy grass, a skeletal leaf
and she said, how beautiful,
and made even death appear to smile.

Durer: Naked Hausfrau

Clark says she belongs to the Alternative
     Convention.
I wish she belonged to me.
I don't think Durer was shocked by her.
He had drawn her too truly
to be anything but not intrigued.
Her small breasts and generous yet
     neither
bloated nor shrunken limbs.
Her deliciously plump yet not potted
belly. Her generously proffered
mons. Her shyly arch face.
All these offset the functional modesty
of slippers on the bare feet,
turban on the head.
She is the epitome of all sexy hausfraus
now or five hundred years ago.
Venus would have approved of her.
I certainly do.

Pamela Bell

No Willow-Cabin for Me

I read in a book a poem once . . .
'I'll build a willow-cabin at your gate
And cry upon your soul within the house.'
The world was full of sad silly women like that. Look
He may have been a real man, and such a mouse
Was never a match for a man like that.
He may have been born with a map
In the dark that lies between heart and brain. A Cook
With a desperate voyage to make. She too
Could have taken her chance to drown
Or dance, using the willow-wood best
For a barque, finding the courage to follow
On the same blue billow, the chart keyed into her life.
With a hollow head and a timid heart
She'd make a bad wife for a sailor!

Some men I suppose would choose such a wife,
The quiet fair head and the thought of tears
On a lonely pillow in a safe home, more to their taste.
I'd make of her wasted wood a ship of my own,
Or a quiver and arrows,
And a bow to go hunting my quarry—
Up on the flanks of impossible mountains his equal belongs,
Where the stones are sharp and the path so narrow
One slip would mean death,
Saving my breath for the chase not for singing sad songs!

R. F. Brissenden

Another Place, Another Time

Writing to me from London in summer,
The season of love and terror,
You say you are lost, homesick — ask:
'What shall I do with my life?'

And I, *nel mezzo del camin*,
In the middle of the safe road,
Where there are no riots in the blood,
Or blood in the streets, remember

Your voice in the iron-cold, Calvin-haunted
Melbourne darkness whispering,
'Nothing matters, nothing at all.'
While each night your bare

Beautiful sullen body, heavy
With guilt and longing, hunted
With mine in terror for the love
We lost but could not kill.

A River Remembered
(With Two Pictures)

'Tell me about the river.'
                                        'It was green
Like glass, or ice, and glittered in the sun
like the grass beside the water or the leaves
that hid the bird above our heads
                                        like glass.

And the stone house was old, and the rooms huge,
Filled with light and air. And in the morning
The tiled floors were cold beneath my feet.'
'Tell me about the river.'
                                        'It was green
and bright with flowers beneath the bare dancing
feet
      like glass. And the old woman spoke
No english
                and in that picture three on the soft
grass with linked hands
                              staring at me
As if she thought I was a whore
                                        dancing
And I looked across the water
                                        or the small
precise waves green in that other ocean lapping
Each day to the further shore, that is,
To Europe
                the great shell where venus rides
Which I saw but never reached.'
                                        'Tell me.'
'I remember it was green. And I came back
Alone
          naked with long heavy hair
and light feet treading the great shell of love'

Nectarines

Full moon: the smell of nectarines floods the air.
It is the tree's first crop: its branches, aching
With fruit, bend, breaking, to the ground;   the
                    leaves
Stir in an agony of ripeness—a girl sighing

In her lover's arms.   *Only a rose*
My parents sang together, her soprano
Blending with his tenor in the songs
Of Hermann Lohr. We heard the soft piano

And their voices as we stood beneath their tree
Touching each other in the fragrant dark.
That tree is dead. Alone I breathe this nectar
And watch the moon, half-sleeping, half-awake.

'Parfum Exotique':
Remittance Man and
Governess in Landscape

Grass-seeds caught in its purple velvet cover
Gems from Shakespeare lies beside them open
At the lines she read to him last night: 'I know
A bank where the wild thyme grows'—but no wild
    thyme
Grows here. Skeletal grey dead thistles prick
The air that quivers underneath the long
Cry of the crow, and ragged willows straggle
Along the creek. By its brown waters now,
Among the cow-pats and the rabbit-pellets,
They lie together in the willows' shade.
Sunflecks dapple her high-necked blouse, her straw
Hat with its red ribbon, her parasol
And her tall black buttoned boots, heaped where they fell
Beside his moleskins and his white silk shirt.
Her thick dark hair, unpinned, is damp with sweat,
Ses deux yeux sont fermés. 'My God, what have
We done,' she whispers, 'what have we done?' Slow tears
Well out beneath closed eye-lids. '*Je respire
L'odeur de ton sein chaleureux*, old girl,'
He says, his voice insistent as his hands.
'We've made the jolly two-backed beast—and you
Must pray that we've made nothing else.' Her tears
Taste salt beneath his searching tongue. Her arms
Tighten around his shoulders and her mouth
Opens as she moans and bucks under him
Like a brumby.
             Late in the afternoon,
Beneath an arching sky where luminous rose
Merges with blue, they wander back across
The dim drought-withered paddocks. 'There is a vale,'
He says, 'in Ida, lovelier far . . .' 'Stop it,'
She cries. 'Oh, stop it—there is just one thing
I want to hear you say.' He smiles: 'Sweetheart—
Of course—I love you: *je t'adore, guidé
Par ton odeur vers ces charmants climats.*'
The bone-white moon, huge, irresistible,
Begins to rise. Dogs bark. In the distant
Homestead someone lights the yellow lamps.

Peter Porter

Sex and the Over Forties

It's too good for them,
they look so unattractive undressed—
let them read paperbacks!

A few things to keep in readiness—
a flensing knife, a ceiling mirror,
a cassette of *The Broken Heart*.

More luncheons than lust,
more meetings on Northern Line stations,
more discussions of children's careers.

A postcard from years back—
I'm twenty-one, in Italy and in love!
Wagner wrote *Tristan* at forty-four.

Trying it with noises and in strange positions,
trying it with the young themselves,
trying to keep it up with the Joneses!

All words and no play,
all animals fleeing a forest fire,
all Apollo's grafters running.

Back to the dream in the garden,
back to the pictures in the drawer,
back to back, tonight and every night.

Old-Fashioned Wedding

It was for this they were made,
The great present of their childhood
Kept unopened, the hard rules obeyed
And the grudged honey of being good:
A pure reward,
Better for being stored,
And, reached at last, seeming like the sea
Stretching after a dream of ice toward
The edge of reluctance properly.

So that the stunned moment now
When talk falls in the bright marquee
Is an elevation of hope, the drinks a vow
Naming everything which is to be;
And after this
The subtly twinned kiss
To start a carnal journey, and the night
Offering shining emphasis
Like crystal gifts emboldening the light.

To which the cynical, caught up
In the flurry of guy ropes let down,
And crushed flowers in delicate cups,
Pay tribute as sexual clowns.
After this huge
Joke, a terrible deluge
The speeding innocents know nothing of,
Mad hours, silence, subterfuge
And all the dark expedients of love.

The Easiest Room in Hell

At the top of the stairs is a room
one may speak of only in parables.

It is the childhood attic,
the place to go when love has worn away,
the origin of the smell of self.

We came here on a clandestine visit
and in the full fire of indifference.

We sorted out books and let the children
sleep here away from creatures.

From its windows, ruled by willows,
the flatlands of childhood stretched
to the watermeadows.

It was the site of a massacre,
of the running down of the body
to less even than the soul,
the tribe's revenge on everything.

It was the heart of England
where the ballerinas were on points
and locums laughed through every evening.

Once it held all the games,
Inconsequences, Misalliance, Frustration,
even *Mendacity, Adultery* and *Manic Depression.*

But that was just its alibi,
all along it was home,
a home away from home.

Having such a sanctuary
we who parted here
will be reunited here.

You asked in an uncharacteristic note,
'Dwell I but in the suburbs
of your good pleasure?'

I replied, 'To us has been allowed
the easiest room in hell.'

Once it belonged to you,
now it is only mine.

A Chagall Postcard

Is this the nature of all truth,
The blazing cock, the bride aloof,
The E-string cutting like a tooth,
          The night that crows?

The cock has seen the standing grain,
The bride is shrouded by her train,
The violin is strung with pain,
          A cold wind blows.

From earth to sky the cry ascends,
What breaks will threaten where it mends,
Proud lovers end as pallid friends,
          These feed on those.

Bruce Dawe

Dial WX 4500

She was a blonde, but the bright planes of her face
     at rest, or fluid in laughter
          have left no trace.

The porcelain hand, Etruscan curve of arm,
    have lost their inexplicable power
        to heal or harm,

And no more in sleek moonlight will I ponder
    the soft niagara of her hair and eyes
        of constant wonder.

My pace was slow, and inevitably she out-ran it —
    gone blazing on into another's darkness
        like a chic planet . . .

O lucky the lives within her orbit, and luckier far
    those who may watch her light turning
        from star to star,

And know, as one knows, spinning back into space
    that he winning her shall have
        no resting-place . . .

The Raped Girl's Father

The buzz-saw whine of righteous anger rose
murderously in his throat throughout the night,
long after she had watched her mother close
the door to, and the honeyed wedge of light
was eaten by the dark, his voice whirred on,
and in that darker dark in which she lay
she felt his jaws rasp on the naked bone
of time and place and what she'd need to say
and how, if he were judge, by Christ, he'd cut . . .
She knew that glare of blindness that came down
upon him like a weather-wall and shut
him off from pity — hunched inside her gown
she shrank from what the morning held, the fresh assault
of reason that his manic shame would make,
the steady rape wished on her for her fault
in being the unlucky one to take
the fancy of another man who'd said:
'OK, this one will do . . .' and swung the wheel.
Somebody sobbed. Grief mimed out in her head
the ritual she did not dare to feel.
Bones, she was dice-bones, shaken, rolled on black,
wishing her frenzied suitors might re-pass,
and at this stage be merciful, take her back,
and leave her, shuddering, blank-faced, on the grass.

Suburban Lovers

Every morning they hold hands
on the fleet diesel that interprets them
like music on a roller-piano as they move
over the rhythmic rails. Her thoughts lie
kitten-curled in his while the slats of living
racket past them, back yards greying
with knowledge, embankments blazoned
with pig-face whose hardihood
be theirs, mantling with pugnacious flowers
stratas of clay, blank sandstone, sustaining them
against years' seepage, rain's intolerance.

Each evening they cross the line
while the boom-gate's slender arms constrain
the lines of waiting cars.
Stars now have flown up out of the east.
They halt at her gate. Next-door's children
scatter past, laughing. They smile. The moon,
calm as a seashore, raises its pale face.
Their hands dance in the breeze blowing
from a hundred perfumed gardens. On the cliff of kissing
they know this stillness come down upon them like a cone.
All day it has been suspended there, above their heads.

The Affair

(For Melbourne)

On the train rolling north I thought of you
as of an older woman I could no longer afford
— it was July and the cold weather
said: 'It's all over, sport, and don't think
it hasn't been fun . . .' and I couldn't come up
with a single retort, I felt browned off and bored, looking bleakly
out at the West Footscray sidings, the night moving personally in
(although I could still remember when
you weren't half so expensive, but
we were both younger then, ah yes: the streets with straight seams
like stockings, the skirts of your suburbs
predictable and entrancing,

and cool, cool, your business premises those magnificent pillars
I would have embraced in broad daylight if it weren't
for the typists and stock-brokers . . .). Twelve years down the line,
what's left of our love? Very little. Only in dreams
do I wake up and say: 'I can afford you now!
I'm on my way! I'm on my way!'

Evan Jones

Ode: The Beautiful Girls

I

Two or three hours after we kissed good night,
On my own hand I caught the faintest trace
Of perfume, maybe powder, and your face
Flickered abruptly in the abstract light
Behind my eyes; but a half-hour's trying
Brought nothing further but a sense of dying.

II

Quite beautiful, withdrawn, utterly pleasant,
Your eyes fixed always past where I was standing,
Offering almost nothing, and demanding
Nothing at all, you were not of the present:
God knows what sullen or insulted past
Was whipped into such elegance at last.

III

Alas, the beautiful girls have hidden terrors—
Their passion is a dancing poise, their love
A haunted walking in a world of mirrors
Which tells them that they move, and do not move.
Just so they pass, chilled to the finger-tips,
Waiting the touch of more abstracted lips.

Nursery Rhyme

(For Peter Steele)

When they first jauntily agreed
the bells, the vows, the rice, whatever
to marry, make themselves one indeed
witty, touching, deft and clever
did the stars shiver, did the earth bleed?

One two three their children were born
bells, holy water, precious gifts
clever, stubborn and all alone
handsome their habits, handsome their shifts
and the wide, wide world was green.

She wandered that way, he went this
tickets for all the fairgrounds cheap
looking for whatever was.
and all the springs were bitter and deep
Their children learnt that life is loss.

> Go to sleep, my pretty one, sleep:
> nothing that is is just as it was:
> nothing will keep, nothing will keep:
> cross your true heart and weep for its loss.

Philip Martin

Tombs of the Hetaerae

(After Rilke)

In their long hair they lie, and with their brown
Faces gone deep into themselves, their eyes
As if in front of too much distance closed.
Skeletons, mouths, flowers. And in their mouths
The smooth teeth set in ivory rows
Like pocket chessmen. Flowers, beads, slender bones,
Hands that lie on a dress of fading weave
Over the heart, a building fallen in.
But there under those rings and talismans
And eyeblue stones (so many favourites' keepsakes)
The silent crypt of sex
Standing unruined, brimmed to the vault with petals.

Yellowing pearls, unstrung and rolled apart,
Bowls of baked earth adorned under the lip
With the painted beauties of their mistresses,
Green shards of unguent-vases smelling of flowers,
And little gods, and household altars showing
Delighted gods in heavens of hetaerae.
Gold clasps, and metal belts that seem burst open,
Scarabs, small figures of gigantic sex,
A laughing mouth, shapes of runners, of dancers,
Amulets, crockery, ornamental pins.
And again flowers, and pearls rolled far apart,
The bright loins of a small lyre, and between
Veils falling below the knee like mists,
As if it crept from the chrysalis of the shoe,
As light as air the ankle's butterfly.

So they lie filled with things,
With precious stones and toys and bric-à-brac,
With broken tinsel (all that fell into them),
Darkening like the bottom of a river.

And riverbeds they were.
Over them and away in swift waves pressing
On to the next life and the next, the next,
The bodies of many youths rushed in a torrent,
And the full rivers of men.

And sometimes boys broke from their childhood mountains
And came down in a hesitating fall,
Played with the things on the riverbed until
The fall and its momentum seized them. Then
They filled the expanse of this broad watercourse
With clear, still-shallow water, eddying
Where it grew deep, for the first time reflecting
The banks, the distant birdcalls, while above them
The starred nights were a heaven that nowhere closed.

Such riverbeds they were.

Among long hair they lie, brown faces secret,
The crypt of sex now barred with funeral petals,
The precious eyes now closed on too much distance.

A Certain Love

There's no gainsaying this:
We're blessed. We know it.
And if God came to me today and said
'You must give her up', I'd answer
'Ridiculous. Why contradict yourself?'

Laid in Earth

After love, and still
Loving, we walk this morning
At rest in this old churchyard:
Traffic hushed away,
Dew on the grass and headstones.
When we are laid in earth,
Each in our separate graves,
Our kissed lips, of course,
Will melt away, and the skin
You touched last night, your fingers
Whispering over my back,
My neck, my shoulders: music
You sent into my spine.
Then, surely, as I wait
There in that private place
To be once more united
With my most private parts
And yours in the general marriage:
Though skin, though flesh are gone,
Long gone to others, surely
These bones will remember.

Jennifer Strauss

What Women Want

Without in any way wanting
to drop names or big note
the heaviest heavies,
I've news for Freud
and for Pontius Pilate:

even in jest,
they were much too abstract.
Here is something
that women want
specifically, truly:
to lie with a lover
a whole afternoon
so close that the skin
knows boundaries only
by knowing contact
and the mind surrenders
managerial fuss,
until to murmur
'What are you thinking?'
is only a game, words
breaking light
and unimpressive
as the quietest of waves
on tide-washed sand.
It is a truth:
time and desire can stand still
although it is also true
that clocks tick faster
than the light's slow glide
across floor and walls
and that sometimes the tongue
does not touch tenderly
but flares into speech
to set division
sharper than any sword
between sleeping bodies.
Perhaps separation's essential,
like sleep, or like sex,
but women want
sometimes still to lie
truly together
a whole afternoon
awake, without wanting.

The Nightside of the Holiday

I wake sweating, still running the track of the dream,
The road a tape, a ribbon fringed with nondescript fur,
Such indeterminate bundles, possum, rabbit, bandicoot,
God knows what—I'm no zoologist, but can't deny
The kangaroo bloating, blood on its snout. 'It wasn't me,
It wasn't us,' I plead 'we drove so carefully.' The room's
A box black with the noise of catastrophe. Moanings,
Visceral thuds, screeches pitched too high for the ear's reach
But fracturing nerves. I want the light, I want
To watch your warrior's face smoothed with sleep and love.
Yes love, that reckless destination that we drove to
So conscientiously, taking such scrupulous rights of way—
And still it's pain I'm hearing, unattended, dragged to a dark
    corner,
Whimpering and whimpering its way towards silence. Silence
    at last.
I lie here quiet on the nightside of our holiday, cold,
Waiting for sunlight and your voice to warm me.

Fay Zwicky

Cleft

One night she headless gave away the
old world, dreamed anew. Men tall and
small and pretty thin slid in
and out of her like
maddened trombones, blasting
her scales. The emptied armour
lay wherein she trusted, tranced,

The hollow vizor's chamber breathed
its last guffaw before
matters got really serious
even at a pinch you might say out of
hand at which nice point the
severed head, wide-eyed with loss
danced towards her orchestrated

Trunk, ready (as ever) with a few
home academic truths: 'Deluded and
unconscious woman! Enact your matey
operations, revisit life, visit the
dead, forage the skull, the skin
the skin,' it moaned, 'but shot you
are of my sublimity.' The groaning

trombones strained in *Leibestod* and,
thickening on her tongue, the dream
did in the dawn.

From *A Tale of the Great Smokies*

2 Penelope Spins

and there she wept for Odysseus

Turn from the word
turn away, he said, schooled in silence.
Made a true wheel, then easy
as breathing, moved down the river
poling his skiff into mist.
                              Thin neck
stiffening, set up to catch the winds of this world
in the long hot shaft of our dying summer.

Loving too much, not enough maybe, hardly a
seeker but cheerful. He had his illusions —
we were one of them.
Things went much as usual.
Maybe the stars had a hand in it,
or the one fixed star of my own
grim seeking whose light
blurs my sight like a
drunkard's candle.

Tread air, tread light
silent as dust riding darkness.
Treadle and turn,
black bobbin fat in my fingers.

Soft as moth's breath,
threads slip through tides of my handling,
wordless to wait on his coming,
fixed in my longing for speech.

Compost   black currant
fodder   horse urine
hickory   smoke
              Breath lives,
wavers within.
              Far below, wide
over the valley burn farmlights
through fog. Dusty signals from
neighbouring hearths.

Tread air, tread light
silent as sleepers in darkness
treadle and turn, unlearn
the bulk of our being, unwind
the tight bobbin. Stand
naked as two spindles saying
in one deep-drawn breath
'I am.'

Tread air, tread light
turn again, little wheel.
Darkness has secrets that
light never owns.

Akibat

I said I can't imagine life without you
as the coconut man passed our window
tapping his shell in the dust

          toc toc   toc toc

I said I'd stay with you forever
as we ate our first meal by the window
(tiny ayam, beans and carrots), sunlight pouring in
on the terrazzo floor. The air so still,
the babu's brown feet splayed soft beneath her sarong,
smiles enveloping our joy:

Njonja muda tuan muda, she would chuckle
young Mrs young Mr—how could she know
that we were only children?
At our age she'd given birth to eight:

At night we laughed and rolled on rice grains
pimpling the mattress. She wanted to make sure
we'd have a child, young njonja and young tuan.
Outside the window the kebong's twig broom
whispered over gravel like a blessing

    sh sh   sh sh

You told the story of your ruined childhood
as if it happened to a stranger: I was torn
with pity under the hammer blows.
Ashamed for outliving you, I can't forget,
a long way from that house, that window.

Akibat: 'outcome' in Indonesian

David Malouf

easier

Easier after a time to speak
of what we share together
as four rooms and a garden
plot, where all the weeds in seven counties
congregate; a view
in spring, of pink horse-chestnuts, and in winter
of black playing-fields.
Also a common interest in Jean Luc Godard,
and the I Ching, and Marx.

Easier to allow the gilt plunder
of junk-shops in the King's Road, a weakness
for last month's papers,
to show how we make room
for each other's oddities; a bowl
of cherries on the night-table, your green travelling-clock
set always ten minutes
east of Greenwich meantime,
and nearer the sun.

Toothbrushes, red and black,
your muddy wellingtons among egg-boxes
and daffodil bulbs
in the dark of kitchen cupboards,
your thinness in my shirts . . .

Easier, I mean,
than to speak of what we share
beyond all this: night-journeys hand in hand

across distances like Russia—
homecoming at dawn, pale sunstalks in our hair . . .

Margaret Scott

From *New Songs for Mariana*

Lies

The night you left you lied to me for hours,
cutting the heart out of every word you spoke
until we floundered and slipped
knee-deep in lifeless language.
Such bloody lies. They whopped on the kitchen floor,
Spouting red till you looked like a butcher
and I was stained and spattered to the elbows.
Only my hands were clean,
mechanical in the water, peeling carrots.
I dropped the carrots one by one,
stiff, orange, phallic,
to cringe and soften
in the steriliser.

We screamed the obsequies from room to room.
Meat and vegetables cremated nicely.
I wept in smoke and threw away the saucepans.
Only your dead lies still putrefy and stink.

Chris Wallace-Crabbe

The Amorous Cannibal

Suppose I were to eat you
I should probably begin
with the fingers, the cheeks and the breasts
yet all of you would tempt me,
so powerfully spicy
as to discompose my choice.

While I gobbled you up
delicacy by tidbit
I should lay the little bones
ever so gently round my plate
and caress the bigger bones
like ivory talismans.

When I had quite devoured the edible you
(your tongue informing my voice-box)
I would wake in the groin of night
to feel, ever so slowly,
your plangent, ravishing ghost
munching my fingers and toes.

Here,
        with an awkward, delicate gesture
someone slides out his heart
and offers it on a spoon,
garnished with adjectives.

The Path

Autumn of the fractured spirit.
The legend has been stood on its head
and stripped back to the bone.

It was you, brave heart,
who went stumbling down to hell
in order to drag me back
from dripping stalactite and malachite.
Hangdog, I blink at the light.

Thin rain, like anxiety, whips the trees;
they seem a thick fugue of black sticks
yet orchestrated quite outrageously
in lemon, crimson, tangerine and gold
(Even Solomon in all his glory . . .)
and they speak for life, obscurely.

Dearest of all imaginable friends,
how could you,
urban comedienne,
witty as a dandelion,
have known the wet track back from hell?
Did you read it in a book?

Beside you
in the mud and rock-jags,
ever so gladly beside you,
I am not worth a tinker's curse
let alone your leafy blessing
which you are (sensibly)
not going to give me, of course.
Marvellous leaves, like little banners,
flap to the ground.

A damp squib
in a rotten firework shop,
I fizzed with neurotic wanhope,
green as mould.
Only you, little spark, were bold.
And only you can bid the rain to stop.

Katherine Gallagher

Surf-Lore

She slipped the bridle
   over a wave
     and rode in like an expert.

Her lover, there already
   swimming up to his eyes,
     refused to be hurried.

He'd hardly noticed
   that the sky was wild
     and gestured coolly—
       no hint of theatre or props.

She led his gaze
   to the curtain of the sky—
     the stage was set,
       they chose their masks.

Waves melted and rose
   lining their voices—their story tracing
     the waves' white fronds, curling whispers
       into the sky.

Premonition

He splintered his songs—
they flew about, brittling the air.
She hovered, a moth in his way.

As he left early again, with excuses
she saw him freeze-framed—
silhouetted against her day.

Rodney Hall

Fountain and Thunderstorm

The playing fountain is your love
wistful narrow well-controlled.
It rises, wavers at the height
you've authorized, then crumples back
to shiver round your bright upsurging.
Over your ornamental passion
clouds collide, sound splits
the air. My love rides down upon you.

Crisscross gutters curb and witness
my devotion. Empty streets
recline beneath me. Steeples shine.
My ecstasy hangs pearled on windows
roars off roofs and saturates
facades of granuled stone and weeps
to swim a statue's metal eye
and greyly seeps through warping wood.

And yet when all is calm again
when thunder passes out of hearing
(barely managing to stir
a transitory drowning ghost

in drains) when people re-emerge
and the sun unshutters heat and glares
emotionless, your fountain plays
as inexhaustibly as ever
still as true to measured limits
sparkling upward—alone yet constant.

How far away my rain has blown.

Thomas Shapcott

From *The Litanies of Julia Pastrana (1832–1860)*

I

The Lord's name be praised
  for the health that keeps me performing my tasks each
  day without faltering.
The Lord's name be praised
  for my very tidy figure and the good strength
  of my spine
  to keep me agile in dancing.
The Lord's name be hallowed
  for the sharpness of my eyes and the excellent
  juices of my digestion.
I am in debt to the Lord
  for all things even my present employment—
  I who could
  have withered on
  the dustheap of the high village am enabled to travel to
  the curious and
  enquiring Capitals of Europe—
I am in debt to the Lord for all things
  even my present expectations
  for my Manager has made me a proposal of marriage. He
  loves me for my own sake.
I am indebted to the Lord of all things.
  My body covered with hair that made me cringe in the
  dark from the
  village stone throwers has earned me true fortune and
  undreamt of advantages,

my double row of teeth set in this bearded thick jaw that frightened even
myself as a child looking in the well with its cruel reflections the Lord has
made for me to be a wonder to the learned physicians of London,
my wide thick nostrils that they called me ape-baby for in those terrible
village days are no more strange in the Lord's eye than the immensely
varied noses I see in the gaping audiences who are compelled to suffer
without any rewards,
The Lord's name be hallowed and praised
for I have been instructed to consider all my born qualities as accomplishments.

In my own tongue I sing a soft theme to the Lord,
In my own heart I dance with quietness—
not so loud that the sightseers will hear me;
yet when I have a
new dress I remember its price and its prettiness, I hold myself
straight and proud—the Lord knows there is beauty in the long
black hair that covers my body. Let them see, let them stare. The
Lord knows that. He gives me pride in that. They pay their pennies
and I dance snappingly for their pennies and for the money my Manager
is keeping for me and for the Praise: the praise I say, of the good Lord
the brother of understanding
who was himself many days in the desert and was jeered at and has my
heart in his dear keeping.

From *Life Taste*

XI

If this is the fabled middle age
let us sprawl and spread and be full of it,
let's not concern ourselves with the mirror
but catch the light in the eyes of each other.

Rubens knew much of it; I salute Rubens.
The Italians knew matrons as well as madonnas.
Think of the music that flutes play together.
We still have the breath to do most things entire.

On the turkish carpet you reach down, touch toes.
More than that, your whole hand covers patterns.
'Now your turn!' I crawl out of bed, rather
stiff and prepared for your laughter.

What value are boyish buttocks now
with my tendons stiff as the knots in the floorboards?
Middle age is a fable. What we've learned though is better
than make-believe—here and now, our own moisture.

Stiff in parts, bulky, subtle,
careful of knots and the meaning of patterns
we can stay in the middle or sprawl like most people:
in the big bed we bounce and are buoyant, believable.

Randolph Stow

Endymion

My love, you are no goddess: the bards were mistaken;
no lily maiden, no huntress in silver glades.

You are lovelier still by far, for you are an island;
a continent of the sky, and all virgin, sleeping.

And I, who plant my shack in your mould-grey gullies,
am come to claim you: my orchard, my garden, of ash.

To annex your still mountains with patriotic ballads,
to establish between your breasts my colonial hearth.

And forgetting all trees, winds, oceans and open grasslands,
and forgetting the day for as long as the night shall last,

to slumber becalmed and lulled in your hollowed hands,
to wither within to your likeness, and lie still.

Let your small dust fall, let it tick on my roof like crickets.
I shall open my heart, knowing nothing can come in.

Robin Thurston

Gifts

And these were your gifts
     these
five bright stones; I count them dying
of love. I come into your room still counting.

One is brown
    naturally
it is the earth, the pitted, growing-old
earth, the body of you. Awkward-
       shaped
it is smooth with river's work. I hold it
roughly. It gentles into my palm; a breast
a brown nipple, it touches my tongue
       now.

Another reddish. Moonblood. The secret well
of life that leaves you. My eyes see only the well.
This is not death,
    the pause,
death is not this.
The red stone murmurs blood-tide queer
rustlings. Red ochre. Red strains of silt
and vein-valves so red they are almost blue.

A third, tinged green and gold, the gift of autumn.
The slow, rich, heaped harvest, neither spring cruel
nor summer foolish, the hills sodden with early rains
and the late grain more yellow than yellow. Mature
(the early birds have gone) a slow procession of us
gypsies, laughter-heavy, wends its evening way
collecting autumn gradually into our baskets,
clotting and clustering by the wild blueberry
left green by the others. The leaves fall into your hair.

The fourth is round and cream. It is a bride.
      Not the bride
you were, but the bride of a night still sleeping.
Not cream satin, but the cream
rising frothy and cool in a bucket,
      the farmer
tasting it slowly and nodding
    knowing

all there is to know about cream,
knowing that cream against clean steel
is a truth he need not explain, that
cream brings him a reason
for his toil.
A separator miracles it
into a smaller can
                    and he whistles.

Five:
        had no colour, no special tone, no sound
but waited
like a long hard
seed, clear and clean
                    like plasma,
like egg-white, like jellyfish, or like what odd children
examine long after school's out. They know
bright colours are fools; only fools hear them.
The first scientist to isolate life will see this
in his tube, and marvel. This *is* death, it lives in my loins
and we drink it across a table,
                        a gift,
last of the five.

Sylvia Kantarizis

Time and Motion

Once upon a time, time
had a woman's shape,
and men could lay an hour-glass on the sand
and stop time horizontally with love, still,
or set the sands in motion at their will
to fill an hour before the next oasis.
Clocks stop for no man,
only for themselves, at the
wrong times. Helplessly
we revolve on a clock face,
making love clockwise,
timing eggs.

A Warning

If I were real I would come to you now, naked
in the half-light of your love.
I would simply smile and ask this or that of you,
would hold you, gently,
not wildly, crazed, wanting to
crush you into my bones,
dry, dry dust on the dead earth.
Perhaps I shall take you with me
into my tomb. Perhaps I shall
strangle you with my cold need. The green
has left the trees, the earth
dried, barren. The wind
takes all that is given, all. You,
I shall fade your colours. I shall
suck you dry, dry dust in my grave.
I shall lock you in bone unless
you are very strong, unless
you are so strong and green, flooding
river of life, and I can drink,
drink endlessly and grow new and real
on your earth.

Judith Rodriguez

Penelope at Sparta

So this is Helen. I used, she says, to be
so fine — such skin, such a waist, a really tiny waist!
her blue eyes looping through wine. She surfaces bewildered,
her fingers flap their exclaimings — she is half-seas over.
And my belly — I was beautiful; my belly, it was white,
        smooth, tight.
Just one baby it took to spoil it, you can't imagine.

She needs no Troy. Simple-stepping Menelaus
has the boys a-shout on the back slope and keeps filling
        glasses.
All she requires is a hearing. Odysseus, she says, Odysseus,
your wife's very clever, very definite. You're a lucky man.
She understands you; anybody can see it.

And I too, going downhill I've discovered I have something
    to offer;
with people, just humanly, I've talents; they say I'm quite
    managing.
I've always known you had depths, impossible to get at,
now you must tell me. You must sit here, on the floor,
come on, I can see it suits you.

Menelaus and I are well-trained, we have that in common.
I sit at my handwork through the harem visit, archaically
smiling at intervals, making small-talk with some kind of
    house-friend.
She's got him facing her now, his back is somnolent,
heavy with uncritical contempt. From getting no depths,
she's progressed to getting no sense. His mind slowly sorts
tools, weapons, cordage, decking, bartered for in foreign
    places.
Her hand on his shoulder, she's thrashing about re-living
(blonde hair cleaving and parting) her divine self,
her daringly innocent prime. He's past seeing it.
Ithaca has nothing like it. Of course we pleaded harem
against the nuisance of molesters. But now with my son
    in charge
women of rank as well as peasant women
go about free-striding, frank in talk and enticement.

I sit with crochet, as long since, keeping an eye on it,
seeing it through. Unexceptionable. Till in the minutes
of absence and opposition, his turned back and unmoving
    head
blank as sea-swilled crags to her rudderless veering
—from her wheedling to her argumentative—
I sense the depth of rock, wind-fed with privateers,
that I shall never speak of, and he half-forgets;
those years of shores, send-up of the long-resolved landfall,
the crews and peoples, quaysides and stranger hearth-
    welcomes
where sacred above droves of men he embraces, most
    honoured,
the ancient royal witch of her bitter island—
beast-attended Circe bronze-eyed, with strong ankles,
his one-time Aeaean woman.

The Mudcrab-eaters

Nothing lovers in their forties do together
    that they don't, you'd say, repeat.
    But then, this day, what others here
    so feast, rising on the lean threat
    of the night apart? or so taste
    and toast their exquisite lot?

    Who else at Gambaro's is happy?
    With dolphin glances serving
    each other, the lovers sit, sea-delight
    lightening air. And though
they night and morning years-long sat down to mudcrab,
    they have never eaten mudcrab before.

In-flight Note

Kitten, writes the mousy boy in his neat
fawn casuals sitting beside me on the flight,
neatly, *I can't give up everything just like that.*
Everything, how much was it? and just like what?
Did she cool it or walk out? loosen her hand from his tight
white-knuckled hand, or not meet him, just as he thought
*You mean far too much to me. I can't forget
the four months we've known each other.* No, he won't eat,
finally he pays—pale, careful, distraught—
for a beer, turns over the pad on the page he wrote
and sleeps a bit. Or dreams of his Sydney cat.
The pad cost one dollar twenty. He wakes to write
It's naive to think we could be just good friends.
Pages and pages. And so the whole world ends.

Norman Talbot

Lovetime Monologue

(For Jean)

'Time past doesn't come again'
        I said when I could use truth
'so let us bite days while they're sweet
because they will dry as grassblades do.

> Before we see the middle of the rose
our lips touch young & true
& we can love, forgetting when
>   words like this will be mere youth
tripped by Time—who is fast on his feet,
>   who makes us see the middle of the rose.'

'Lonely as a shallowshadow fen'
>   I said, & half recognised,
'later our bodies won't meet
with this heartstopping sheer love.
>   Lying by the pulse in your arm
I'll look at the dark above
your open eyes.' I didn't know it is then
>   love has to start—when we're surprised
to find a love in the defeat
>   that lies by the pulse in your arm.

I said, 'it's the same with all men,
>   all of us processed by time
find loving & knowing retreat
till what were couples find themselves alone
>   & feel the moonlight altering & cold
& hear no password's trusted undertone.'
You see I thought we'd never join again
>   & yet we feel our bodies rhyme
not with a clinging fear, but as we meet
>   repealing moonlight's altering & cold.

Tristan in Dawn

> He wakes & feels much better
the last of the moon
swings & wavers deeper
into the palegreen water
& heavily soon it disappears
the ripples step in & out of the reeds
but the centre is quiet.

He splashes his face
the soft mirror wrinkles wildly
recalling those ill nights—
his mind is fine &
she comes much brighter into his mind . . .

'Shining, that's the word—
her light swift
rising & lilt—
no ghast mystery in dark
(that was me) but stir
yes stirring like an ivyfull of birds
dark leaves catching light—

her mind's a ringing song
located by a wingflash
tree after tree—her mind
lightbone softbeat feathering
the whole dawnshine
& entirely she's swanwingstrong
entirely she is quick . . .

Now the water is unmoved
I will not look in
but let her beware of me
take her flight beyond
my heavy drownman eye.'

Philip Roberts

Poem to Mike

It's the ashtray packed with butts
starts my mind on you. So full
of darkness, gravid, sassy. I seem
to want to straighten you out.

The gear's dead wrong. In future
wear torn jeans and sneakers; on top
an army shirt or something.
But leave the beard and hair as is.

And why don't you drop that fix-
ation with Greek mythology?
My head can't take all those names!
Longer periods of silence, please.

You don't do sport—which is why
the arms and vacant chest. You
come swimming with me for a month,
get a tan—what transformation

there'd be. And finally, like a mate,
you'd have to agree to speak only
to the half of my mind that cares,
be simply the world's best buddy.

But
how could a person put up with
someone with so little backbone?

Now you say what you want from me.

Mudrooroo

(formerly Colin Johnson)

Calcutta in the Evening

On the verandah, I stand thinking of my love:
Against a dark wall, the black shape of a palm bends,
Countless voices drone the tamboura of the city,
　　　Above weaves the sitar of a poet.
To my right a baby cries, to my left a mother sighs,
Before me the husband shouts, and Grandfather mutters
　　　While I stand thinking of my love
In the evening raga uniting in a sudden quietness:
The palm sways as supple as her body,
And the flute of my sigh adds its magic
　　　To Calcutta in the evening.

Love Song

I have no need of love songs,
Rani is my wife,
She works beside me in the fields,
She is black but comely:
That is what they say.

Rani is my life,
Young and lithesome,
Strong to plant the paddy,
She might have borne me sons,
But she was black and comely:
At least that is what they said.

Rani was my wife,
They took her away one day,
I found her naked in the field,
Black but ugly,
Her terrified mouth stuffed with dirt.

Now I sing my love song,
How long, My Lord, how long?
Rani was my wife,
Now I sit beside the roadside,
Singing: Rani, my life is gone.

There Is Love

There is love around the bend,
Where the forked lightning splits;
There is love around the bend,
Where the kangaroo inclines in obeisance;
Where men sit intent in their thoughts,
Thinking while the women's ceremony unfolds
Beyond their gaze—in their thoughts,
Though beyond their thoughts, beyond their vision.

There is love around the bend,
Lost in the haze of a smoothed escarpment;
There is love, intense and straight,
Where the women conduct their ceremonies,
Beyond the vision of men, beyond their thoughts,
Where the earth turns into female ground,
Where the grains of dust cling and cling;
There is love there—forces of attraction,
Beyond where the men sit intent in their thoughts.

J. S. Harry

The Moon and the Earthman

Cast out
from the moonman's bed
and unable to hide
her wild grief on his chest,

behind the black
almond-shaped
forest of the leaves,

the moon is spinning moonlight
down a dark lake
for earth's men — There — where the mullet slap —

she is calling him with her tide
she is filling the lake for his song
she is singing the earthman in (He will walk to the mouth
    of the creek,
he will plant his salt tongue in the tide)

This, of her, he would speak —
the hooked man, earthling, as
he spits
barb, blood, and jagged flesh
and follows gleams of light — lost deep

as the diver whose
airline — between walls of sunken coral —
parts, at the mouth of a shell:

still he follows the gleams of her light —
(He will plant his seed on the moon, he will
sleep, with her child, at his side)

Manfred Jurgensen

philatelist

your affections are
issued like a rare
stamp from another
land my hands gather
in awe of its age.

touch is sacrilege,
a threat to the thin
paper of your skin,
the fragile teeth of
your being, the love
you date to invest
as the very last
code to give away.

collected, i buy
myself into your
images of power,
your set's mystery.

if you opened me,
your forceps would find
the letter contained
a lover's lament.

it was never sent.

on time

some commute
between home and work
others between
wives and mistresses

we bought a season
ticket of departures

nothing is
as punctual
as absence

love in front of the computer

it's easy, see:
turn to TEXT, the quick reference guide
explains it all:
just remember the correct sequence:
FIND
SUBSTITUTE
ADD/REPLACE
FORMAT
MERGE

just like any other
love
stored in memories
until the disk can take no more
and DELETE precedes another FIND

Geoffrey Lehmann

Furius

At first your servant boy didn't want it,
but now you're stuck with him, Furius,
handing you a bunch of carnations in the morning,
sleeping outside your bedroom door at night,
enraging your wife, bugging you.
'I want to be with you all the time,'
he says and apes your opinions.
Serves you right, Furius.
The tan track's not all roses.

Lenin's Question

'As Lenin said, "What is to be done?"' Your words
were naked like our bodies as we lay,
mid-morning on a working day, the sheets
rolled back, your long black mane of hair undone.
The bed was like the Russian steppes. The horse
on which we rode veered unpredictably,
its spirited hooves took us beyond all landmarks,
and looking back, all we could see was wheat.
That day we planned children, the bourgeois response
to Lenin's question. But we could not plan
the vehemence of the young bones you would carry,
voices demanding, small fists grabbing breasts
years after they were weaned. The farm we planted
was older than collectives or kibbutzim,
it could survive these fires and summer storms,
monogamy, our oldest cultural unit,
where women own the gate and men are guests.

Kate Llewellyn

Diaries

Is there an end to this plot? that end could not be ethical
since ethics is an illusion of men, not of inscrutable Gods
Jorge Luis Borges

There they are twenty years of them
on the new shelf and one missing
the year of my daughter's birth
lost in some cupboard somewhere
or in a plastic bag with dresses I can't throw out
any more than the past or all those thousands of words
and names of lovers
each one hurt like a knife at the time
I remember hanging off a bed in a pale blue silk kimono
half dead with someone there
he was blond I can't remember his name
don't talk to me of love you say
what else is there to discuss
we are all waiting to die
sometimes we have ethics we always have love
it changes like the moon
with men's whims or reasons or mine
or desperation
desperation you say? yes what is love
but a recipe for desperation or a dreamed-of peace
it returns again like hope and grass
inevitable embarrassing
faithful old dog love
hanging on till the bitter end

The Fish

In the morning
the fish remember the night
how they swam
in the warm dark sea
over and over
sliding together
then resting floating
their tender gills blowing

the seaweed went past
but they didn't see it
waving at their sleeping gills
safe from all Japanese divers
and small biscuits served with a gin

when even the seaweed
feels safe as this
the fish begin to dream
they dream they are silver
and their scales have become skin

their fins grow into arms
they put their beautiful arms
around each other
and lie in the dark
face to face stroking
smiling and murmuring
words only fish know

He

The poem
is not a polite husband

arriving
when you're sitting in bed

in your best nightdress
no it strikes like a shark

it prods your dreams
with its snout

it won't wait
it wants to come

right now
in the middle of lunch

or kissing
it's a brute

Jan Owen

The Kiss

I love the way
a Pole will take your hand
in both of his
and straighten with the merest hint
of a military click
and bow his head
and tighten his grip
and press his moist and fervent lips
to your skin,
also the gentle after-caress
of his moustache.
Most, I love the dark
and frankly soulful look
(still holding your hand)
he'll fix you with
for exactly three seconds after;
the look that says
this we understand means nothing
and everything —
you are a stranger I salute
across this vast uncrossable abyss,
you are Baila, my first love
in her blue cotton dress,
you are my mother
holding back her tears,
you are garrulous Mrs Majewski
who gave us eggs,
you are all our grandmothers
waving after the train,
you are woman,
we may never meet again.

Geoff Page

Love at the End

Forty years . . . our bodies quiet,
thin sheets an easy load for spindle bones,

a window pales towards dawn and the general
catastrophe seeping in over the skyline.

So, in a private end of night, we listen
for the light capricious flicker of our hearts,

hollow and dry, like ping-pong balls, clicking
towards and then away from unison.

Fingers linked, we float towards that last
stopped moment when one will hand the other through

alone
to disbelief   and silence.

Ideal Couple

By counterpoint
they speak one mind

the makeshift world
no longer tempts them

and two who grow
from such a bond

are blonde and full of promise.
Life it seems

is a workable substance
shaped by the steady will

plans drawn up
proceed to their fulfilment.

Strange whispers of the skin
if they occur will draw them inwards

never split the seal.
Meeting them at parties

couples from the outer world
and slightly broken by it

will see them as a measure
of their failure

and driving home
be no less happy

under the uncertain stars.

Craig Powell

Short Message for Cupid

Drove so fast I hardly saw them—
parked on the main highway in peak hour,
her knees uplifted and his
buttocks bobbing in the front seat . . .

Passed them so quickly that I hardly remembered,
except to chuckle a bit and think
of two that had abruptly turned from the traffic
in obedience to an earlier book of rules.

Stupor Amoris! Lewd angel of Volkswagens,
larrikin seraph, patron saint of the quick one—
regard them for a moment,
consider his deep writhing and

her legs deliciously apart
(trying hard to ignore
that gap between the seats,
the hand-brake in her left kidney

and the entire joke of being human).
So the dashboard squeaks, the shock
absorbers stutter, there is still
all of that good oil in the

SUMP! and they are all we dream of being, angel.

Andrew Taylor

Developing a Wife

In the one cool room in the house
he held her face two inches under the water
rocking it ever so gently
ever so gently. Her smile
of two hours earlier came back to him
dimly at first through the water, then with more
boldness and more clarity.
The world is too much with us
on a hot day (he thought); better
this kind of drowning into a new degree,
a fraction of a second infinitely
protracted into purity. Her smile
free now of chemical and the perverse
alchemy of heat dust and destroying wind
free from the irritation, the tears
and the anger that had finally driven him
down to this moment,
was perfect, was
irreversible, a new reality.
Is it, he thought, that there is truth
here which she imperfectly embodies?
Or is it that I'm developing here —
my dream, my vision of her,
my sleight of hand?
Perhaps, he thought, our marriage is like this? —
flimsy, unreal, but in its own way real:
a moment, a perfection glimpsed, then gone, gone utterly,
yet caught all the same, our axis, stationary,
the other side of drowning?
                              He bore
her smile out in the heat to her, as a gift.

The Beast with Two Backs

Only the clouds were new
scenario out of the best pens
(all of them) and the setting
straight Manet

But the clouds
newly born of the sewage farm
the water treatment section of the steel mill
the heavy hydrogen plant etc.
found those first
fumbles of adultery
novel enough to rain on

at least they *came*

while the orchestra in the pit
well it was an old tune on
new instruments

and we drove back through rain
only we we said
would attempt the moon in a deluge

After the flood we had our memories
beasts coupled in the cabin of a car
nothing was changed and nothing was the same

From *Travelling to Gleis-Binario*

V

A walk in the Black Forest. We proceed
from the house you lived in once, turn left
to the station, cross by the iron footbridge
and enter another world. A Romantic world
of gushing streams, fallen trees and pines
by Altdorfer, light by Grünewald and paths
by the Landeswildschutzamt
which lead us back to the car. For two years
you walked there, and you lead me back
also to the Cathedral, stunningly filled with song.
An hour from Frieburg on the autobahn
to Basel, and to hell out of all that
jealousy. You'll never love me
as you loved then, the fever, the indulgent landscape
and adventures with the motorbike and now
all that in the past. That's just as well.

Julian Croft

Amica

As the flower blooms without the bee,
the wave can break without a beach.
The tree can bend without the wind,
yet the apple stay forever out of reach.

The lamp may burn without the moth,
and my hand need never touch your hair;
my mouth gives body to your name,
but my lips kiss nothing but the air.

Like someone watching from a cliff
the thousand smiling ocean sprawl,
I see the light play in your eyes,
but know, this time, I need not fall.

So friendship is another kind of love,
engrafted to that ancient root,
unworried by the chafing bee,
or the bruised tongue on salty fruit.

Lee Knowles

Boomerang Gorge

That year returns
as they return to this, a cave on which,
thousands of years before, the roof fell.
Rock settled and the old tribes gathered.

All her family are here as they were
that year they rented a tram, perched above the gorge.

That holiday her brother stalked kangaroos.
A playmate completed her sister's fun
while she, twelve and getting angrier by the year,
read in the bush, kept constant unnecessary watch
and, between nibbles, planned a spell-binding life.

There is marriage in the air. The celebrant
has unpacked their future with the required papers.
The children leap from rocks, brigand chiefs
of this bend. The champagne picnic is rolled out.

She is getting married, is happy. Still her eyes
watch the gorge wall as though expecting
that unfinished girl with her unsuitable dreams,
her cropped head and boots full of stones
to scream down the track and wreck everything.

Jennifer Rankin

Gannet Dreaming

They found the bird dead on the beach.
They carried it into the room.
Its long slender neck lay limp on the table.
Still warm in my arms I caressed it.

And tonight your fingers fit gently about my spine.
There is laughter in the room. And a naked light.

The dead bird stares from its table.

How the feathers shine at its neck!

Tale

Rotund, stubby fingered
I feel him fumbling
stumbling his body against mine.
But where is his head?
Over there, discoursing with Aristotle
on the mantelpiece.

Nigel Roberts

She is becoming

She
is becoming / a poem
as she cuts through
the eager & ordinary
through
the busking sex
to the bar
of the William Wallace Hotel

She is becoming a poem / where
we drink & patrol
for the new
where / we poll & market
second favourite & the left
or speculate in
the alchemical futures of
Dope Sex Rock'n Roll

She is becoming a poem, &
I read her out —
Anna / contained
controlled
critical
& cruising

She is becoming a poem / a policy
for / & a prescription against
lust & panic

She is becoming a poem / or copy
for Blake's Chariot?
whatever —
she is / anima
& flesh enough
to test desire's mileage

She is becoming a poem / she
says
because you love something
doesn't mean
something will love you back.

She is becoming a poem / that
   which is a born thing
         like the morning's hardon
   that which gives life
            to life / & is a construct
of heart & breath

She is becoming a poem / in
      the manner
   a poem becomes a poem —
               from the flash
 the one singing idea or line
            that demands
      form

      She is now / she
      who has become
      a poem.

Lee Cataldi

History

of the notches on my belt which are
the legends of women
you are one

                  cold sunlight   grey uniforms   shadows
                  smoking behind the kindergarten
                  nameless offences
                  sex and success at dancing classes   I didn't
                     like

                  small boys whose gestures had no meaning
                  but when my love
                  looked old and frail and female in the
                     daylight
                  I went into hiding

I'm still on the run
every time
I have to climb
all those stairs

I dive for the door hoping
no-one
will witness our unusual liaison

> when I open
> the door you're alone
> I wasn't mistaken
> at sixteen I put it straight in the vein

the stage is gone
where we played to each other
electric firelight
in an obscure corner of the set
two women
gazing at each other
as if their lives depended on it

From *Fairy Tales*

1

there was once a princess who fell in love with a handsome young prince, and together they wandered in the wood. but the prince got lost in pine needles, and the princess searched for him, disconsolate.

she met a toad who said, 'come with me and I'll give you shelter.' so she went with the toad.

later the toad said, 'will you sleep in my bed?' so the princess did, but the toad remained a toad.

the princess continued to live with it because it was kind, because she was fond of it and because she was used to it.

one day, along came a handsome young prince. as the princess went off with him, she said to the toad, 'I did so wish you'd turned into a handsome prince,' and the toad said, 'it's all in the mind, lady.'

your body

your body is on
the tip of my tongue

your entire physiology is on
the tip of my tongue
your personal and social history
your psychology
your metaphysic and the structure
of your phantasy system are on

the tip of my tongue

your family
your relatives near and distant
by blood or marriage
the places you've been
the movies you've seen
the houses and apartments you have inhabited
are all
now on
the tip of my tongue

sometimes I imagine
our souls
the way nameless and formless
the tidal wave
ebbing and flowing under the universe
god
the spirits of our ancestors
the holy trinity are on
the tip of my tongue

alas
I do not have
the federal government
the financial times
queensland
shell oil
the royal family
the pentagon or any other
thing it would be better
to obliterate with a lick
of the lips on the tip

of my tongue

Robert Adamson

Action Would Kill It/A Gamble

When I couldn't he always discussed things.
His talk drew us together;
the government's new war, the best french brandies
and breaking the laws. And it seemed
a strange thing for us to be doing;
the surf right up the beach, wetting our
feet each wave.

On that isolated part of the Coast, counting over
the youngest politicians.
Huge shoulders of granite grew higher
as we walked on, cutting us from perspectives.
He swung his arms and kicked
lumps of quartz hard with bare feet, until I asked
him to stop it . . .

He didn't care about himself at all, and the sea
just licked his blood away.
The seemingly endless beach held us firm;
we walked and walked all day
until it was dark. The wind dropped off and the surf
flattened out, as silence grew round
us in the darkness.

We moved on, close together almost touching;
he wouldn't have noticed, our
walk covered time rather than distance.
When the beach ended,
we would have to split up. And as he spoke
clearly and without emotion
about the need for action, about killing people,
I wanted him.

The Home, The Spare Room

I am the poet of the spare room
the man who lives here

with television's
incessant coloured noise

between the ads keeping the children
at bay

At night I walk the seagrass
down the hall

my head rolls before me
like some kind of a round dice

which room tonight?

I think of my wife-to-be
who has thrown herself down

into a foetal shape onto her bed

I am a hard man, a vicious seer
who simply wants

to go on living—love is beyond me

if it exists—my heart,
so called, is as efficient as a bull's

and as desperate
for the earth's treasures—

I turn into the spare room
begin to write a poem of infinite tenderness

Songs For Juno

I

My lies are for you, take them utterly, along
with the truth we are explorers for.
An old skiff mutters, pushes up Hawkesbury mud—
The image comes in, drifts, sinks, disappears:
shape changing gods we dream in separate bodies,
a part of it, we want feathers for sails;
the rivers we are, dance standing upright in sky,
distance between them—though at headlands
fork, touching mix, become ocean.

II

Wind and the sails full in dreaming with you.
We talk of great deserts, old chalk cities,
ice language and its lava. Then imagination darts,
Tasmania appears filling our bedroom. Sails

are wings of geese, homing ocean, white tricks
of the distances. How do we depart our tiny pasts?
My love, time fragments, blows into space —
we ride, fly, sail in every way we find there is
to now. Bring us a new language, to re-make
these questions; into dream, the gale, I whisper
to you softly.

III

How long in these secret places from childhood —
the old embers smoulder on, the lowlands
laced with fire-lines: Long spokes turning
in sky. Were we at play or were the games more,
half remembered charms, songs? We inhabit,
are rocked by still those innocent passions.
Dressed up for the new ritual, we move
the circle more than dance it. Take the moment,
hold it to you, the new, my brave and frightened
lover is a sacramental kiss. Our dreams touch —
warm with light. Give me your nightmares too.

IV

Paint flaking from the belly of an old clinker.
The boys with their rods, prawns
and blood-worms rubbed through their hair,
tasting the westerly around Snake Island —
and you sleeping, curled around the stern.
The mountains everywhere, skirts of the mangroves,
then at Danger's jetty, an octopus
sucking for its life at the end of a line.
Blue-wrens hovering for invisible insects, a shag
hunched on a wing. The trim park
patched there amongst the scribbly gums,
houses, a wash-shed, and in a backyard there
Lemon-grass drying in the sunlight.

V

The new list begins.

Harriet Westbrook Looks at the Serpentine

We reached Edinburgh
and were alone
a few days together
from then it was always

some bitch, some poet
or another. The days
flowed into days,
nights like dark moths

fell about me. Your
dream of perfect love
betrayed us Bysshe
you took it not me

then blew us away, threw
my love in the air
and watched the wind
float it off like paper.

How many times I tried
folding it up, holding it
for sheets to write?
You'd use it for kites

to fly with our fights
in the Scottish weather.
Bleak days after
crazed nights; now there's

no God like you said,
no harbour to shine
brilliant with bright sail,
it's black mud, a slimy

stream, fit place for
the Mad Woman of Queen St.
Your once radiant wife
is skipping out

with the dragon's tail—
though not for you, this
is mine, taking one
last lesson from your strife,

know with me Shelley, how to die.

John Tranter

At The Piccolo

Sitting in the jazz café at four a.m.
plotting a future in another country and a change of heart
I see a friend walk past with a 'striking woman'
I happen to know has syphilis. His last girl was a lesbian
the one before that slit her wrist
four times in a week. Sitting at my table
with a Spanish coffee and a diary of despair
scribbling its lunatic message in my eyes
I think of two foreign girls with brutal inclinations
grappling on the gymnasium floor with their legs
awkwardly apart, smelling of stale perfume, honest toil
and a frank desire to please.

The girl thinks she might make the coffee
'on the house'. I'd back out of such a contract
on principle, remembering the advice of a friend
now married to a bitchy hag who used to be 'affectionate'.
Don't shit on your own doorstep, he said. Outside
the street takes on a pale radiance and a hint of mist.
My friend walks in, alone, and we talk
carefully avoiding references to women, love, despair
and the pale carnage of the street.

From *Crying in Early Infancy*

46

Two figures: the great physicist idles homes
across the golf course late in the evening.
Sweat glitters on his forehead, rich executives
pause to let him pass—he is puzzling
how to tell his wife the facts of life.
The wife—nubile, sick and sexy
and like a foolish puppy in her eagerness—
is dreaming of the queer brothels of Singapore

which she has never seen. She will never travel
to enjoy the queer brothels, we note, as she is stupid
and soon to be demoted to the rank of baggage.
The proud scientist coughs and dies of money,
suddenly. This Marxist poem is called *The Futility
of the Emotions of the Majority of the Proletariat.*

Crocodile Rag

Hearing your song again on the radio
late at night reminded me to write my
schoolgirl fan letter at long last,
but your boy-friend's face in the photo
you sent, that pale flesh, made me
hate you for what you'd turned into —
please don't *tell* me those things.
I see your groupies throwing up,
sick with disappointment at the door.

You're right — your husband has a role:
literature's dentist. And if we disregard
two land masses and the South American
novelists, he's the seventeenth-
most-important person of his type
this side of the Equator. Honest.
He looks like a plump young Cary Grant,
when you make him cry, and you do that,
don't you — teasing like a piranha.

I feel confused and hostile about
my position as a recent house guest.
He was hanging about in the hallway
when your drunken party friends broke in
just as we were making love on the rug,
but I guess you wouldn't remember that.
Whatever the emotions you may have wished
to convey then, sweetheart — tenderness,
migraine, whatever — you blew it. Sorry.

Are you going to settle down now, like a
good wife? Your reputation can only
decline if the attacks get worse.
And they will. I know I'm capable of
wicked things — I'm not a Nice Girl —
but I loved you once. Now your
'Crocodile Rag' frightens me, frankly.
It's in the fingering, the heavy chords.

But hearing your voice last night
on the radio, hoarse with sorrow
brought it all back. Maybe—why not?—
we could try it one more time.

Caroline Caddy

Past Love

Primordial whole—
two heads   four arms   four legs
                    as Aristophanes described—
we had a creature like that
                        but more beautiful—
svelte as a leopard
            playful and gentle
                    always coming to its name.
We fed it   kept it warm
                    strong as the sun
                            and clever.
One day it came home
                its feet muddy
                        coat rough and starred.
After that we often found it
sleeping in doorways
                or stalking small helpless animals
in the street—
                a life of its own
                        mortal then immortal
roaring in the good times
                        then sick and irritable
and us so hurt
        we said
        with it fawning and dying at our feet
it isn't ours.
After the dissection
                having traced veins
                        named the organs
and classified the beast somewhere between
                            knowledge

and ignorance —
we look away
            keeping whole the perfect head
                            and dark thumbed pelt
falling back on surer centuries
when any variation
                from Galen's description
                                was because
that specimen
            had changed since the master's time
not the ideal.

Joanne Burns

and you say yr not an easy rider

and you say yr not an easy rider
keeping yr friends hanging round
                        in yr back pocket
                        convenient like small change
                        that you jangle so efficiently

and you say yr not an easy rider
that's why yr bed
                    is jam packed
                    with a dozen dangling feet
                    rubbing callouses

                    that's why you hitch hike
                    from one matress to another
                    thumbs up all the way

you say yr not an easy rider

lucky babe

                there's a transport strike tomorrow

Diane Fahey

The Pool

He has given her this room of mirrors, in which she is bored;
she may speak to him only when he speaks to her.

He spends most of his time by the pool. What is it he sees,
staring down at its tiled floor—some classical coin

with smooth bronzed face? He is as beautiful as a dolphin
but never swims. She often does. She likes the splashing cry

of the water as her long arms slice through vivid green.
Why does he never look at her? He is always looking down—

even into his glass as they sit in the evening by the pool.
'Have you had a nice day?' (he stirs and pokes his ice);

'. . . a nice day?' she echoes, desolate.

                                    Oh, but she loves him!
Once she swam the pool's whole length to surprise him,

curving up to where he gazed soulfully, teardrops pocking
the chlorine. At first he did not see her face, then,

when she was almost out of breath—but still smiling—
those clear eyes glazed with shock and he looked away.

She did not hear the slapping of her feet on concrete
as she walked inside then dripped up the long soft stairs

to her room. 'With only mirrors to keep me company
I shall waste away, waste away . . .' she thought

but could not say—as usual, the words stuck in her throat.
And she curled into herself, hiding from all those faces.

Stretched out flat by the pool, he too loved and wasted,
had not even sensed her moving away, her stifled sigh.

Psyche and Eros

'I am your darkness—*trust me.*'
So said her unseen lover, cupping her
like a fruit. In the breathless room, Fear
whispered its tingling fantasies: 'He may be

monstrous—or worse, smoothly revolting.' She found
strange growths upon his back, the bed
became lopsided, overburdened,
then it swayed . . . Sea-sick, love-sick, she turned

the lamp on while he slept and saw, beneath
its gold, a youth whose skin fused peach
with ivory, those wings that must have reached
towards her, unable to bequeath

their mystery. 'He is everything I desire,
yet would have kept me here
in blind faith!' Her hands trembled in anger,
spilling oil from the lamp—a hard spiral of fire

into his flesh.
           She had no words during the ordeal
that followed: her lover's panic, his spiteful
look when he abandoned her—left as the fool
of other gods with hurtful whims. That oil—

one drop—had burnt a deeper wound
in her: such a long time before she felt whole again.
On Mount Olympus, Eros regained
his strength quite soon, flew questingly abroad.

Yet new stirrings troubled him.
              Only years later,
when they were long-married, did she refer
to that lost time: he'd known who she was, or
thought so—had he ever considered *her*?

He was vague at first, until her finger
pressed that old scar: 'Then, you were a mirror
for my power. Now we are dancers circling a fire,
earthed within a space that grows warmer, brighter'.

Gillian Hanscombe

From *The Charms*

8

Hecate asked me,
when you are waiting for a lover to come
do you adorn yourself
or do you lie panting

or do you sit composedly reading Wittgenstein
or do you walk around with a domestic air
or do you idle with a poem?

I said
it depends on the kind of lover.

13

I lamented to Hecate
when men write poems they are all about
sex
they say how
the twentieth century has liberated
pulse of heart with pulse of orgasm

Hecate said
the ways of woman are too
dank too fecund altogether

I said
are the arcs of mountains muscle?
are the tides actually orgasm?
are the trees thighs?
are the rockets, automatics, Gothic spires,
phallus?
are the hearts and houses merely holes?

Hecate argued the traditional argument
Hecate said
we must invigorate the language
Hecate said
we must use the language of the common people
Hecate said
take this down:

for imagination read id
for love read eros
for style read sublimation
for satire read sadism
for lack of love or money read masochism
for vision read hysteria
for faith read fixation
for ambition read obsession
for purpose read sex

I said
and for death read death

Peter Murphy

Jane Eyre Extensions

Things only end outside of pages.
Jane will always walk down an echoing hall
to laughter in a distant room.

A project beyond time—
that dark face by a bed in flames:
Rochester's perverted temptress
playing with a bridal gown.

A young lord cursing God in Jamaica
drenched in a storm of lashing palms
is master with an ugly bride
excusing himself in a little church.
The infinite circle loses its source in artifice.

Thornfield Hall in flowers, a crimson curtain, and charades
is Thornfield Hall when the walls are lightning:
is a creole lady turning into fire.

Nothing begins.
On the fringe of Miss Eyre—Rochester.
In the wine-glass of an English peer
the Carribbean and insanity.

No distinguishing the unborn from the dead

while in Jane's quiet reproving eyes
pianos explode in red soliloquies
and doors smash out of being

which always a virgin governess in white
drifting endlessly in a rotting hall
drawn by vile laughing from her sleep

is forever about to open.

Mark O'Connor

The Pairing of Terns

Human lovers know it only in dreams
the wild mating flight of the terns;
riding the weird and unguessable surf of the air
though flung round the compass they hold as one pair.
Firm as if locked by invisible steel; wings taut
as the sharp stretched skin of a pterodactyl.
Now criss-crossing moon-high in an evening sky
and now outskimming the wind on the waves of a twilit bay
now rising, now falling tumultuous heights
and cackling their random delirious laughter.

Sometimes they hover
motionless, high in a half-gale torrent of air
unmoved yet sustained by the stream that surrounds them;
then, with no effort involved,
sudden and sharply they break
quick as a kite
when the string snaps
plunging down and across the sky.

And now low against wind they row back hard
plying with swift strokes their strong feathered oars,
beating into curd the thick vortices of the air;
then turn and take the gale under their wings
running fast as the wind without moving a feather
driven miles from their haunts, yet unworried,
they know there is nothing they cannot do.

Their love is everything for which we have only metaphors,
peaks and abysses, stallings and dizzying speeds
wild oceans of distance, and feathertip closenesses,
and wingbeats that answer so swiftly none knows
which struck first, which called and which answered.
They were circling the globe when our fathers still
cringed from the monsters beyond the next hamlet.

Bobbi Sykes

From *Love Poems*

I

I
like the look of you/
moving easily in the street/
   stopping to notice the clouds/
      the flowers/
      the cut-price clothes
in store windows;
Eyes slipping stealthily sideways
to catch your own image in the windows/
     as you pass
to make sure you look
as good as you feel.

I noticed you yesterday/too/
   and a time or two before that/
But then/
   I was in haste/
   doing my thing/
And you just flashed into my mind and vision
     looking GOOD
But today/
   you look good/
    and available.

Sins of Omission

Omitted to tell you . . .
   how often you were on my mind
    while you were away,
   and on my lips,
   and how I trembled to hear your voice . . .

Told you '*no*' . . .
   but omitted to tell you why,
   but then . . . you omitted to ask,
   and in our long conversation on
     communication

we omitted to communicate—
to put into the air
anything of ourselves
and today I know as much as I knew
                            yesterday
which wasn't much . . .
But better than nothing at all,

You are easy to be with
            despite your efforts to say nothing
            your hand reaching out
            speaks eloquently
            and your lips speak a language of
                            their own . . .
            but I'm a woman of more earthly fare

And very wary of current trends
                            of taking without knowing
                            of hurting without realizing
                            of using without needing

And I would rather regret
                        that I omitted
            than regret
                        that I'd committed!

Aboriginal Song Poetry

(Translated 1946
by Ronald M. Berndt)

From *The Goulburn Island Cycle*

Song 11

They saw the young girls twisting their strings, Goulburn Island
    men and men from the Woolen River:
Young girls of the western clans, twisting their breast girdles
    among the cabbage palm foliage . . .
Stealthily creeping, the men grasp the cabbage tree leaves to search
    for their sweethearts.
Stealthily moving, they bend down to hide with their lovers among
    the foliage . . .

With penis erect, those Goulburn Island men, from the young
    girls' swaying buttocks . . .
They are always there, at the wide expanse of water . . .
Always there, at the billabong edged with bamboo.
Feeling the urge for play, as they saw the young girls of the
    western clans,
Saw the young girls hiding themselves, twisting the strings . . .
Girls twisting their breast girdles, making string figures: and men
    with erect penes,
Goulburn Island men, as the young girls sway their buttocks.

Song 27

With its keen eyes, the gull saw the small tracks of the mice,
Mouse tracks, leading into the grass and the lily foliage . . .
The gull circles around, flapping its wings and crying . . .
It is always there, at the wide expanse of water, at the place of the
    Sacred Tree . . .
Diving down, probing about with its beak . . .
The sound of its flapping wings, as it swoops on a mouse . . .
It is always there, that bird, among the western people . . .
Its cry spreads over the country during the wet season, the time of
    the new grass . . .
And the squeaking cry of the mouse . . .
It is mine! [says the gull] I spear the mouse on its track, holding it
    in my beak . . .
The squeak of the mouse, and the cry of the gull, echoing up to
    the sky . . .

From *The Rose River Cycle*

Song 9

They arrange the branches about the *nonggaru* shade, and the
    sacred shade of the women . . .
Branches to screen the women's shade, at the *nonggaru* place,
    among the clumps of bamboo . . .
They are building the screen, arranging the branches . . .
Thinking of women's vaginas, and of coitus.
They are always there, people with moving buttocks:
Clans with subincised penes, clans of the barramundi . . .
All the southern clans, assembled together . . .

Towards the place of the Snake, the place of the Crab, the place of
 the Catfish . . .
Arranging the screen to hide the women within, with a wall of
 branches.
We saw the heaving chests of the southern clansmen, arranging the
 branches . . .
Building a screen of branches, beside the *nonggaru* . . .
They have made it well, covering the top of the shade with
 branches . . .
Shaking the branches, making the shade . . .
Men of the southern clans, in the spirit country, making the
 shade . . .
Thinking of play, of the *mandiela* dancing, and of the *kunapipi*.
They are always there, people with moving buttocks, men with
 subincised penes . . .
Men of the southern clans, men of the barramundi . . .
Making the screen to hide the women within, at the sacred shade,
 and arranging the branches . . .

Jeri Kroll

Man Holding Cat as Woman

(For Rick and Adelaide)

She looks up unabashed
 blinks once
 arches her neck
eyes close to his rhythm
 stroke   stroke
gliding downstream in his arms

          (she could be a baby
          but they both know better).

    Whiskers tingle like spray.

She knows if she opens her eyes
they will hit the rocks.

        Be my servant forever, she purrs,
        and the river will run for you, too,
        carry you past yourself, to me.
        The pool at the rapids' bottom
        swirls by my tail alone.
        The stone at the pool's heart is my eye.

Shelton Lea

he came to her as a birthday gift

he came to her as a birthday gift.
her friends had chipped in to buy him for the night.
they knew that she loved him with an uncommon passion
despite the fact that he was a male whore and she knew it.
they knew that even to have to buy him for her was,
if necessary,
better than not ever having him at all.

The Daily News

what sort of news do we really want to hear?
that the sky has fallen,
that everything about us is motorised;
that your hair falls upon the pillow
in cascade,
that busts of lenin are being remaindered
and while the berlin wall's torn down
others more subtle are being raised;
that in iraq there's a giant gun of god
half assembled
that your hair is red, burnished like a raphael,
and beirut has fallen to its knees.
clouds frog march across the sky.

you lie like a question mark upon the sheets.
as smooth as stone.
the tea steams lazily.
you sip dreams.
at wodonga a thick fog has covered the hume
and you are an ocean,
rolling waves in my head
that has tossed you naked
washed up on my bed.

K. F. Pearson

From *3 Versions of Sleep*

1   A Formal Sonnet

When we lie separate at verge of sleep
I remember my being entered you
that well I'd have you remember our prow
-ess of my cock and your clitoral tip
whilst you are slipping down to sleep as well
my love for I'd have entered you far in
to reaches of the dream and have you moan
as you have moaned your pleasure with me full
-y and have your dreaming lips again pronounce
and cry my name my name—oh I'd have done
to you as you have done to me, made green
my general drab and blue the sky for once
to such effect I hear a deep song or
know our times the origin of colour.

Eric Beach

poverty is a monologue

when she feels that something with
someone it just so happens/times
you realise you don't want a woman
instead/

> & anger makes cruel & women
> have more reason to be angry
> & fear makes nothing & women
> have more reason to be nothing
> & I am nothing, not a door, not
> a garden

each leaf a birthmark on my skin
th rain connects us like nails
in th rented houses/those
who hate landlords become landlords

—women hang all on th same fences—

not for th gossip of money in pockets
nor for th clink of promise in the sideways look

what is our freedom/now she's gone
th years stare back with their unused faces
she says she's suspicious & gives me her hand
then she takes it away & blames me for
th other man/well you're only one more
                    girl I adore

I wish I was with you on another day
I wish I was with you on another day

untitled

now that there's too many love songs
                    all i can think of is you
too many people been done wrong
                    believe that th sky will turn blue
can a minute/
            last an hour?
                        can a flower/
                                    sting a bee?
has a lover/
            any power?
                        can a cannon/
                                    shell a pea?
now that my heart has been broken/
                        all i can hear is th clock
sent you th hands as a token/
                    believe if I want that you'll knock
can a minute/
            last an hour?
                        can a flower/
                                    sting a bee?
has a lover/
            any power?
                        can a cannon/
                                    shell a pea?
I know there's too many sad songs
                    there's a blues in every hue
too bad so many been done wrong
                        assistant librarian dues
can a minute/
            last an hour?
                        can a flower/
                                    sting a bee?

has a lover/
        any power?
               can a cannon/
                       shell a pea?
what's a lawn with
        -out a mower?
               what's a you with
        -out a me?
what's a dawn with
        -out a lover?
what's a shoedo
        onnashoetree?
shoobedooboo
        shoebeedeebee

Kristin Henry

Late Life Interview

What if I'm wrong
and years from now
those who decide these things
decide that you were brilliant
instead of merely mad.
They're sure to find out about me.

Suppose I'm interviewed
half-reclining on a brocade couch
wearing—
yes—
dove grey silk
and a semi-wistful smile.

'At one time you and he were
very close, is that correct?'

(a shade more wist here)
'We . . . knew each other . . . well.'

'In those days were you aware of his
genius?'

Having been of course
prepared for this
I will recall
behind a knowing nod
your lack of punctuation
and the depths of your shallowness;
my inadequacy
in the light of your obscurity,
and I'll tell them
you were always one who
explored the possibilities of language.

Billy Marshall-Stoneking

The Cost of Love

Maybe if she'd brushed her teeth before going to bed;
Maybe if she hadn't hung her stockings up in the bath;
Maybe if she'd faked orgasm more often;
Maybe if she hadn't put all her eggs in one basket;
Maybe if she'd gone for a guy with bad eyesight;
Maybe if she hadn't set her sights so high;
Maybe if she'd been blonde;
Maybe if she hadn't been so short;
Maybe if she'd been more realistic;
Maybe if she hadn't trusted men at all;
Maybe if she'd had a degree in business administration;
Maybe if she hadn't told him about her old boyfriends;
Maybe if she'd met him two years earlier;
Maybe if she'd had bigger tits;
Maybe if she hadn't tried so hard;
Maybe if she'd thought more about his feelings;
Maybe if he hadn't had an ex-wife;
Maybe if he hadn't been a musician;
Maybe if he hadn't been so shy;
Maybe if he had been younger;
Maybe if she'd been younger;
Maybe if he'd been a Catholic;
Maybe if she hadn't been Catholic;
Maybe, maybe . . .
Maybe if she'd let him tie her up;
Maybe if she'd set fire to herself;
Maybe if she would've died for him,
Just maybe . . . maybe
they might've still been together.

Graham Rowlands

The Letter

Found a queer. Put him in my pocket
to flash as conversation piece.

Liked his monologues and jokes.
Always liked a pretty face, he said.

Didn't proposition at first. Asked if he should.
Our recent reading had to substitute.

Rather be queer than straight, he said.
I said Because you're queer.

Had it coming he was so frank, wilful,
nothing could be counted confidential.

Grew in love with a woman—dropped
him cold with my own handwriting

when there'd been no need for words
before I grew up, outgrew puppy love.

I didn't think he'd think it rape, mine,
that penned few lines too many. He did.

Wrong. He didn't know that not writing
proved the more difficult of to or not to.

Always wanting to avoid my own puppylove
I never told him the reason for my words.

He'd unzipped me before I saw
tolerance as a comeon. I zipped.

We're friends now. He's reconciled.
Never mentions try or letter.

I do, virgin, coy not coy I don't know
although not for no one's trying.

Guilt still gnaws through that intolerable note
grinds like bottles up my arse, imagined.

Michael Dransfield

dread was

Dread was, in the winter,
week-old snow without a foot-print.
In spring, it was
a great web woven by
spiders
across the doorways and upon the door.
Summer sped the
frail ship of my love
to no safe harbour.
When autumn came,
it came alone
and the only presage
was dead leaves, and a
bare page in the
volume my heart had once begun to write.
Rain returned
sometimes
but she did not.
Even
beyond the moat of retrospect
she is not so far I can forget.

pas de deux for lovers

Morning ought not
to be complex.
The sun is a seed
cast at dawn into the long
furrow of history.

To wake
and go
would be so simple.

Yet

how the
first light
makes gold her hair

upon my arm.
How then
shall I leave,
and where away to go. Day
is so deep already with involvement.

parthenogenesis

Must be the best way. Loving
isn't worth its weight in hangups. Either
to be with someone altogether, or not at all.
To have been too near her, her lips mine for a moment
then pulled into the frown of a problem.
Now, concentrating on a particular abyss,
I find myself more alone than I thought I'd been
when we were together, watching her eyes
flicker in and out of my being with her.
At least in the monastery there had been nothing to think
        about,
nothing but crucifixion.
Wintry summer night,
walls ceiling floor these remote six surfaces,
touch in a corner as many as three they will not respond
bodyheat means nothing to stone that old.
The wind, is it calling a name?
Does it not know they have all gone away,
leaving Him nailed to unalterable realisations and the
        knowledge
that He needn't have bothered.
Three trees' geometry on a dust hill,
a town out of focus, olive groves, a window of proconsuls,
        a skyful of begotten sons.
A Rimbaud proclamation:
'Hell is closed for the season.'
Doubt cancers,
prophets die better at a distance
clad suitably in thorns and stained robes,
seeming not overconfident, not reluctant.

Jeff Guess

She Smells the Rain

she smells the rain on me again   behind
   the still warm stove   I have brought winter though
in to her   my eyes full of the loose robe
   that all the dark way here   through the long climb

I have imagined   using the dark pine
   for cover   the fragrance of her soap I know
and wanted   all the evening down the slow
   back roads   of trying to recall the time

a year ago   when my feet crunched the gravel
   drive   by the broken swing   where a car that drove
past   turned   her first words then were of the rain

upon my coat   and mine   the pine   the soapy smell
   of her loose robe   laid by the still warm stove
for us   she smells the rain on me again

Tony Lintermans

The Custom of Kissing Eyes Observed

Beside the road, against a flaring Mallee sky
how tenderly he kisses her eye.

She laughs and strokes his back beneath the shirt.
Afternoon rears above the red, red dirt

and minutes wheel; the whirring of distant wings
could be galahs or other, closer things.

Then, stirred to a moist surprise
she kisses lightly his stopped blue eyes.

'Keep your eyes on the road,' she says,
'But your mind on me, on this edge . . . '

She walks towards her car, gets in, goes home.
He sets off for the coast alone

absorbing this connection like a rock
hurled against the windscreen in the dark.

Irina Grigorescu Pana

Your Eyes

Dry crescents about your eyes
Remind me of block lettered inscriptions
At the camp gate: we serve the country,
The scent of thickening ink
Makes my head reel. Is this exile?
A ride in style every night after sleep
Revisiting. Plaster façades, acacias, tulips
Signatures facing a clock, in a dance
Reinvented on these happy journeys.

In sleep we stand next to each other
On the shelf. You give me tulips
But my hands sleep in rainy weather,
My bones are nothing but memories,
And I am drawn to the gate of Bucharest
In a burst of recognition. Rationed summer
When I lack not the music but the words.

John A. Scott

From *Confession*

Relationship

You fall and everything is falling through the dark. Your
fingers comb the air. This final time I look upon you for the
absolution of excess. The scar-lines where clothes once were,
grow faint in nakedness; your white body draped across the
chair. And I would be with you now, for the moment that might
justify my own obscenity. But now you are revealed. The subtle
lesions of speech appear; the flesh wax-dull in trance. And after
all, the waste. The waste possesses you. The theft of useless
words, the electricity and the humid air. This final time I look
upon you with desire. Each moment a disease. Society continues
to minister to its sick. It will burn you.

John A. Scott

Breath

1

In windows he sees
women comb their hair: light failing
in distance, horizon light.
Women combing hair against the light.
    And 'against' might mean
'they fight the darkness' or 'provide
a counter motion to the darkness'
or 'their bodies lean out from
darkness'; there is no way to be sure.
Only that he sees their hair spiral
from the clouds; the faces of visitors
caught in light, vague as lost sailors,
and the light trailing like
        women's hair.

2

        and now rain.
And now rain ceasing.
He sits in a room. He feels that gentleness
has been lost from the circumstances
of his life. He wonders at its 'peculiar lack'.
He wonders how it is that things change
unaccountably. 'Change' meaning
'to grow different' or 'to take another
instead of'. What he feels
compressed to this word. What
he sees compressed to the contents
of this room. What he hears.
Outside, a road already half-dry
        with traffic.

3 *(Breath)*

He hears her breath.
This trace of presence: air rustling
distance, horizon air,
the faintest assertion of being.

Once he heard
her fight for that same air
against the rush of former lives
and saw her come to life.
Now he lies awake,
the closest he will ever be to her.
And from the sounds that might
name this place, or give it shape
and sense when all is dark, there is
only her, breathing.

Smoking

She 'owed him' too much,
her wild and ugly man. Her violent man.
Swapping that mute endurance for something
ten years ago; she'd never say. And if you asked
her how things were, she'd take a little long
to say 'they're fine', or light a cigarette—
her waking hours saved for cigarettes—'. . . fine';
and the nervous catapult of ash: all you ever
know or guess about people.

                                'I was thinking of
the pelicans,' she said, her fingernail catching at
the linen in *Italo's*, 'the gravel pits, the city
hills at night'—that meagre range of life they
shared, beyond sex. And holding out her arm,
without the slightest shift in tone she said
'He burnt me.' Then she turned to face the menu
and ordered, as if the waiter were there.

                                        It was
late afternoon. She picked up a box of matches;
noticed the sift, the brittle percussion.
She stared through the blue smoke, layered in
the room like an expensive drink. 'I really must go.'
A chinaman from the fifteenth century dreaming
of immortality; a leather book of handmade papers:
her eyes letting go of civilisation. Blowing out
the flame. Smoking. 'You *could* stay, if . . .'
But she was mad. She would never surrender.
Never let go his betrayals (not for peace),
the scotch, the Parramatta Ford (not for love).
She wouldn't leave her wild man, her violent man;
she would never leave her ugly man.

Alex Skovron

From an Interview with a Faded Juggler

In those days she was lapsing rapidly
  Into liquidation. You see (and here
    The voice dropped) she'd make me fumble silly
      With impatience half the night, my fever

Rising crude within me, then she'd pipe
  The need for an *impératif* before the usual course
    So I'd splosh the glass again—she wiped
      It clean in one enormous gulp—and toss

The bottle, wait, until she'd done
  Sketching yesterday's fresh sign of early
    Menopause, so by the time we'd finally begun
      I'd feel the grim morning's surly

Tap on shoulder, but still squeezed the last drop
  Of night into the paling pillows, while
    My none too canny at best of times timing flopped
      Once more, and she'd destroy me with a smiled

Alas my love you do me wrong, to the tune
  Of the original. And my flushed quick try to link
    Wit with revenge by some keen countercoup soon
      Would evaporate absurd, would sink

Her merely to such lusty fits of silent piercing
  Laughter that it tore my blood adrift
    As day finally cracked the curtains, kissing
      Her black velour piano-seat with a grey mist

That always somehow scared me. So, as before,
  A vow: the last time, this. But listen: then
    It was the lastness of it moved me more!
      And I knew I'd be returning to her—maybe when

My funds ran low again, I rationalized.
  And so, despite succeeding daily wrestlings
    With myself, where gingerly I clean surprised
      The Id of me, started to glean caressings

Of a wisdom more autumnal, perhaps some clear
  Approach to purge the woman, I understood
    What no-one in his righter mind would know (here
      He cocked his face): she was rich food

For a glutton soul so frail and poorly travelled . . .
 Thus disexcused I'd hoist the phone and blithely start
  Afresh; and all that day I'd dream the sweet Devil,
   Greedy old whore after every man's heart

  And after mine after all.

Vicki Viidikas

The artist without his body

  A long gloved hand
with broken fingernails inside the cloth

  A message
in magic chalk on a woman's slate

    You have forgotten my face/how
a voice persisted, pushed us silently through nights

   You have forgotten
as the flowers of your words grow old,
fade broken stems/linkages of rhetoric
  meaningless without their bodies

  Whatever art you forged
was away from physical closeness/an escape
  somewhere bodiless without your sex

  Broken vessels and poems
scatter around my feet/love letters without scent/
  advertisements without faces

    And you live somewhere with a mother
holding you in ancient bondage
    Live afraid of your skin's demand/
phantom lover who always looks back

  You remain an artist
with a legend to maintain/and suddenly I'm an ogre
giant sorceress to kill your image,
  laying claim to your life of fame.
I want my pen filled with gold
I want your tongue paying back what it stole
I want clean sheets, an honest bed

So tell me you're out of jail,
that I exist beyond walls of your mind/
Pain was the motivator
pain your pale muse/without suffering you stand defenceless

Now I'm outside your walls
reading poems and looking for noise/waiting past your silence
for the lovesong you swore existed

Alan Wearne

Roger

No one, Charley, reads an article or book
to think yes, that's the way to run it.
At least I don't. Those reasons some Cleo-hack
gives in How Affairs Succeed? We'd all begun it,
whatever 'it' was, generations before.
The early-to-mid twenties of this family man
slotted into an inevitable mosaic, sure;
but Barb liked me. She never, *per se*, planned
to share another's words breath body farewell-kisses:
which seemed the silliest events on earth,
at the time. For me simple 'going at it'
wasn't simple. I'd other ways to please the missus
if not excite her. Don't try them? Then you're not worth
that pinch of proverbial. No, something better mattered.

Yet, she's seeing someone. Doesn't need a barrage
of love-bites to be hit, for one more crater
to pock the moon of your marriage.
Oh you always hear from clever men, years later,
what they would do. Stay very single, forget
if any kids were ever hatched.
But Barb, I and Jack lived what we had, for *that?*
Pragmatics are too passionate. Try it detached,
you still need to conceive (italics/
capital H) *Him.* Enough contenders bound
from the blocks, most you'll never meet (the price
of a good imagination). This issue, the smart alecs
know, requires a more soluble state. They pound
the problem (yes, you have one) with advice.

So when friends mind your business it's an art
to wear their blunt moralising:
man-to-man, Rog, you married a tart.
A skill, sure, like Barb disguising
not *Him* but her despair: the hocus-pocus
affairs need to continue. (Or love, who knows?)
I'd get myself asleep hardly rousing notice
at the hour she might return, stoned I suppose.
By Spring Barb seemed caged to the haywire pulley
of infatuation. Near Christmas, she came clanging
back: their trysts, assignations, dates
had closed. And I'd the future: enough to sense *bully-
the-lot-of-it:* sharing her round, hanging
out for what's thought martyrdom, by mates.

For most times we'd adjust. Those nights I'd end
on some past-the-heal edge of the city:
or her quotation marks round 'catching up', 'friend'
(fugues that curled out and back to routine). Self pity?
Less happier men can't tell themselves,
'She's fucking this guy it doesn't matter much
because I say this someone else
is only lucky now . . .' (He was as clutched
to what us kids, for we were kids, believed.
And that was passing.) '. . . with all their perks
of love a highly probable grand finale
approaches.' So much for those ghosted entries heaved
into Open Marriage: How It Works.
I never over-dupe myself on books, Charley.

Laurie Duggan

From *The Epigrams of Martial*

VI xxxiv

When I want you to kiss me
you ask how many times.
Would you have me enumerate asteroids?
count the salt grains of Lake Eyre
or the microbes in Walden Pond?

I want no number less
than a figure eight laid flat.
If you wish to table the meeting
            of our lips
you can count me out.

XII lxv

After a night of love
and a deep alcoholic sleep
I was considering making you a gift,
when you woke up,
inserted your tongue in my ear,
and whispered huskily:
'Where's my white wine and soda?'

Obsession

The pilot in his ejector seat nose-diving
through smoke, the starved man in his cell,
the drugged old man in hospital, the hermit
in the desert, think like me, like a hobo
trudging across a dreary boulevard,

of women, of dark blonde women,
of their smell, of their mother-of-pearl fingernails,
of the blonde hair of dark women, sleepless
and pale, who think of the saint in hospital,
of the diver on his straw mattress in the desert,

think fleetingly of the hobo,
muttering, on his way to the river,
thinking of nothing but women, dark women
who think perhaps of him as he staggers,
hungry, across the bridge and into the darkness.

After Hans Magnus Enzensberger

Alan Gould

The Burying

I died, fell forward in the creek
and held the water like a lover.
Crayfish feasted on my forearms:
sixty nights I lay unburied.

The hiker found me, took a shovel,
dug a hole beside a river,
laid me in with care and effort,
piled some stones and went away.

I slipped into his dream and said
'Your harvests will be mostly happy:
this my promise to you. Yours
to give me half of all your joy.'

He prospered as the quiet do,
farming an acreage near a river.
Lilacs purpled at his door
and black snakes hung by string on fences.

Each evening he would ride and banter
with his neighbour's eldest daughter.
She mocked him gently, rich in humour:
creaturely she watched his gestures.

Bride and bridegroom crossed the doorstep,
lay embrangled on a sheet.
I slipped into his dream again.
'A half of all your joy,' I said.

He looked beyond his window deeply
where the moon, a bone, had bleached.
He looked at scattered roofs and lights:
'A half of all my joy,' he said.

He watched where she was smiling, sleeping
on the whiteness at his side,
and in that dreaming calm he murmured
'Half my joy I give you freely.'

There could have been no better answer.
I showed the darkness in his joy,
a black snake writhing on that whiteness
in its blind material fury.

Behind its head I seized the black snake,
took it far beyond that doorstep.
In the sunlight when he woke,
beside him lay his human bride.

John Jenkins

Why I Like You

Just let me say
that I like you because
your are beautiful as a tropical
avalanche in a glass full of gold.

Another reason,
your energy.
It often happens . . .
Before I've slept after breakfast
you've showered, walked the dog,
and made little aeroplanes out of an icecube.

Should I also mention
that you remind me
of starlight pulsing
between the spokes of a bicycle?
You whir so fast it leaves me breathless!

Or say, 'I like you because
you celebrate the motors of flesh and air'.
Should I also say *that*?!
Well, I couldn't imagine you earnest or dull!

And is it really
a coincidence
that *le douceur fleurie des étoiles*
(a quote from Rimbaud),
also reminds me of you?
Just a coincidence
in the back of our husky sled
that we could wake up *any moment* in Cuba!

And really, I'm wild too
about your 'trick'
where you dip the entire universe
into a can of blue paint
such that everything is my favourite colour!
Yes, I think that's a good one.

I also like you
for your teeth
which are useful for untying knots

and because of Tasmania,
the love-shaped island
between your thighs

and for your eyes
which rhyme and are green
tiny traffic lights
saying *yes* when we kiss!

Kate Jennings

Met a Man a Fine Man

*Paul gave birth to Ella, the naive Ella.   He destroyed in her
the knowing, doubting, sophisticated Ella and again and again
he put her intelligence to sleep, and with her willing
connivance, so that she floated darkly on her love for him, on
her naivety, which is another word for a spontaneous creative
faith.*

Doris Lessing

I want to celebrate
explain a new love
I want to be with him live with him be looked after
by him
even marry him
and make public in a traditional
way our love
and have children by him
landscape my heart

singing
I've found a new love he is a true love
I've found a new love to last me all of my life
oh I'm

weak and stupid
(I love him
for what it's worth)
what I ought to do is
give him the shove
jackbooted tell him
to kiss his own ass because only I can
lie in the bed I've made

met a man a fine man
wanted to write love lyrics
instead I wrote obscenities
(he'd rocked my soul)

I don't want to marry
I want to be barren and spinsterish cold proud alone
in a house on a hill I'm in love with a
wild & beautiful
woman writer called Djuna Barnes
she is either eighty-one years old
or in a heaven for broken women
don't trick me kiddo
a man's love is a man's love

Jennifer Maiden

Circe

The rain stops.
Her gate's pink lichen of iron,
where hearts ripen on the vines with grapes,
dries like the scab from a fall.
I swing its maze of rust until
the heat stills my hand.

Her weird steep laugh:
so welcoming—but what?—
& an edgy whiff of sulphur in the hall,
perhaps from the floor polish, or her cat.

She always says 'You trust too much
. . . you never will be told . . .'
'Well, no, but then my innocence
is purposeful: ignominious but chosen . . .'
I relax, with my sleek head

bent to touch the wood,
grunt into my handkerchief, scared
to be understood & broken.
I needn't talk tonight.

She'll watch
the saccharine whirl in her coffee,
never offer to tell my fortune
now, as she used to do.
I thwart her trade—which is to listen—too.

She still thinks that I should need more
than sex & pillows & a phenobarb
to satisfy my famine for the sea
beyond her garden & this ample trough.
One night again to calm her I'll pretend
humanity & lie it was a loss.

Doings

'I lied to the G.P. & told him
you had fallen through a plank
in the footbridge which had rotted.
                    We agreed
something should be done about
that footbridge & he seemed to believe:
or a man who knew what not to ask.'
                    In the laundry
your mac's pockets are heavy
with pebbles from the riverbank & glass.
I had a private fiction, when a boy,
that I saved Plath & nursed her, knew
alone the healing words & doings, but
when you tried you made so sure
I wasn't there. I was waiting
at the garden gate, your garden, knowing
you were too late back & knowing
I knew why, but too slowly
since you said in the note:
it would just be a walk & to wait, & you do
walk so long & often to the river or the sea.
And you shuddered home: 'I didn't . . .'
at dusk, dank & icy with green mud.
The small cuts didn't bleed until
your hot bathwater stung them.

By the radiator, I dry
& brush your hair myself although
you've always brushed it alone because
your mother when you were a girl
brushed it each morning cruelly. I've
a photo of you, pretty, in the
crooked plaits that smarted on your scalp. I said
it wouldn't hurt you if I held your hair.
So I steady the strands near your head
with my left hand, use the brush with
my right.   And you uncurl, unsolved,
in an easy married doze. And I have
exhibits of my fantasy: one brush
that needs no untangling & enough
mossy stones for the border by the gate.

A Summer Emotion

jealousy is a summer emotion
when the skin is hard to handle
and friendship is intimate
as the stain in the armpits
of the dress worn to impress
a judging rival. It is a long
slow urge like a silkworm
spinning. Now softly it emerges.
Its wings have been folded
badly like sheets crowded back
on a shelf. It uncreases them
slowly with grublike patience.
Once again I have left things
too late to roast it for silk.

Vicki Raymond

The Witch Sycorax
Addresses Her Lover

Perhaps you were thinking of leaving.
Don't try. You see, while you were asleep,
I stole some hair from you. It's buried—

where, I won't say—and it will tighten
round your throat and draw you back to me,
or choke your life out while you're sleeping.

Perhaps you fancy someone else:
if so, I have bad news for you.
There is a candle one can make,
obscene in shape, not made of wax
but something else—I won't say what.
As it melts, so melts your manhood.

Perhaps you are bored with me.
Here is a nice black milkshake,
will make you play the satyr.
Come: that is only a branch
scraping the window. Nothing
can harm you. I'm here. Relax.

Love Poem

Here is a small love poem
to squat on your bedside table.
Be careful! In the dark
it will squirm under your hand.

Its brain is smaller
than a dry lentil.
The red points of its eyes
are lidlessly fixed on you.

Keep it where you can see it.
If you are lucky
it will unwind silk
from its belly for you.

It is gathering itself
to spring on to your shoulder.
It extends one feeler.
See! It likes you already.

Chat Show

'You never married.' 'No,' he said,
'Relationships were not my *forte*.'
'Any regrets?' 'Ah . . .' Here we supply
the bitter-sweet accompaniment.

Of course. But he had higher ends
than procreation. Who could fill
the deep well of his genius? 'Perhaps.'

'You never married.' 'No,' she said,
'I wasn't asked.' Poor thing,
ceaselessly shovelling her work
into that lack. 'Regrets?'
'No, none at all.' Oh well, she would say that.

Edith Speers

From *Tarantellas*

1

Adultery has all the advantages
of seven deadly sins
rolled into one.
Pride, lechery, envy,
anger, covetousness, gluttony,
and sloth
are combined compactly
into an obdurate self-centred mass.
Better than killing two birds with one stone
when you bowl over the 7th commandment
the others go down,
like ten pins if you'll pardon the pun.
Since treachery
constitutes half the rest
you might say it's easily done
but I call it a daring achievement
nonetheless
to kill steal cheat and trespass
so succinctly in a single act.
Try it yourself and you'll see,
it's intractable fact,
you can gutter or score
but you can't retract
or restore the old order
once you've sent your ball
down the alley.

Richard Kelly Tipping

Deep Water

id be myself for you
id stumble through fragmented
bits of speech, quick breatht
grabbing words away from silence
stuttering through pause to meaning
then open to your smile

id be myself for you
aqua profundo (the sign
at the harbour pool)
in weather baked like custard
slurping pineapple frosties
then splash & dive

id be myself for you
difficult enough to be simple
harder to be naive
resurging as if bizarre
wavebreakers of suburbanity
then call us the poets union

id be myself for you
embracing puzzlement id give
silence the right to be heard
dazzled by grace id lay down
clumsy &/or delicate
then smile for you & for myself

Heading North

i love you more than a tree full of frogs or
a bursting creek, because you hear loud ants
the scrape of shaving and the sea
making love with rocks.

you leave rainforests where you walk —
parrots and pythons, intricate orchids
slipping from your freckled shoulders
like embroidered gowns.

you don't stop when it stops.
i'm axle to your wheel: careering magpies,
mottled doves, quick flapping away
from the first car for hours

Jena Woodhouse

The Bride of Byfield

The bride is marrying flamboyants:
see her standing where their limbs
brand her dress with fiery tokens,
nimbus her with crimson fronds.

She is marrying dense forest —
pines that make her drunk with resins,
touching her in dreams
with passions whispered and foregone.

At her elbows in attendance
slender pink grevilleas
offer soft vignettes of feathers —
dark green pigeons; finches; doves.

The bride of Byfield is in love
with angels incarnate as trees,
their great wings shedding
crimson petals, resins, and cicada song.

Philip Salom

He Sees She Sees

He is five foot two, and thin as a paper-clip.
He feels his great shoulders in a white suit,
brown and muscular as a horse.
She is tallish, stooped. She has a Roman nose.
Brings her height down, increases in voluptuousness.
Then, straight and as a model, her face, immaculate and poised.
He notices her admiration, well, what woman could resist him.
In fact she is trying different heads on those shoulders.
She sees his stunned look, hears the catch in his voice.

He worries she is flat-chested, her lips are porcelain.
Gentlemanly, opens the door, his Porsche's red enamel.
She spurs up the horses of her Lamborghini.
They drive like racers, absorbing lust from their passengers.
He goes to his place, she goes to hers.
She's fed up with subterfuge, tears off her clothes in the bed.
He professes knowledge of all kinds, strokes her like a cat.
She is dressed again, in silk, prising confessions out of him.
He makes love as no woman has seen.
She gives in to her lust for another go.
They have oral sex because she loves that special feeling.
They have oral sex because he loves to see it happening.
She's still going, still changing the face of her feelings.
He stops coming — shocked, changes back to himself in
    humiliation.
She screams, seeing him along that awful nose.
Such is her shame she could almost break him.
He chokes, seeing the horse he's been riding, struggles
into his tacky jacket. She scoops into an ancient petticoat.
He roars off in his Holden, she rattles in her Datsun.
Both bend over the wheel, scowling.

Spirit to the Body

When I've kissed you, made love with you
I've kissed the flat surface of the Estuary
where the air is glassy but the sand
shimmers like a warming body. I've tasted
the sun and turned over on its belly,
I've felt the long intimate throat of the sky.
Such is the after-taste. And so I make
the world in the prospensity of love, being
sensuous, lusty, and generous.
And sometimes cold. On sharp nights
I lie down among the sheets of frost
each of us miniscule and white.

I curl up into the Olgas, where the endless
being of the world has worn us down
into these woman-rocks, or the man-bunched
shoulders, the bent knees, outrageous testicles
and I am naked, walked upon by stars,
fed from the intricate surfaces:
crystal, insect, leaf, each at a time
fed into the air, levering upon the sun
to feel each day roll over me.

I wait, imbedded in a southern cliff,
the weight of land behind me, like a great spine,
the wind in my ribs of limestone.
I am the washed and wind-altered
skeleton, harbour of birds from their pushing
ocean-world of air below the constant
moving walls of consciousness, this other ocean
moving in, fold upon fold of the cerebrum.

John Forbes

Missing Persons

the planets line up & nothing happens
beneath the sheltering bowl
of your don't-have-a-clue feelings
as the day goes to pieces & you disappear.
equally indulgent but almost on schedule
in the next life I am Ike
& you are Tina Turner, vibrating
between box speakers on a shelf.
next to me is a water-ball
with snow falling on Sydney Harbour
why not invent
a roll of 20s & 50s held together
by a white elastic band? You know
nothing can keep us apart.

Love Poem

Spent tracer flecks Baghdad's
bright video game sky

as I curl up with the war
in lieu of you, whose letter

lets me know my poems show
how unhappy I can be. Perhaps.

But what they don't show, until
now, is how at ease I can be

with military technology: e.g.
watching their *feu d'esprit* I classify

the sounds of the Iraqi AA—the
thump of the 85 mil, the throaty

chatter of the quad ZSU 23.
Our precision guided weapons

make the horizon flash & glow
but nothing I can do makes you

want me. Instead I watch the west
do what the west does best

& know, obscurely, as I go to bed
all this is being staged for me.

Popular Classics

there's an end to sex
it's like the alphabet but simpler
                    and for you, all there is
and for you too
this gets clearer day by day
and the background music gets louder,
majestic & tender or at least
suggesting you feel that way,
as if you were strapped to a plank
that's floating out to sea—
not riding the surf but less directly mimetic,
a function of tides & currents,
not the waves—
you go where a history of flotsam sends you,
an extended metaphor covered in barnacles
                    and on your way to comic fame
where falling in love
becomes a theory of presence,
as if each bit of sea wrack
whitening above the high-tide line
knew what the flesh is heir to
and why
like a vague rehearsal, you were there.

Susan Hampton

The Queen at the Ice Palace

She is very cold, and glitters at your best regrets;
she is soft about the house like snow.
She wants you, in her way. She is very disturbed
that you feel the loss of me so much:
she would like to kill me. I know her,
I know what she thinks. I am the Red Queen
who hauled you in the nets of my hair
from her harrowing, I am the bitch who couldn't keep
her hands off, I am the red hessian binding
around your old thoughts for her. But at least
she has you back in the palace now, having held
up a prince and a princess to show you
how the Red Queen had made her mad; at least
she can try to rewrap your thin love-wrangled bones
in her hair and her ice-white arms. Silent
and alone, the Red Queen does her knitting, thinks
of casting spells and sending arrows of despair
to the airmail Queen at the Palais de Glace.

Jealousy

Jealousy had loaned her its machete-coloured eyes, suspicion its
crepe cloak, and she herself had plunged a dagger in her heart.
So when she went down to the shops for bread and milk you saw
this woman approaching glaring at you (and everything: the
hibiscus, the Fijian man in his grubby sarong) with steely eyes,
the black cloth flapping out behind her, and the wooden handle
of the dagger bumping up and down on her chest as she walked.
It was certainly an uncanny sight.

Back home she tried to remove the dagger (apparently it hurt)
but when she did, everything inside her started to spill out—old
stories, the leakage of every vein, bits of toast. So she went to
the kitchen dresser and stopped herself up with Araldite, first
mixing Part A and Part B carefully with a match on an old saucer.
Yes she did. And now, the story goes, she has relationships with
great ease, no pain, no blame.

Jenny Boult

i'd like to know about the fruit bowl

because you lived here
but didn't live here
because you kept your own place
(we had agreed on that)
it's difficult to know whether or not
you still don't live here

the cup i gave you for your birthday
is in the kitchen
so is the fruitbowl you won
in the easter raffle
& the thermos i gave you for christmas

but the drill isn't in the laundry
your books aren't in the study
& your trophy's not on the t.v.

your hairbrush is on the sink
there's shaving cream razor toothbrush
your green towel. the bathroom's full of you.
don't you get dandruff at your place?
is the shampoo in the shower a hint?
you've taken the nail clippers

i was feeling guilty
about not feeling guilty
i didn't miss you
maybe it was the small change by the bed

if you'd left the keys & taken the rest
i'd have known exactly what you meant
i would like to know about the fruit bowl
& whether or not
you still don't live here

scene

laid back on a bed of fantasy you
sip champagne, the glass at rest
between your toes.

your long hair moves like roses
blown by summer, dappled
by unseasonal clouds
as they shadow the open window.

the book held in your long fingers
tilts & spreads like fabric on
your naked flesh, the cover
a white rose on a dark background

as i stand here
in the doorway watching you
are unaware i cannot read the title
dare not move

a sharp wind on the rose's stem
would make the petals fall.

' π O '

Love / country style /

on this road, i know no one
i've met no one
& i've come at odd times
to see someone

but i'm sure
no one
comes this way

(the stones lay wet with blood
& sorries
hundreds of sorries
hundreds of sad sorries
like broken pig bones)

not to disturb a thing. pass
thru hell along this road
& not feel a thing

come out & not
exist

but there are always people!
chipping a bit of flesh from the sinews
not seeing you (& saying so) even me
i'm a bit like that

. . & if i could throw, disjoint my tongue
from me
i would (but it's hard
& hell at times)

i never had a house on this road
& i can't understand
what you're saying

all i know is
i have to keep on talking

How to be Polite

when i came inside you last night
you were dry

if i'd stopped to ask you
to talk

. . . but having fucked
anything that i could have said

to explain or
apologise
meant

          . . . needed teeth.

the thing that hurt most
was, you just played along

an ocean inside you, saying NO
and burning at the tip of your tongue
neon bars
of steak joints

and NO
(to say NO, but how to say it, polite)

you had cum, and your vagina was
hot

but your skin
tight

and what came over me
was the thought, rape

not t.v. rape, no torn panties
nor asylum appointments

but the silent
how to be polite, when you're being raped.

Ania Walwicz

Big Tease

She's a big teaser. She took him half the way there. Only one half or a quarter, or even less. Than that. She wore these silk stockings. With a black line down the back. Snakeskin pumps. She's a pretty girl. The only thing she was ever good at. She. She didn't have any men friends. My mother flirts with the tailors. They drop their needles. They laugh with pink, distended faces. She's a big teaser. She's this big tease. Big. She knew what they were after. So she was going to give it to them. Not by a half or a quarter or even less. Not at all. You get some sneaky ways if you can't hit. And angry. He couldn't hardly wait. Broke a box, taking me home. Looked ridiculous. And in one big hurry. You can tell when someone just aims. I was talking to Bruce at an opening. Bruce doesn't like me. And he wants to. I'm talking to this Bruce at an opening. I'm talking. Bruce, this he, drinks this red wine. This claret in a cut glass. Hello Bruce I say and more. Bruce hates me. And he wants to. Bruce doesn't love me. Bruce swings his hand around with a full tumbler. Bruce gets too happy with himself. I watch the hand, the glass describe an arc, and spill the red on someone else's white trousers. I'm this big flirt who put a knife in this man's gut. Made him squirt.

Flip

You make me. Want to take my hat. Off my head. And throw it. Up in the air. I flip. I hot water. Flip my lid. Steam kettle. I jump up and down. Write you letters. I go to Luna Park again. With bright lights and the merry go round. You make me spin. I get so very red. And hot. You turn me inside out. Like my coat I threw on the bed. You make me different. I paint this heart. Red as my lips. You push me over. I fall down. I tip. Arse over. Fall on my back. You make me stand on my head. So I can laugh. Makes all the money fall out from my pockets. I inside out myself. So you know. Exactly how I am. On the inside. I'm red meat out of the mincer. I pumpkin a soup. That was my carriage to the ball. Mixed vegetables in the atomizer. You make me fluid. I feel everything this straightaway for you. High jump. You flip me up like a pancake. Make my fly. Took me on the ferris wheel. On a big dipper ride. That gave me such a lovely look at the lights of the city below. City lights from the highrise. Made the sky so big. Moon shine like a shot through me. Made my night shimmer. All clouds opening out. And a big rainbow in my sky. Make me better than before. This exciting. I get so drunk. Without a drink. Mister Egg Flip. You mix me with your milk. That stands for life. You cut my carrot into thin slices. You light me up. Like a bulb. Make me into a neon girl. I skip in my vinegar sign. I play on my swing under the clock. You made my whole red. You red me sky. Gave me a jacket to wear you. You give me this entry for free. Into how you. And drunk with yourself. I copy what you are. Saw you walk outside. I ran out. Before I even know. What I am doing. So fast. Make my world all shimmer glimmer. You big I love you took me on a big dipper ride. In black night. Made me. Yell.

Tony Page

Sungrowth

Sungrowth
as nebulous as the newgrown hair
surprising your faster flute,
now swelling bold from sleep.
Of course I love you
with your tusk so sharp for play,
but aren't you meant to be
courting Juliet today?

You can't avoid it, Romeo:
we've been stalking in your bed
for three years, hunting nothing but dreams.
Such sport seems pure as flame,
but angers the elders
crushed dry in their youth.
How jealous they'd be to see
our sheets work with such speed.

But you've got to remember,
I'm over twenty, no longer a boy;
and you're fifteen,
tall and sprightly for your age.
Your family will start asking
questions soon, and can you imagine
our kind of love bringing peace
to the warring clans? Never.
Last night in the alley
they laid Shakespeare out cold,
and now he daren't lift the curtain
on such a climax as
our jumbled thighs.

Your father pays me to paint you,
an angel of harmony
above sacred scenes,
but I'm not to sound
your more solid chords.
Don't follow me then
as I slip over the garden wall,
clutching the trellis pierced with dawn.

Chris Mansell

Breakfast

1
do not cut your hair
a woman likes something
to run her fingers through

2
do not talk about your other women
women do not mind queues
when they're not in them

3
cultivate a manly bum

4
do not pick your nose
too obviously

5
do not be very polite
because she's there

6
forget that you and she are enemies
for the duration

7
do not expect her to believe in you
as Number One Mr Super Hero Incarnate And Flagrante

8
remember that she thinks
the sun can shine out of only one arse at a time
and that this week it's hers

9
when she espouses double standards
do not assume too much
she means you to be faithful

10
do not tell her her skin is soft
when it is not

11
refrain from commenting on her thin arms
as she has refrained from mentioning yours

12
do not fuck by numbers
filling in the little squares
with a touch of red or purple
as the chart suggests

13
finally
leave when you're asked to

14
do not expect breakfast

Lady Gedanke rings home

I dial you and you are not there
we talk of poetry and music
as if it is possible to talk at all
meaningfully scraping our chairs

having another cigarette I dial you
and you are not there and I also
have no more than a feeling about
things their place in the world
is no clearer than the position
of a tree or the emblematic half-fruit
half-person conversation has become
more theoretical and so more poetic
but speaks in tunes the way a chair sounds
scraping inwards towards a desk
I dial you and you are not there
it is my own number I am calling this evening
the dark emulsion has branches I try to mimic
the tree at night
I dial you and you are not there I am
alone with a newspaper—the million
poets in America rise early scrape their chairs
inward and begin to deconstruct
the planet into smaller more precise
gestures the planet is oblivious you
are not at home

Peter Bakowski

in my dreams

all the housewives
have put down their shopping, declaring—
'we are now interested in the arcane;
you know—gypsy caravans that crawl with broken axles
here under the fire of heaven'.

the savage in the Guatemalan jungle
walks up to the American engineer and says—
'you can't build a paper mill here,
don't you know anything about punctuation . . ?'
the engineer apologises and offers the savage his wife
and the savage answers as perfect as F. Scott Fitzgerald—
'no thanks, I'm vegetarian'.

presidents have put down their sad weaponry
and have become artists building robot sculptures in parks,
    saying—
'all those bombs were just our mojos not working
and now we just want to research the meaning of "Diddy Wah
    Diddy"'.

all the animals have left the zoo, casually smoking cigarettes,
wearing three-piece suits made from the skin of debutantes, saying
to astonished reporters, 'yeah, Adolf Hitler was our lion-tamer
but we just want to hear Charlie Parker now'.

all the inmates of every madhouse and every prison
are free and dancing the mazurka and the tango
with jailers, tailors, magistrates and thieves
who are so earnestly remorseful, teary-eyed and saying—
'we're so terribly sorry, somehow
we got marsupials mixed up with marzipan, you know how it goes,
anyway here are the keys to our city'.

all the winos and wheelchair cripples are dancing
with Ginger Rogers and Fred Astaire, saying—
'now tomorrow will never be our dungeon;
let's run and watch the sunset make orange love to the ocean'.

and in my dreams
someone says to me
'I love you'.

Kevin Hart

The Beast

Whatever it is you've given me
    it's something I cannot control, something wild
pawing inside me, an animal
swung by the tail and thrown inside a cage.

All day I feel its claws,
    its burning moods; it's broken all I own
and makes me live in a country
lit only by storms,
    or sits up late with me, in a room
pierced by the purest music.

A wolf and lamb in one, the taste
    of honey and gall! I've done nothing,
yet this thing hunts me from within
and my body aches
    as if rubbed with crushed glass.

It has no grace, no manners;
    I've tried to reason, but it backs off
into a corner, snarling. And yet

it's made me know the strangeness
of the seed when the tree inside begins to kick,
    the river's longing
when it feels the ocean's pull.

I've tried to feed it,
    but it grows daily, and when I starve it
I feel it scratching my heart.

You've given me this animal you've bred;
    tell me, can it be tamed?
I cannot live with it or bear to let it go;
already I love it, even its claws.

Midsummer

These are the richest weeks
when light slows to heat, when all that grows
fattens with the sweetest juices —
and the cloudless sky
so heavy, as though we walked through cloud.

Green summer has come —
and you are dressed in white.
Simply to be here, now, in the heat's stunned silence
with all of time ahead, to think of it
as something given, a garden.

Forget the listless nights,
the darkness that will not accept our roots,
the wasp among the poppies,
the soldiers marching past the orchard.
Our day is here, today,

and even tomorrow has begun
though far away from us, in cities still cold,
in grasping hands,
in rooms where spiders dream of lace.
It will be all that was promised,

tomorrow, the new land,
as though I have never touched you before:
another day, as rich as this,
the garden in blossom, the river's hush, the promise
renewed through change: this world.

Four Poems

Going through old clothes
I find a single blond hair—
all I have of her.

Just to be with her
I'd cut off both nose and ears
though not lips or eyes.

That entire summer
we made love, and now she's gone
I still cannot sleep.

Her tongue in your mouth,
her hand just where it should be—
but her mind with him.

Peter Rose

Kitchen

Lesbia, Lesbia, look at me now.
Stop fretting tomorrow night's *boeuf*.
It's only cow! I want to feel those
frantic arms around me, the sun
catching their short blonde hairs just so.
Can't we lose ourselves for a moment?
Can't we wallow and accept,
alone, unmade, like a maniac's bed?
The pores on your face have never
been so exposed. Like myriad
tired eyes they stare at me. So!
Let this sallow flesh sag together.
No one will notice. No one will care.
The world is a prentice decades
our junior, ardent, callow, merciless,

forever cutting his teeth. So come now,
right here, amid the refuse,
amid the bottles and detritus.
Let us consummate what the times portend.
The squalor is playing our song.

Judith Beveridge

Invitation

Cooking oil putters like an engine.
My kitchen is setting its course!
Islands of palms, dishes of singed coconut.
Will you kiss me when the heat steers East?
The pan dips low over soft island music
urging me on past salt and spices
to the ingredients of erotic cooking.
I'm reading the brochures of recipes
to impress with the wide map of my food.
I like the way a carob-bean maps
the Caribbean, I will say, as we overlook
the harbour and Opera House—that rack
of draining dishes. I have bought wine
the colour of betel-nut; all these fruits
are my map-maker's colours. We can stain
our fingers while the moon circumnavigates.
Already in the simmer of a kiss I hear gulls calling
over estuarine landscapes. I try to steer
the flavour, arrange the colours on a plate.
The kitchen is the compass sending us onwards
and it's nearly seven exactly.
Tonight, let's savour the placenames of food;
let's travel through time like a panel of tasters,
we'll follow the tongue, our native-guide
and discoverer; whole tablespoons to tour with.
Islands of figs, oil carefully frying
a wild banana; a breeze gently rocks
and water murmurs like a slow sentence
lifted from the phrase-book.
Whoever owns the language owns the food
though once dreaming paths may have linked
our sites. We will stare into our plates,

call all fares to our table.
I light the candles, their flames
are the soft palms of stewardesses
in the heart's wild, imagined places.

The Bee Keeper

He hunts bees, those workers who dance
for pollen. Like caravans that wander incense routes
East in his garden. They buzz as they scrub out
their cells with the salt and chastity of devotion.

Later, they'll drool honey. Yet sweetness
can turn sour and today they have collected
from the crippled plum and there is bitterness
amongst the roses, mutiny in the hepatica.

He watches them enter petals like vestries
in which to pray. But he knows piety can turn
in a treachery of light. One day, they'll compute
the sun for an exit; a choreography telling them:

left at the rock, three times round the tree.
So he listens for them in their noisy gazebos
and ponders loyalty, servitude. They were hers.
She'd hold a jar of them to the light

small as dried camomile flowers; she kept them
amongst the cheaper daisies. A solitary man,
he remembers how, once close to his ears
they sounded like knives in an attic of terrors.

The air leaked no scent of her betrayal. Yes,
he will rip up those plants. Now, he watches
for the queen. Is she plotting to leave
with the dance of another promised scent?

Any moment they could swarm; like Guy Fawkes
sparking the death of his own effigy.
But amongst his roses is strewn bitter gunpowder.
And now the bees like apprentices hand him

veil and gloves. They hood his fanaticism;
they dress him in the vestments of terror;
they hum him notes of a requiem; they plot
their routes; they are yellow with addiction.

He could burn them, he thinks, remembering
her lips crushed against his, bitter
as saccharine. His passion could tear
like a blowtorch through those racks of honeycomb.

Gig Ryan

Small-Scale

The nazi in your bed arranges you.
The strategy of his time bends like toothpaste.
You're shy and pleasurable. He knots your teeth.
He's got it all lined up.
The nothings you could never put into words.

Sure you look your best. His ugly intelligent face jams
into the sheet. His mouth crooked as a courtroom,
proud of his clumsy flesh
so sure you envy like a patient.
You're inexpressible, you're his way.

And when he's grasping like a dog,
you're not there. His clipped knowledge grinning like a jail.
You're locked, inexhaustible. He will quiet you like a gun
and fail to draw you.

For Grace / And You're So Fine

1

We pull in, early morning.
You are the flower, soft in me,
who goes, pull at the difficult door.
I hear the gate come back
into my bed, the rattle, your pale concern.
You are the final man, distracted and careful.

How grey eyes skid at my retrenched heart
to employ it provisionally, and well.
We kiss. Going down the sorrowing road like strangers,
ephemeral and rare. You're close as a lifetime.

All the sky is rain and tomorrow, running.
We're fixed.
The recent dream we step from like a taxi,
into the usual glass, the familiar financial year.
Your gentle look rifts into my bed.
Your grey forgotten mouth, the illness, how we crumble,
without proportion, delicate and mortal.
You are the element, sheer, the hand jarring
on the white reluctant gate.
You are the flower.

2

And her, with her wise and compact limbs,
smiles like Easter.
In the good room, the man will carry you away
on an ambitious and derelict passion.
The cheap red crying down in you.
His thin flesh hard against the tragic sheet, yours.
He is the sweet bone in you, grieve then, your approximate arms.

She's coming like a saxophone, jazz,
her private inscrutable pain, stay
with the man you don't care for.
His stadium arms, his collector's joy.
She leans in him like an easy-chair, useful and reliable.
She will.

All the shops die, now,
his long grey cloudy eyes wrapped at your neck
like a loss. His kiss before you like an initial,
curious and perishing, weep then, for what we do allow.
Cool the remarkable night, touched on, anonymous, perfect.

3

or dream. Genuine as a ruin, you're
bred in me, your kiss of shadow, contemporary and going.
The long half-light will long for you
in these limited hours, divide the clock, and nurture.
How rare you are, how sorry,
as we take the dark into us, meek in the abstract,
and pass over.
You are the last man, slowed in me.
The door picks at the eye.
Dissolve the awful hands, wept for,
and watch the long light rapping like a trial
it shuts you down.

She Gives Reason

It had to end and so I snapped it
but pain alternated with emptiness swarming in my stomach
and there was a man who wanted me to sing charm
to his clients, to connect, and economically it fits
He gave me masses of the stuff
showered me with it like a wedding
a soft forgetful splint I could at least stand in
and we'd drive. It amused me to draw from each
the right distance, cold or consecrated
and to study the language of exchange. I could cut it
to a tee. He's rising without me,
better, with his cool brain. I couldn't mix it
They'd see beneath the tip soon
and the staggered ice realistically I am.
It was good I made him.
Now I rent it up, the white sheets to be prepared
and weighed, and the heart's wrapped up in its sick cradle.

Donna McSkimming

Ululation for a Red Headed Woman

(For Julia)

if you kiss a red head lick her ears & you'll
hear crimson semitones; the sacred fires lit
& attracting revellers to some dark hill
& dancing, dancing till you fall exhausted
against the old tree shivers/remembers bonfires.

or

if you kiss a red head stroke her hair,
like silk snapping electric. static.
imbedding spark on spark, till the future
detonates along the fey lines of your palms.

or

if you kiss a red head, taste her nipples
translucent & touched lilac—as the core
of the flame—as the space between the
Goddess's breaths. a helix from nipple to;

eyes begin a canticle in blue a scale sliding
finding the spiral through the centre
of an iridescent iris

or

if you kiss a red head like running downhill
through acres of opium poppies. the petals
stinging a skinful of pungent kisses. & poppy
heads—knuckles into flesh already
begging/bursting full. O grip the inner thigh hard
& let the opiates roll like balm across my
stomach.

Dorothy Porter

From *Scenes From a Marriage*

v

Nothing so sweet
nothing so obscene
as my lover and me
will ever be
shown on TV

this fragment,
        from a pop song I imagined,
            stuck in my throat
                helplessly
        during the coldest night
            of the year
when mixed passionate breath
        fogged up
                every window
                every mirror
                every TV set
                    in my house
while I collapsed cosy, trivial
                and tender—

then in coffee's camaraderie
     a silt
  like Lake Eyre parched white
when the night parrot
     questioned my fidelity
when the night parrot
     arrived home.

Tristesse —
     and watching through smudged glass
the wind
     savaging a sapling —

this trapped tyranny
     of watching
          nothing
    and conjuring violence
      from the magic powder
        of boredom, —

I'm a deserted wife
    listlessly watching
       tomato soup
  as if it were 'Gone with the Wind' —

it's the dry season
   the night parrot
    is starving
  and won't mate
    can't nest
  and finds my water
    bitter,
we're fighting
  and I say
      like a whining suburb
      sculpted by salt bush
        and Campbelltown land developers
       this is your desert, not mine!

From *When Desire's Gone*

II

The dance   King David remembers the dance
dancing before the ark   before God
feet   ecstacy   nakedness

dancing before God   the ark gold
moving towards him swarming terrifying
like a plague of burning locusts
this dance before God   dancing before God
I remember   I remember
geriatric David freezing
crawling over the ribs of his teenage concubine
can't dance   can't feel the storm of God in his blood
thorns of dust through the feet
can't desire   can't dance before God.

Cars. Lightning. Rain.

Cars. Lightning. Rain.
Your cheek on my hair.
Strawberries. White wine.
A mess in the back seat.

I drive you home
and we chat between thunder claps
about the fall of Crete.

A bare-breasted goddess
at ease, insouciant control,
holding firmly with feminine hands
two writhing snakes.

Secretly
    I imagine loving you
        like that,
my feet balanced
        apart,
hanging on without fear
        to any pet reptile between us.

But between kisses
    my breath tears like wet paper,
holding you in my arms
    is a tender farce or a blubbering High Mass;
I skid on my wrenched heart
    even more than this old car
        skids on the drenched road.

Cars. Lightning. Rain.
When you leave me
I watch every Minoan fresco
    ever painted and cherished
        drip and burn.

Lionel Fogarty

Love or human nature

Love originator is her koori love's
Glad nearly complete with you
when not sad
possess we personally for the peoples
spirit and goal
bring me to koori cause cos cos
Equally we like to be near bodys
Mother is woman
Nature are from koori scoreness
respectfully comforts me here
Mankind . . . womankind . . .
even when man hypocrites
and black baits at the coloured bar
So love originator thousand
Stir in seen godfully gentle
to her black man now.
Or violent massing greedy boy or girl
will sway
late coming to home
a voice strong aware you
'take relevance and articulate
give strength, pride of a koori language
Share your women brother . . .
Nah . . . nah . . . don't live thata now downing.
The five paces behind . . . now . . .
up front expression desire
desire your own love
original womens.
I'm murri koori aboriginal
loving fresh and bold
see ya, told ya
us humanity
not discovered.
Gladly came
emerging just to our people
making love love love.

Love travels

Love travels
I watch inexhaustibly
Inspiration by
Love travels
visible deep emotions
proves our magic powers
Brightness on memory
comes love travelling
My express sprung
temperate in summer
Camouflage formalized
mimic loving
They believing
We suns in hails
Mountain rain
We spiritful
rythmically
poetry.
Peculiarities in bliss
of solitude
are sharpened senses
learned by
Love travels
terribly depressed them
Crawl crawls
We murries
Love . . . travelling . . .

Fiona Perry

The Cuckoo Wife

At first he made excuses, thought she'd change.
She'd been an only child. Her parents kept
her cloistered, nymphlike, but they died.
She suffered herself for a space, a short unbearable
freedom then gave him her limbs like peonies
her glorious hair, her parents' wealth. He married
to enclose her always. But men came with notched
cocks, clocking up cuckoo wives. And she ran off.

In the items left were the children who gave her
eczema. 'They stole her away.' 'She is in a story,'
they whispered in bed. He tucked them in, their sleepy
heads, tumbling like apricots onto their pillows.
He curled them up, little kernels, his horde
against the winter. She is outside their arms
and his love where the iron wind blows.
Dreams empty and scar her. Frightened
she watches her imperfections grow, conceals
them when she can. His for the asking.

The Unearthed Girl (an archeologist's dream)

I would have carried you
like the stranded dolphin in my arms
past the river Sarno, to the bay
of Napoli.

Waited
until your thirteen years, of stealing navel oranges
dreaming Gods by the leaden fountain
yearned for me.

I would have found you
in the calidarium combing your pubic hair,
your thighs in a cone of serpentine light,
defiled you there.

Instead the oven-tongued Gods spat
lapilli on birds, on the fluted
urns in the viridarium, ash on the sundial,
ash on all Pompeii.

I found your lunging house.
Your mother stuccoed
with fear before the door,
a spent green serpent, 'Let me by!'

But the tongues of the Gods
were inside you, their tongues
of earth in your mouth.

I dream flesh.
A frieze of bones
I will not search for.

Let strangers find
your small wrists
under green pumice stones.

Stephen J. Williams

Love

(perform *allegro con brio*)

when i feel its got to stop its because im afraid of what it might
do to me if it does stop and im not ready to feel that its got to
stop because i might be pulling myself silly and the time when
its got to stop might never come

when i feel its got to stop i take long walks under the sky under
the words i left hanging in the air

when i feel its got to stop i eat bran and read logic so my conversation wont feel like an early mornings constipated pushing and
groaning in the toilet

when i feel its got to stop im too polite and ask if i can interject
your logorrhoea like rubber suppositories or cigarette buts in the
kitchen sink

when i feel its got to stop i tell you i dont love you anymore and
mean it for at least as long as it takes me to say it and when you
do think i mean it i want to die

when i feel its got to stop i call you at three in the morning and
ask for a fuck and you give me the address of a friend whose out
of the country and wont be back till next year

when i feel its got to stop i wont come at to your parties because
i dont like talking philosophically about the aristotelian origins
of wittgenstein and i dont understand how the tractatus can teach
me to say i love you without farting

when i feel its got to stop its because i still love you enough not
to want you to know that i feel its got to stop because when i
feel its got to stop

when i feel its got to stop its because the six doughnuts of our
love affair werent enough and after checking the contents of my
box one last time you guiltlessly replace my sweaty body on the
supermarket shelf between the baked beans and the chicken noo-
dle soup

when i feel its got to stop i get lost in the city mapping the tedi-
ous plan of streets waiting for the place where the pain and sorrow of our last argument will fall out of the night and tear my
guts apart leaving me to survive till morning by licking the remains of our last sensuous rain out of the gutter

when i feel its got to stop its because im afraid of what it might
do to you if it does stop and youre not ready to feel that its got
to stop because you think that the time when its got to stop
should never come

Adam Aitken

Take Me for a Ride

She knew foreigners wanted dope and —
ssshhh the hotel manager is listening —
put two fingers to her lips.

For hours we would mime
                              sweet nothings.
What was my address?
Dissipate handwriting from her
                              delicate hand.
We bring out the little black books —
'Please write your address here.'

Her mother briefed her —
'Make your suffering look
                              charming,
learn the Samba, or at least the Rumba.'

I want to dance,
            the steps are so
                        intricate
while she touches me,
            praises my
                        movements, reckless and foreign.

Catherine Bateson

Persephone Remembers Helen

She got under your skin, that one. Even cool Hades sweated
desire around her. It was a way she had
of walking into a room as though asking permission,
of listening to you as if you were the only person at the party.
When you think of Athena you think of a precise beauty,
an equation in pure maths, a map of the stars.
When you see Diana you remember
the arrow's perfect flight, a long glass of cold wine.

When you saw Helen you thought of sex,
those afternoons and the enveloping smell of sperm.

It wasn't her fault and it was a gift,
in its way, but it was bound to turn out badly.
Melelaus was a good enough man, not what you'd call
    passionate —
methodical and kind.

Paris — there was a boy — skin like peaches,
the muscle definition of an athlete — and we all know he could run.

Poor Helen. Impossible to describe her beauty.
A Monroe, that's what she was: forever trying to hold down her
    skirt
with all that pouting innocence and yet a knowledge,
deep as Eve's
locked in her eyes.

From *The King of Spain Poems*

1

The king of spain drove out of a romance magazine
in his 4-wheel drive. He's the high school dream,
he's the one I cleave to. He turned up
in my Tarot cards — bright king of pentacles —
and ruled there.
The king and I were inseparable.

The king of spain has left for interstate. His phone's
off the hook. He's sleeping in at the Hilton, ordering
    room-service,

pinching the waitress's arse.
My doorstep is covered in autumn leaves
and the wine has gone sour.

The king of spain has forsaken me.
I was no more than a caption in his life.

The king of spain is dead.

I've given up on royalty.

2

The king of spain is dead

but he turns up in every man I love, sly
jack of hearts, bitching up my patience deck.

He tattooed passion into my pale bones, he coloured
me in. We taught each other—we were blank canvases,
new languages,
we were all we could get
of each other.

The king of spain is dead
but he turns up in every man I love.

Dipti Saravanamuttu

Nageen Lake

You journey through the heartlands
with your hair cropped, and the chaos
comforts you like a welcome.
Kashmiri musicians play the water-pot
like a drum while Akbar's fort
looks down at the water lilies.
We're disco dancing to forties music
on one of the houseboats.
I'm dancing with a friend, I
close my eyes and dance intensely
missing her.
He sings to me, we both sing:
'I'd like to take you
on a slow boat to China'.

It's like philosophy, or the Bhuddha's sermon
when he held up a lotus flower
and perceiving the lesson in this
only Kasapa smiled.

View for a Mirror

You don't send her the *Dharmapada*
as though wishing her happiness

is enough. Time stopped like a young cat
soft-boned and final, at 4 am.

'Self is one's refuge', O Bhikku.
'I am taking back the illusion

with which I strengthened you.'
The wise teacher explains

the meaning and the text, and that
is the poem, separate of you.

Still she lives within you
like a sense of sunlight.

Charmaine Papertalk-Green

Wanna Be White

My man took off yesterday
with a waagin
He left me and the kids
to be something in this world
said he sick of being
black, poor and laughed at
Said he wanted to be white
have better clothes, a flash car
and eat fancy
He said me and the kids
would give him a bad name
because we are black too
So he left with a waagin.

Waagin: East Coast word for 'white
woman', derived from 'white gin'.

Alison Croggon

Lyric

As brazen as the naked day
he came and stole my heart away
though I was wanton, sly and fey:
merry meet and merry part
my heart.

No modest ban, no practised play
could keep his gentle hands at bay
for all my armours fell away:
merry meet and merry part
my heart.

And all my blood grows on his bone
and in his ribs my heart is sewn
when one and one make only one:
merry meet and merry part
my heart.

And if one day the ruthless sun
wakes us to show our love has gone
then of us two there will be none:
merry meet and merry part
my heart.

From *Howl*

1   Betrayal

my lover is not here
to touch the child
rolling in my womb

o unbearable innocent
how will you smile
in this hive of lies

Seduction Poem

I want the slew of muscle, a less
cerebral meeting place; no word
but your male shout, the shirred
unpublic face and honest skin
crying to me, yes,
the mouthless, eyeless tenderness
crying to be let in.

Unbutton all your weight, like a bird
flying the night's starred nakedness:
put down your grammatical tongue, undress
your correct and social skin:
come white and absurd
all your language one word
crying to be let in.

ACKNOWLEDGEMENTS

We wish to thank the copyright holders for permission to reproduce the following material:

Charles Harpur: 'Country Lovers'; 'Rhymes to a Lady with a Copy of Love Poems'; 'The World-Birth of Love'; 'Self-Liberty' from *The Poetical Works of Charles Harpur*, Ed. Elizabeth Perkins, Angus & Robertson, 1984. James Michael: 'Fallen'; 'Said the sunlight to the moonlight' from *Songs Without Music*, Sydney, 1857. Charles Thatcher: 'Colonial Courtship, or Love on the Diggings' from *Thatcher's Colonial Songs*, Coles Book Arcade. Reproduced The Library Board of South Australia, 1964. 'Colonial Courtship' first published in *The Colonial Minstrel*, Charlwood, 1864. Henry Kendall: 'Ulmarra'; 'Campaspe'; 'Rose Lorraine' from *The Poetical Works of Henry Kendall*, Libraries Board of Adelaide, 1966. Emma Frances Anderson: 'No Room for the Dead' from *Colonial Poems*, Marlborough, 1869. Ada Cambridge: 'A Wife's Protest' from *Unspoken Thoughts*, Kegan, Paul, Trench & Co., 1887. Reproduced English Department, University College, UNSW-ADFA, 1988. Victor Daley: 'Elizabeth' from *Wine and Roses*, Angus & Robertson, 1913. 'Lachesis' from *Victor Daley*, Angus & Robertson, 1963. W.T. Goodge: 'Love and the Cycles' from *Hits! Skits! and Jingles*, Bulletin Co., 1899. Reprinted, Pollard Publishing, 1972. George Essex Evans: From 'Loraine: Part I' from *The Collected Verse of G. Essex Evans*, Angus & Robertson, 1928. Mary Gilmore: 'In Poverty and Toil' from *Marri'd and Other Verses*, George Robertson & Co., 1910. 'Down by the Sea'; 'Eve-Song'; 'From the Spanish'; 'In Life's Sad School' from *Mary Gilmore: Selected Verse*, Ed. R.D. Fitzgerald, 1948; 2nd ed., Angus & Robertson, 1969. William Gay: 'Love's Menu' from *The Poetical Works of William Gay*, Lothian Publishing, 1911. Inez Hyland: 'Jilted' from *In Sunshine and Shadow*, George Robertson and Co., 1893. Barcroft Boake: 'A Wayside Queen' from *Where the Dead Men Lie and Other Poems*, Ed. A.G. Stephens, Angus & Robertson, 1897; 2nd ed., 1913. Bernard O'Dowd: 'Lust' from *The Poems of Bernard O'Dowd*, Lothian Publishing, 1941. Henry Lawson: 'The Watch on the Kerb'; 'He's Gone to England for a Wife'; 'Taking His Chance'; 'The Sliprails and the Spur'; 'The Shearer's Dream' from *Henry Lawson: Collected Verse*, Ed. Colin Roderick, Angus & Robertson, 1968. 'E' (Mary E. Fullerton): 'The Selector's Wife' from *The Breaking Furrow*, Galleon Press, 1921. 'Travellers'; 'Lovers' from *Moles Do So Little With Their Privacy*, Angus & Robertson, 1942. Christopher Brennan: From 'Towards the Source: 2'; From 'Lilith: XII'; 'It is so long ago!' from *The Verse of Christopher Brennan*, Ed. A.R. Chisholm, Angus & Robertson, 1960. 'Sydney Partrige' (Kate Margaret Stone): 'The Lonely Man' from *The Lie and Other Lines*, Koolinda Press, 1913. John Shaw Neilson: 'You, and Yellow Air'; 'Love's Coming'; 'Song be Delicate'; 'The Worshipper' from *John Shaw Neilson: Poetry, Autobiography and Correspondence*, Ed. Cliff Hanna, University of Queensland Press, 1991. C.J.

Dennis: 'A Spring Song' from *The Songs of a Sentimental Bloke*, Angus & Robertson, 1915. Reprinted in Australian Pocket Library Edition, 1945. Hugh McCrae: 'Song of the Rain'; 'Gallows Marriage'; 'Names' from *The Best Poems of Hugh McCrae*, Ed. R.G. Howarth, Angus & Robertson, 1961. 'Furnley Maurice' (Frank Wilmot): 'Praise' from *The Gully*, Melbourne University Press, 1929. Reprinted 1945. 'Brian Vrepont' (B. A. Trubridge): 'Night' from *Beyond the Claw: Poems*, Angus & Robertson, 1943. Ethel Anderson: 'Orchard Secret' from *Squatter's Luck*, Melbourne University Press, 1942; 2nd ed., 1945. 'Doubtful Lover' from *Sunday at Yarralumla: A Symphony*, Angus & Robertson, 1947. 'William Baylebridge' (Charles William Blocksidge): From 'Love Redeemed: XXXIX'; From 'Life's Testament: III' from *Collected Works*, Ed. P.R. Stephensen, Angus & Robertson, 1963. 'Anna Wickham' (Edith Hepburn): 'The Man with a Hammer'; 'The Resource'; 'Song of Ophelia the Survivor' from *Selected Poems*, Ed. David Garnett, Chatto & Windus, 1971. Dorothea Mackellar, 'The Heart of a Bird'; 'Riding Rhyme'; 'The Other Woman's Word'; 'Once When She Thought Aloud' from *The Poems of Dorothea Mackellar*, Rigby, 1971. J. Alex Allan: 'The Bride Wakes' from *Revolution*, Bread and Cheese Club, 1940. Zora Cross: 'My Muse'; 'Thou Shalt Not'; 'Night-Ride' from *Songs of Love and Life*, Angus & Robertson, 1917. Nina Murdoch: 'Warbride' from *More Songs of the Open Air*, Robertson & Mullens, 1922. Lesbia Harford: 'I can't feel the sunshine'; 'The Folk I Love'; 'A Bad Snap'; 'I'm like all lovers'; 'Grotesque'; 'You want a lily' from *The Poems of Lesbia Harford*, Ed. Drusilla Modjeska and Marjorie Pizer, Sirius/ Angus & Robertson, 1985. Elsie Cole: 'The Slayers' from *Children of Joy*, Lothian Publishing, 1928. Leonard Mann: 'Girls and Soldiers Singing' from *The Delectable Mountains*, Angus & Robertson, 1944. E. M. England, 'Incompatibility' from *The Happy Monarch*, Carter-Watson Co., 1927. 'Bush Girl' from *Queensland Days*, Dymock's Book Arcade, 1944. Jack Lindsay: From 'Clue of Darkness: Release' from *Clue of Darkness*, Andrew Dakers, 1949. Kenneth Slessor: 'Earth-Visitors'; 'Polarities' from *One Hundred Poems*, Angus & Robertson, 1944. Re-issued as *Poems*, 1963. R.D. Fitzgerald: 'Her Hands'; 'Of Some Country'; From 'Moonlight Acre: IX'; 'The Waterfall' from *Forty Years' Poems*, Angus & Robertson, 1963. Mary Finnin: 'As You Like It' from *Look Down, Olympians*, W.A. Hamer, 1939. 'For a Picture of Lovers In Stained Glass'; 'Approach' from *Royal*, W.A. Hamer, 1941. A.D. Hope: 'The Wandering Islands'; 'An Epistle: Edward Sackville to Venetia Digby' from *Collected Poems 1930-1970*, Angus & Robertson, 1972. Eve Langley: 'Among Wild Swine in the Woods' from *Jindyworobak Anthology*, 1942. Ronald McCuaig: 'Sydney, A Fine Town'; 'The Hungry Moths' from *Quod Ronald McCuaig*, Angus & Robertson, 1946. Elizabeth Riddell: 'The Letter'; 'Here Lies' from *From the Midnight Courtyard*, Angus & Robertson, 1989. '"Autobiography"', *Overland* 115, 1990. Walter Adamson: 'For Non-Swimmers' from *Adamson's Three Legged World*, Abalone Press, 1985. Hector Monro: From 'Don Juan in Australia: Canto Two, XXI to XXIV', Hawthorn, 1986. John Bray: 'Lust and Love' from *Poems 1972-79*, Australian National University Press, 1979. Margaret Diesendorf: 'Modigliani Nude' from *Light*, Edwards & Shaw, 1981. Selections from 'Holding the Golden Apple' from *Holding the Golden Apple*, Phoenix Publications, 1991. Barbara Giles: 'Eve Rejects Apple'; 'In the Park, Looking'; 'Oh I will cut him up on little stars' from *The Hag in the Mirror*, Pariah Press, 1989. Roland Robinson: 'The Water-Lubra'; 'Gymea' from *Selected Poems*, Angus & Robertson, 1989. John Blight: 'Conversation' from *The New City Poems*, Angus & Robertson, 1980. Flexmore Hudson: 'Waiting for a Letter' from *Ashes and Sparks*, F.W. Preece & Sons, 1937. 'The Sorrow of Earth' from *With the First Soft Rain*, Economy Press, 1943. 'The Kiss'; 'A Sleep of Grief' from *Pools of the Cinnabar Range*, Economy Press, 1959. Joyce Lee: 'Double Wedding' from *Abruptly from the Flatlands*, Pariah Press, 1984. Kenneth Mackenzie: 'How Full Kate is'; 'Tripoli'; 'The Moonlit Doorway'; 'In this pain-enchanted place' from *The Poems of Kenneth Mackenzie*, Ed. Evan Jones, Angus & Robertson, 1972. Douglas Stewart: 'As the Crow Flies' from *The Dosser in Springtime*, Angus & Robertson, 1946. J.M. Couper: Selections from 'Letters to Aunt Welch in the Year of Her Death' from *In From the Sea*, Wentworth Books, 1974. Patrick Hore-Ruthven: 'In Palestine' from *The Happy Warrior*, Angus & Robertson, 1944. Dorothy Auchterlonie: 'A Problem of Language'; 'Present Tense' from *The Dolphin*, Australian National University Press, 1967. '"The Hollow Years"' from *Something to Someone*, Brindabella Press, 1983. David Campbell: 'Come Live with Me'; 'We Took the Storms to Bed'; 'Lovers' Words'; From 'Two Songs with Spanish Burdens: A Grey Singlet' from *Collected Poems*, Ed. Leonie J. Kramer, Angus & Robertson, 1989. John Manifold: 'The Griesly Wife'; 'Song' from *Collected Verse of John Manifold*, University of Queensland Press, 1968. David Martin: 'Geometry' from *The Gift*, Jacaranda, 1966. Judith Wright: 'Woman to Man'; From 'The Blind Man: Country Dance'; 'The Man Beneath the Tree'; 'Dove–Love' from *Collected Poems 1942–1970*, Angus & Robertson, 1971. 'Eve Scolds' from *Fourth Quarter*, Angus & Robertson, 1976. From 'Four Poems from New Zealand: The Beach at Hokitika' from *Phantom Dwelling*, Angus & Robertson, 1985. James McAuley: ' When Shall the Fair'; 'Canticle'; 'One Thing at Least'; 'Father, Mother, Son' from *Collected Poems 1936–1970*, Angus & Robertson, 1971. Jack Davis: 'Tribal Girl' from *Jagardoo*, Methuen, 1978. Anne Elder: 'At Amalfi' from *Crazy Woman*, Angus & Robertson, 1976. Nancy Gordon: 'The Lady and the Pheasant' from *The Inner Courtyard: A South Australian Anthology of Love Poetry*, Ed. Anne Brewster and Jeff Guest, Wakefield Press, 1990. Rosemary Dobson: 'The Rape of Europa' from *Selected Poems*, Angus & Robertson, 1973. Gwen Harwood: 'The Wine Is Drunk'; 'Carpe Diem'; 'Fever'; 'Carnal Knowledge I'; 'Iris'; 'Meditation on Wyatt II' from *Selected Poems*, Rev. ed., Angus & Robertson, 1990. John Millett: From 'Tail Arse Charlie: VII' from *Tail Arse Charlie*, South Head Press, 1982. Oodgeroo of the tribe Noonuccal, Custodian of the land Minjerribah (formerly Kath Walker): 'The Young Girl Wanda'; 'Gifts'; 'My Love' from *My People*, Jacaranda Wiley, 1970; 3rd ed., 1990. Lex Banning: 'Moment in Time' from *Apocalypse in Springtime*, Edwards & Shaw, 1956. 'Touts les Chats sont Gris' from *There Was a Crooked Man*, Ed. Richard Appleton and Alex Galloway, Sirius/Angus & Robertson, 1987. Alister Kershaw: 'The Gift' from *Collected Poems*, Angus & Robertson, 1992. Nan McDonald: 'The Mountain Road, Crete, 1941' from *Selected Poems*, Angus & Robertson, 1969. Dimitris Tsaloumas: 'Girl Riding' from *Falcon Drinking*, University of Queensland Press, 1988. Geoffrey Dutton: 'Love Song' from *Antipodes in Shoes*,

Edwards & Shaw, 1958, © Geoffrey Dutton. From 'A Body of Words: 2, 3, 8, 9' from *A Body of Words*, Edwards & Shaw, 1977. Dorothy Hewett: 'Country Idyll' from *Windmill Country*, Overland, 1968. 'Psyche's Husband' from *Selected Poems*, Fremantle Arts Centre Press, 1991. From 'Alice in Wormland: 10, 21, 38' from *Alice in Wormland*, Paperbark Press, 1987. Nancy Keesing: 'Sydney Domain: Lady and Cockatoo'; 'Sailor and Lady' from *Three Men and Sydney*, Angus & Robertson, 1955. Eric Rolls: 'Akun' from *The Green Mosaic: Memories of New Guinea*, Thomas Nelson, 1977. David Rowbotham: 'Like a Gnome of Grimm' from *Maydays*, University of Queensland Press, 1980. Vincent Buckley: From 'Late Winter Child: I, II, VIII, XXV from *Late Winter Child*, Oxford University Press, 1979. 'I have you poised in the mind' from *Last Poems*, McPhee Gribble/ Penguin, 1991. Laurence Collinson: 'The Lover, on Returning from the Wars'; 'The Room' from *The Moods of Love*, Overland, 1957. Jill Hellyer: 'The Puzzle' from *The Exile: Selected Verse*, Alpha Books, 1969. Joan Mas: 'A Death'; 'The Water Pool'; 'Haiku: Love' from *The Fear and the Flowering*, Edwards & Shaw, 1975, reproduced with permission of Heather Cullen. Grace Perry: 'The tulip' from *Within the Hill: A Collection of Erotic Verse*, Ed. Alan Gould and Paul Balnaves, Canberra Poetry, 1975. 'Eros in Moss Vale' from *Be Kind to Animals*, South Head Press, 1984. Bruce Beaver: 'Death's Directives XI'; 'Durer: Naked Hausfrau' from *New and Selected Poems*, University of Queensland Press, 1991. Pamela Bell: 'No Willow-Cabin For Me' from *Poetry 1947–1989*, Thomas Rowland, 1990. R.F. Brissenden: 'Another Place, Another Time' from *Winter Matins*, Angus & Robertson, 1971. 'A River Remembered (With Two Pictures)' from *Building a Terrace*, Australian National University Press, 1975. 'Nectarines'; '"Parfum Exotique": Remittance Man and Governess in Landscape' from *Sacred Sites*, Phoenix Review, 1990, reproduced with permission of R.L. Brissenden, c/o Curtis Brown (Aust.) Pty Ltd, Sydney. Peter Porter: 'Sex and the Over Forties'; 'Old-Fashioned Wedding'; 'The Easiest Room in Hell' from *Collected Poems*, Oxford University Press, 1984. 'A Chagall Postcard' from *Possible Worlds*, Oxford University Press, 1989. Bruce Dawe: 'Dial WX 4500'; 'The Raped Girl's Father'; 'Suburban Lovers'; 'The Affair' from *Sometimes Gladness*, Longman Cheshire, 1983. Evan Jones: 'Ode: The Beautiful Girls' from *Understandings*, Melbourne University Press, 1967. 'Nursery Rhyme' from *Left at the Post*, University of Queensland Press, 1984. Philip Martin: 'Tombs of the Hetaerae'; 'A Certain Love'; 'Laid in Earth' from *New and Selected Poems*, Longman Cheshire, 1988. Jennifer Strauss: 'What Women Want'; 'The Nightside of the Holiday' from *Labour Ward*, Pariah Press, 1988. Fay Zwicky: 'Cleft' from *Kaddish*, University of Queensland Press, 1982. 'Penelope Spins' from *Ask Me*, University of Queensland Press, 1990. 'Akibat', unpublished, reproduced with permission of the author. David Malouf: 'easier' from *Bicycle and Other Poems*, University of Queensland Press, 1970. Margaret Scott: From 'New Songs for Mariana: Lies' from *Visited*, Angus & Robertson, 1983. Chris Wallace-Crabbe: 'The Amorous Cannibal' from *The Amorous Cannibal*, Oxford University Press, 1985. 'The Path', unpublished, reproduced with permission of the author. Katherine Gallagher: From 'Surf-Lore' from *Poet's Choice*. 'Premonition' from *Fish-Rings on Water*, Forest Books, 1989. Rodney Hall: 'Fountain and Thunderstorm' from

Selected Poems, University of Queensland Press, 1975. Thomas Shapcott: From 'The Litanies of Julia Pastrana: I'; From 'Life Taste XI' from *Selected Poems 1956–1988*, University of Queensland Press, 1989. Randolph Stow: 'Endymion' from *Counterfeit Silence: Selected Poems*, Angus & Robertson, 1969. Robin Thurston: 'Gifts' from *Believed Dangerous*, University of Queensland Press, 1975. Sylvia Kantarizis: 'Time and Motion'; 'A Warning' from *Time and Motion*, Prism Books, 1975. Judith Rodriguez: 'Penelope at Sparta'; 'The Mudcrab-eaters'; 'In-flight Note' from *New and Selected Poems*, University of Queensland Press, 1988. Norman Talbot: 'Lovetime Monologue'; 'Tristan in Dawn' from *Find the Lady*, South Head Press, 1977. Philip Roberts: 'Poem to Mike' from *Selected Poems*, Island Press, 1978. Mudrooroo (formerly Colin Johnson): 'Calcutta in the Evening'; 'Love Song'; 'There Is Love' from *The Garden of Gethsemane: Poems from the Lost Decade*, Hyland House, 1991. J.S. Harry: 'The Moon and the Earthman' from *Poet's Choice*, 1976. Manfred Jurgensen: 'philatelist' from *The Skin Trade*, Phoenix Publications, 1983. 'on time' from *Selected Poems 1972–1986*, Albion Press, 1987. 'love in front of the computer' from *The Partiality of Harbours*, Paperbark Press (1988?). Geoffrey Lehmann: 'Furius' from *Nero's Poems*, Angus & Robertson, 1981. 'Lenin's Question' from *Children's Games*, Angus & Robertson, 1990. Kate Llewellyn: 'Diaries'; 'The Fish' from *Luxury*, Hale & Iremonger, 1985. 'He' from *Honey*, Hudson, 1988. Jan Owen: 'The Kiss' from *Westerly No.3*, 1991. Geoff Page: 'Love at the End'; 'Ideal Couple' from *Selected Poems*, Collins/Angus & Robertson, 1991. Craig Powell: 'Short Message for Cupid' from *A Country Without Exiles*, South Head Press, 1972. Andrew Taylor: 'Developing a Wife'; 'The Beast with Two Backs'; From 'Travelling to Gleis-Binario: v' from *Selected Poems*, University of Queensland Press, 1988. Julian Croft: 'Amica' from *Confessions of a Corinthian*, Angus & Robertson, 1991. Lee Knowles: 'Boomerang Gorge' from *Dial Marina*, Fremantle Arts Centre Press, 1986. Jennifer Rankin: 'Gannet Dreaming'; 'Tale' from *Collected Poems*, Ed. Judith Rodriguez, University of Queensland Press, 1990. Nigel Roberts: 'She is becoming' from *Steps for Astaire*, Hale & Iremonger, 1983. Lee Cataldi: 'History'; From 'Fairy Tales: 1' from *Invitation to a Marxist Lesbian Party*, Wild & Woolley, 1978. 'your body' from *The Women who Live on the Ground*, Penguin Books, 1990. Robert Adamson: 'Action Would Kill It/ A Gamble'; 'The Home, The Spare Room'; 'Songs for Juno'; 'Harriet Westbrook Looks at the Serpentine' from *Selected Poems 1970–1989*, University of Queensland Press, 1990. John Tranter: 'At the Piccolo' from *Red Movie and Other Poems*, Angus & Robertson, 1972. From 'Crying in Early Infancy: 46' from *Crying in Early Infancy: 100 Sonnets*, Makar Press, 1977. 'Crocodile Rag' from *Under Berlin*, University of Queensland Press, 1988. Caroline Caddy: 'Past Love' from *Conquistadors*, Penguin Books, 1991. Joanne Burns: 'and you say yr not an easy rider' from *Ratz*, Saturday Centre Poets, 1973. Diane Fahey: 'The Pool'; 'Psyche and Eros' from *Metamorphoses*, Dangaroo Press, 1988. Gillian Hanscombe: From 'The Charms: 8, 13' from *Hecate's Charms*, Khasmik Poets, 1975. Peter Murphy: 'Jane Eyre Extensions' from *Poet's Choice 1976*, Island Press. Mark O'Connor: 'The Pairing of Terns' from *Selected Poems*, Hale & Iremonger, 1986. Bobbi Sykes: 'Love Poem: I'; 'Sins of Omission' from *Love Poems and Other Revolutionary Actions*, University of Queensland

Press, 1979. Aboriginal Song Poetry: From 'The Goulburn Island Cycle: 11, 27'; From 'The Rose River Cycle: 9'. Translated Ronald M. Berndt, *Three Faces of Love*, Thomas Nelson, 1976. Jeri Kroll: 'Man Holding Cat as Woman' from *Death as Mr Right*, Friendly Street Poets, 1982. Shelton Lea: 'he came to her as a birthday gift' from *Palatine Madonna*, Outback Press, 1978. 'The Daily News' from *Overland* 123, 1991. K.F. Pearson: From '3 Versions of Sleep: A Formal Sonnet' from *Messages from Things*, Friendly Street Poets, 1981. Eric Beach: 'poverty is a monologue' from *a photo of some people in a football stadium*, Overland, 1978. 'untitled' from *The Inner Courtyard*, Ed. Anne Brewster and Jeff Guess, Wakefield Press, 1990. Kristin Henry: 'Late Life Interview' from *Slices of Wry*, Pariah Press, 1985. Billy Marshall-Stoneking: 'The Cost of Love' from *Southern Review*, 1990. Graham Rowlands: 'The Letter' from *Dial a Poem*, Friendly Street Poets, 1982. Michael Dransfield: 'dread was'; 'pas de deux for lovers'; 'parthenogenesis' from *Collected Poems*, Ed. Rodney Hall, University of Queensland Press, 1989. Jeff Guess: 'She Smells the Rain' from *Leaving Maps*, Friendly Street Poets, 1984. Tony Lintermans: 'The Custom of Kissing Eyes Observed' from *The Shed Manifesto*, Scribe Publications, 1989. Irina Grigorescu Pana: 'Your Eyes' from *Meanjin* 48, 1989. John A. Scott: from 'Confession: Relationship' from *The Quarrel with Ourselves & Confession*, Rigmarole Books, 1984. 'Breath'; 'Smoking' from *Singles*, University of Queensland Press, 1989. Alex Skovron: 'From an Interview with a Faded Juggler' from *The Rearrangement*, Melbourne University Press, 1988. Vicki Viidikas: 'The artist without his body' from *Condition Red*, University of Queensland Press, 1973. Alan Wearne: 'Roger' from *Meanjin* 48, 1989. Laurie Duggan: From 'The Epigrams of Martial: VI xxxiv, XII lxv' from *The Epigrams of Martial*, Scripsi, 1989. 'Obsession' from *Blue Notes*, Picador/Pan, 1990. Alan Gould: 'The Burying' from *The Pausing of the Hours*, Angus & Robertson, 1984. John Jenkins: 'Why I Like You' from *Chromatic Cargoes*, Post Neo Publications, 1986. Kate Jennings: 'Met a Man A Fine Man' from *Come to Me My Melancholy Baby*, Outback Press, 1975. Jennifer Maiden: 'Circe'; 'Doings' from *Selected Poems*, Penguin Books, 1990. 'A Summer Emotion' from *The Winter Baby*, Angus & Robertson, 1990. Vicki Raymond: 'The Witch Sycorax Addresses Her Lover'; 'Love Poem' from *Holiday Girls*, Twelvetrees, 1985. 'Chat Show' from *Small Arm Practice*, William Heinemann, 1989. Edith Speers: From 'Tarantellas' from *By Way of a Vessel*, Twelvetrees, 1986. Richard Kelly Tipping: 'Deep Water' from *Domestic Hardcore*, University of Queensland Press, 1975. 'Heading North' from *Nearer by Far*, University of Queensland Press, 1986. Jena Woodhouse: 'The Bride of Byfield' from *Eros in Landscape*, Jacaranda Press, 1989. Philip Salom: 'He Sees She Sees' from *Sky Poems*, Fremantle Arts Centre Press, 1987. 'Spirit to the Body' from *Barbecue of the Primitives*, Fremantle Arts Centre Press, 1989. John Forbes: 'Missing Persons' from *The Stunned Mullet*, Hale & Iremonger, 1988. 'Love Poem'; 'Popular Classics' from *New and Selected Poems*, Angus & Robertson, 1992. Susan Hampton: 'The Queen at the Ice Palace'; 'Jealousy' from *Surly Girls*, Imprint/Collins, 1989. Jenny Boult: 'i'd like to know about the fruit bowl' from *Flight 39*, Abalone, 1986. 'scene' from *The White Rose and the Bath*. 'πO': 'Love / country style /'; 'How to be Polite' from *πO Revisited*, Wild & Woolley, 1976. Ania Walwicz: 'Big Tease'; 'Flip' from *Writing*,

Sirius/Angus & Robertson, 1989. Tony Page: 'Sungrowth' from *They're Knocking at My Door*, Pariah Press, 1986. Chris Mansell: 'Breakfast' from *Head, Heart & Stone*, Fling Poetry, 1982. 'Lady Gedanke rings home' from *Redshift/Blueshift*, Five Island Press, 1988. Peter Bakowski: 'in my dreams' from *Verandah*, 1989. Kevin Hart: 'The Beast'; 'Midsummer'; 'Four Poems' from *Your Shadow*, Angus & Robertson, 1984. Peter Rose: 'Kitchen' from *House of Vitriol*, Picador/Pan, 1990. Judith Beveridge: 'Invitation'; 'The Bee Keeper' from *The Domesticity of Giraffes*, Black Lightning Press, 1987. Gig Ryan: 'Small-Scale'; 'For Grace / And You're So Fine' from *The Division of Anger*, Transit Poetry, 1980. 'She Gives Reason' from *Excavation*, Picador/Pan, 1990. Donna McSkimming: 'Ululation for a Red Headed Woman' from *Moments of Desire*, Ed. Susan Hawthorne and Jenny Pausacker, Penguin, 1989. Dorothy Porter: From 'Scenes from a Marriage: v' from *The Night Parrot*, Black Lightning Press, 1984. From 'When Desire's Gone: II'; 'Cars. Lightning. Rain' from *Driving Too Fast*, University of Queensland Press, 1989. Fogarty, Lionel: 'Love or human nature'; 'Love travels' from *Ngutji*, Cheryl Buchanan, 1984. Fiona Perry: 'The Cuckoo Wife'; 'The Unearthed Girl' from *Pharaohs Returning*, Penguin Books, 1991. Stephen J. Williams: 'Love' from *A Crowd of Voices*, Pariah Press, 1985. Adam Aitken: 'Take Me for a Ride' from *Letter to Marco Polo*, Island Press, 1985. Catherine Bateson: 'Persephone Remembers Helen'; From 'The King of Spain Poems: 1, 2' from *Pomegranates from the Underworld*, Pariah Press, 1990. Dipti Saravanamuttu: 'Nageen Lake'; 'View for a Mirror' from *Statistic for the New World*, Rochford Street Press, 1988. Charmaine Papertalk-Green: 'Wanna Be White' from *Inside Black Australia*, Ed. Kevin Gilbert, Penguin Books, 1988. Alison Croggon: 'Lyric'; From 'Howl: Betrayal'; 'Seduction Poem' from *This is the Stone*, Penguin Books, 1991.

INDEX OF FIRST LINES

INDEX OF AUTHORS AND TITLES